Hitler's War in Africa 1941–1942

There's a Devil in the dawn—
See him fawn on those who served him well,
Who blinded, deafened, breathed the cordite reek,
Fed the ravening guns, and swore that it was hell.
F.E. Hughes, Bombardier

There are flowers now, they say, at Alamein;
Yes, flowers in the minefields now.
So those that come to view that vacant scene,
Where death remains and agony has been
Will find the lilies grow—
Flowers, and nothing that we know.
John Jarmain (51st Highland Division)

Hitler's War in Africa 1941–1942

The Road to Cairo

DAVID MITCHELHILL-GREEN

Pen & Sword
MILITARY

AN IMPRINT OF PEN & SWORD BOOKS LTD.
YORKSHIRE – PHILADELPHIA

First published in Great Britain in 2021 by
PEN AND SWORD MILITARY
An imprint of
Pen & Sword Books Limited
Yorkshire – Philadelphia

ISBN 978 1 52674 436 4

A CIP catalogue record for this book is available from the British Library.

Typeset in Times New Roman 11.5/14 by
SJmagic DESIGN SERVICES, India.
Printed and bound in the UK by CPI Group (UK) Ltd, Croydon, CR0 4YY.

Pen & Sword Books Limited incorporates the imprints of Atlas, Archaeology,
Aviation, Discovery, Family History, Fiction, History, Maritime, Military, Military
Classics, Politics, Select, Transport, True Crime, Air World, Frontline Publishing,
Leo Cooper, Remember When, Seaforth Publishing, The Praetorian Press,
Wharncliffe Local History, Wharncliffe Transport, Wharncliffe True Crime and
White Owl.

For a complete list of Pen & Sword titles please contact
PEN & SWORD BOOKS LIMITED
47 Church Street, Barnsley, South Yorkshire S70 2AS, United Kingdom
E-mail: enquiries@pen-and-sword.co.uk
Website: www.pen-and-sword.co.uk

Or

PEN AND SWORD BOOKS
1950 Lawrence Rd, Havertown, PA 19083, USA
E-mail: Uspen-and-sword@casematepublishers.com
Website: www.penandswordbooks.com

Contents

Acknowledgements

I am indebted to many individuals for their valued assistance in this project. Veterans, now passed, and their families, kindly provided personal diaries, post-war recollections and wartime snapshots – gritty and imperfect, yet sober and realistic in their depiction of the Desert War. Thank you: Richard Weston, A.C. Fletcher, F.M. Paget, Frank G. Perversi, J.H. Flak, Heinz Becker, Kurt Sawall and Melanie Ashfield. Other individuals who assisted through their expertise in the Second World War include: Richard Hargreaves, Honza Kase, Bertram Nold, Peter Jason Lai, and Suranjan Das. A special thank you to Akhil Kadidal for allowing me to use his maps of the North African campaign and Mr Owen Niall for providing an insight into contemporaneous surgery. To the individuals working in archives and libraries in UK and Australia, I am most grateful. My heartfelt appreciation is extended to Roni Wilkinson, Heather Williams, Amy Jordan and Matt Jones at Pen & Sword for their enthusiasm in bringing this book to life. Finally, I dedicate this book to my exceptionally supportive family – Jenny, Harvey and Hana.

Abbreviations

ADC	Aide-de-Camp
AFS	American Field Service
AIF	Australian Imperial Force
AWM	Australian War Memorial
BBC	British Broadcasting Corporation
BEF	British Expeditionary Force
C-in-C	Commander in Chief
CIGS	Chief of the Imperial General Staff
CRA	Commander of the Royal Artillery
DAK	*Deutsches Afrikakorps* (German Africa Corps)
DCM	Distinguished Conduct Medal
Div	Division
GOC	General Officer Commanding
GHQ	General Headquarters
HQ	Headquarters
NZEF	New Zealand Expeditionary Force
OKW	*Oberkommando der Wehrmacht* (High Command of the German Armed Forces)
PoW	Prisoner of War
RAF	Royal Air Force
RASC	Royal Army Service Corps
RHA	Royal Horse Artillery
RN	Royal Navy
RTR	Royal Tank Regiment
RVNR	Royal Volunteer Naval Reserve
SAAF	South African Air Force
SAI	South African Infantry
VC	Victoria Cross

Foreword

Signal was a popular illustrated German propaganda magazine produced during the Second World War. In mid-June 1941 a diary account of fighting along the Egyptian frontier was published:

> The last golden glow of the setting sun fades…Everything fine. Am fit and well. I'm glad I was there when the British were given the thrashing they deserved at Sollum.

The piece was later translated and circulated in a British Army publication with the comment from General Sir Claude Auchinleck: 'These fellows are good soldiers; they know their job and mean to do it… I hope we'll have him under the sand or in the bag before long.'[1]

This is the story of these soldiers, fighting across North Africa from late December 1940 until the beginning of November 1942. It begins with Hitler's decision to intervene and reinforce Mussolini's vanquished army, and concludes with the defeat of the Deutsche-Italienische Panzerarmee at El Alamein in early November 1942. It explores the experiences of the Axis and British coalition armies – conspiring to kill, while simultaneously battling rampant disease, fluctuating morale, technological disparity, leadership shortfalls, and a hostile environment.

We follow an ill-prepared German army thrust into an unforgiving desert landscape for which its European machinery was never designed, its diet compromised, its ally reeling from recent defeat. Driven in part by a sense of adventure and the lure of the Nile, its commander, Generalleutnant Erwin Rommel, boldly led his men across vast swathes of empty desert in an ambitious quest to drive the British from Egypt. But in a theatre of secondary importance, Rommel would become increasingly reliant upon captured vehicles, weapons and stores. Supply would be a constant headache. In this arid arena, bitterly contested battles, won or lost without a decisive outcome, forced victor and vanquished back and forth many hundreds of miles across the Western Desert's coastal plain. Here the rules of desert warfare intervened – bringing one side closer to its supply hub; its enemy's lines of communication correspondingly overextended. Eventually a bloody war of attrition ground Rommel's coalition army to a halt just 160 miles from Cairo – the zenith of Hitler's war in North Africa.

*****

Although it may be offensive to some today, I use the term 'British' in its contemporary context to represent Commonwealth and Empire troops drawn from India, Australia, New Zealand and South Africa. Specific formations are identified by their country of origin. Imperial measurements will be used, in keeping with the period for British forces, as will inconsistencies in spelling and grammar that feature in quotations. Contemporary labels such as 'Wog', 'Wop' or 'Hun' – derogatory and hateful to today's reader – have been retained for historical accuracy.

David Mitchelhill-Green, 2021

Chapter One

Rommel's African Sideshow

When marching through the desert heat,
With burning throat and blistered feet,
Amid choking dust and blinding sand,
You curse the day you saw this land.

–Anon

May 1940. Oberst Heinz Heggenreiner, assistant to the German Military Attaché in Rome, visited Libya to observe the Italian colony's preparedness for war. 'Everywhere' he visited 'the gloom of an impending war was only too apparent – a war which people did not desire and for which they saw no reason… Why have a war that jeopardised everything, and for which the country was not prepared?' Having met with Maresciallo dell'Aria (Air Marshal) Italo Balbo, commander of the Italian forces, Heggenreiner foresaw defeat, writing: 'I could not shake off a premonition of disaster.'[1]

Seven months later, a British Hussars officer surveyed the astonishing scene before him. In a makeshift camp holding thousands of Italian prisoners of war he estimated some 'twenty acres of officers and a hundred acres of men'.[2] Similar scenes of Italian troops laying down their arms beside masses of abandoned military equipment were a familiar sight in the aftermath of Mussolini's ill-fated invasion of Egypt. Having secured a toehold, only some sixty-five miles across the frontier, his encamped army was attacked by a British raid on 9 December 1940. Sudden victory precipitated a full-blown British counteroffensive, one that threatened to trounce the Italians and eliminate them from North Africa altogether. The prospect of such a calamity, on top of Italian misfortunes elsewhere, pushed Adolf Hitler to dispatch an armoured 'blocking force' to Libya – at best a sideshow to his forthcoming invasion of the Soviet Union.

'What about our mail?'

Mussolini's rout in Egypt arose from his lofty vision of a new Roman Empire. The Italian dictator longed for a time when his country would have 'free access to the oceans' since 'Italy is in an inland sea which is linked to the oceans by the Suez Canal…and by the Straits of Gibraltar, dominated by the guns of Great Britain.'[3] To achieve his ancient imperial ambitions, he would prise open the 'bars of the Italian prison' and challenge Britain's control of Egypt, Gibraltar, Malta, Cyprus for dominance of the Mediterranean.[4]

10 June 1940. Having waited in the wings since Germany invaded Poland in September 1939, Mussolini opportunistically declared war on France and Britain, urging the 'Italian people, rush to arms and show your tenacity, your courage, your valour'.[5] Awarded only a meagre slice of territory at the Italian – French armistice talks, the Duce set his sights firmly on Cairo. North Africa would be *his* theatre of war since Hitler, as specified in the original 1936 Axis agreement, harboured no plans of expanding south of the Alps where Mussolini would independently re-establish a 'Roman Empire in the Mediterranean'.[6]

Mussolini's proclamation of war received a lukewarm response from his army in Libya. *Tenente* Paolo Colacicchi (platoon leader in a Tenth Army machine gun battalion) summed up the prevailing lassitude:

> The main reaction among the men was 'What about our mail?' … They had no aggressive feelings… We realised that the British Army we were facing in Egypt, even though considerably smaller than ours, was better trained and better equipped, especially in transport, tanks and armoured cars.[7]

Italo Balbo, too, understood the folly of thrusting mostly non-motorised and poorly equipped infantry against the well-equipped British in Egypt. News of hostilities made him 'so angry that he picked up the billiard balls and smashed all the glasses… He was absolutely furious because he knew the position there and he had a lot of friends in Egypt among the British.'[8] Unfortunately Balbo died on 28 June when his aircraft was shot down in a freak friendly-fire incident.[9] His successor, Marshal Rodolfo Graziani, was equally dispirited about marching on Cairo.[10]

For all his bellicose thunder, however, Mussolini bided his time. He awaited news of the Wehrmacht crossing the English Channel in

Unternehmen Seelöwe (Operation *Sea Lion*) before entering Egypt. Triumph over the British, he explained to Graziani, would provide an overland passage to Italy's Abyssinian colony and (no less than) seal the fate of the British Empire. Sensing a 'total disaster', Graziani offered his resignation.[11] The British, in opposition, acted immediately. General Sir Archibald Wavell, Commander in Chief of the Middle East, at once issued orders for aggression along the Egyptian frontier, what British troops called 'the wire'. On 11 June the 11th Hussars (7th Armoured Division) forced their 1924-pattern Rolls Royce armoured cars through the barbed wire entanglements delineating the Egyptian frontier. A number of one-sided skirmishes developed; after three months the combat tally stood at 3,500 Italian casualties against 150 British.

Goaded by Mussolini, Graziani's Tenth Army finally crossed the frontier at dawn on 13 September 1940. A remarkable letter from the Italian dictator a month earlier spelt out just how little was expected: 'I repeat that there are no territorial objectives, it is not a question of aiming for Alexandria, nor even Sollum. I am only asking you to attack the British forces facing you. I assume full personal responsibility for this decision of mine.'[12] Having done his best to forestall the invasion, Graziani pessimistically penned: 'For whatever evil may occur, I, before God and my soldiers, am not *responsible*.' Hitler's military attaché in Rome, General Enno von Rintelen, was likewise unconvinced of any success. He foresaw 'no immediate prospect of [Graziani] capturing Alexandria, the Delta, or the [Suez] Canal...'[13]

The invasion force advanced a mere sixty-five miles – in almost ceremonial fashion – across worthless desert before halting at Sidi Barrani, a non-descript small town some eighty miles before the major British base at Mersa Matruh.

Sergeant Emilio Ponti, an Italian tank gunner, recalled how 'the British Navy came close to the beach [that night] and put a few shells in, and damaged quite a few of the lorries belonging to the Blackshirts [or *Camicie Nere*, Fascist Party militia in a combat role], and killed some of them. The day after, we said, "That could have been us. But as they get much more pay than us, it serves them right." You become really cruel when you are in the army.'[14]

Graziani's encamped army set to work constructing a series of lavish fortified camps, independent and not mutually supporting, while the Italian propaganda machine worked overtime. The offensive, Rome pretended, '[had] exceeded all expectation'! Sidi Barrani's trams were again running, 'thanks to the skill of Italian engineers'; the shops were open; even the nightclubs were flourishing.[15] Scarcely a reward, Graziani had taken a dusty town of twenty homes, which never had, nor needed, a tramway. Mussolini fumed powerlessly at his Marshal's refusal to advance. Time, he realised, was running out. The invasion must resume.

Far from idle, the British continued to badger the Italians. Major Ralph Bagnold formed a scratch force from a group of New Zealander servicemen (later complemented by Rhodesians and British troops) and ventured deep into enemy territory. 'We captured a small Italian convoy; took half a dozen men without a shot being fired… When the group was increased in size it had to have an official name, so we chose the Long Range Desert Group [LRDG].'[16] The LRDG would prove to be of enormous value in both sabotage and covert reconnaissance functions. Other irregular units to harass and stage hit-and-run operations against the Axis were the so-called 'Jock Columns', named after their founder Lieutenant J.C. 'Jock' Campbell, the Special Air Service, and, later, 'Popski's Private Army' – officially No. 1 Demolition Squadron.

'The Italians are in no position to achieve anything on a decisive scale'

On 21 July 1940, the Führer directed his army C-in-C, Generalfeld-marschall Walter von Brauchitsch, to prepare plans for conquering the Soviet Union – *Unternehmen Barbarossa*. At the same time, Britain remained a dogged foe. Since the Luftwaffe had failed to achieve aerial superiority in the Battle of Britain – a fundamental prerequisite for an amphibious operation across the English Channel – Hitler's senior army and naval commanders turned to the Mediterrenean and Middle East.

Berlin had already investigated the dispatch of an armoured corps to North Africa since little was expected of Italian endeavours. Generaloberst Franz Halder (Chief of Staff of the Army High Command – OKH) noted: 'The offensive in Egypt will accomplish no decisive results if executed by the Italians alone. Handicapped by their economic straits and their ineffectualness, the Italians are in no position to achieve anything on a decisive scale.'[17] Generalmajor Wilhelm Ritta von Thoma visited Libya in October 1940. His damning report decried Graziani's performance to date and sluggish preparations for resuming the advance. Highlighting Rome's reluctance for military assistance, von Thoma deemed supply as crucial in a desert war and recommended four or more armoured divisions to overwhelm the British and reach the Nile. Irritated by the report, Hitler was further annoyed to learn in private that von Thoma valued one British soldier at more than a dozen Italians.

Mussolini, on the other hand, was incensed over the prospect of unsolicited German formations operating within his sphere of influence: 'Hitler always faces me with a *fait accompli*,' he grumbled to his foreign minister (and son-in-law) Count Galeazzo Ciano.[18] Notwithstanding recent bungled operations, he needed to even the score: 'I shall pay him back in his own coin. He will find out from the papers that I have occupied Greece.'[19] The following day, 13 October, senior Italian officers were tasked with drawing up a new invasion plan. In keeping with his 'private war', Mussolini emphatically rejected any offer of German aid. His refusal of assistance, much to the Führer's annoyance, was followed on 28 October by news that Italian forces had invaded Greece. Mussolini's latest foray, however, soon stalled in the face of stiff resistance. In yet another military débâcle, the valiant Greek defenders would push the invaders back across the border and liberate a third of Albania by the end of 1940.

'Fox killed in the open'

Back in Egypt, the reluctant Graziani postured defensively while Wavell opted to 'sally forth and strike'.[20] Britain's first desert operation, codenamed Compass, would also assist the Greeks in their fight. On 9 December 1940, General Richard O'Connor's Western Desert Force (WDF), comprising the Infantry of the 4th Indian Division and the heavily armoured Infantry 'I', or Matilda II tanks, of the 7th Armoured Division, undertook a raid that was expected to take four or five days.[21] In O'Connor's words, 'the operations were to be in the nature of a big raid which, if successful, was to be exploited as far as our meagre administrative resources would permit.'[22] During the interwar period, British officers had studied a similar scenario, when the highly mobile German Eighth Army had defeated two much larger Russian armies in 1914.

Compass began with the Royal Navy and Royal Air Force bombarding the Italian camps on the night before the assault to mask the clatter of British columns moving forward. Daylight, an officer in the 7th Armoured Division wrote, revealed:

> a wonderful sight, the whole desert to the north covered with a mass of dispersed vehicles – tanks, trucks, and guns all moving westwards with long plumes of dust rolling out behind.[23]

11 December. British troops were astounded how easily their two divisions had traversed the desert unseen. They now assaulted the Italian camps from the rear. Alf Davies, 1st Royal Tank Regiment, remembered his surprise: 'We were expecting to see Italian tanks or infantry. But instead of that we saw about three hundred men, they all had candles – they were attending Mass. Well, you know, there is no law and we just opened up with machine-guns.'[24] Many tank crews were killed before they could reach their vehicles. The Italians, according to Captain Bob Hingston (Royal Horse Artillery) were 'utterly lamentable. We were pretty green, but they were …appalling soldiers.'[25]

Sidi Barrani was swiftly retaken, with 38,300 prisoners, 237 artillery pieces and 73 tanks. British losses stood at 624 casualties. Anthony Eden, Winston Churchill's foreign secretary, borrowed the prime minister's famous Battle of Britain phrase to crow: 'Never has so much been surrendered by so many to so few.'[26] Even Mussolini acknowledged that 'the Italians of 1914 were better', ridiculing his people as a 'race of sheep'.[27]

The Italian PoWs, Lance Sergeant Ian Sinclair (South Notts Hussars) observed, were 'hopeless, shattered – the last thing they had expected, I think was to be attacked. I don't know what they thought they were there for, quite frankly! They certainly didn't give the appearance that they'd come to fight. They were so dishevelled, so dirty.'[28]

The horror of war confronted Bombardier Ray Ellis (South Notts Hussars), who was charged with the 'horrible job' of burying the dead.

> After the first day or so, these corpses were beginning to swell and smell. We found some big meat hooks in the cookhouse, so we used those. You stuck it under the shoulder

6

and dragged them. We made no attempt at all to identify anybody, we were treating them like carcasses… There was no reverence or respect at all. The main thing was to get them under the ground.[29]

Across the Mediterranean, King Victor Emmanuel bewailed his country's military misfortune: 'For much too long in Italy a chair is being called a palace. But the fact remains that a chair is only a chair. Likewise, our divisions, thin and poorly equipped, are divisions in name only.'[30]

News of O'Connor's assault, Ciano recorded, hit 'like a thunderbolt'.[31] Mussolini was gripped by panic. He cabled Berlin on the morning of 23 December, in desperation, to procure 'tanks and artillery at any price'.[32] Il Duce would salvage honour from defeat! Meanwhile, the British charge quickly evolved into a staggeringly successful campaign. O'Connor resumed the offensive in the New Year, this time with the unblooded, volunteer Australian 6th Division in place of the Indian Division, which was withdrawn for service in Eritrea. Crossing the frontier into Libya, his next objective was the heavily defended coastal fortress at Bardia, which General Annibale Bergonzoli declared 'impregnable'. The assault began on the morning of 3 January 1941. In his first experience of combat, an Australian infantryman secured one of the perimeter defensive posts. As he disarmed the emerging defenders,

I found a grenade in the pocket of one of them… He snatched it back, saying something in his own language. Thinking he was going to blow us both up, and the safety catch on the rifle being on, I was just resigned to having to use the bayonet on him. When the grenade came apart, it was full of cigarettes instead of explosives much to my relief.[33]

Bardia fell a little over two days later. The 'resistance of our troops was brief', Ciano lamented, 'a matter of hours.'[34] In his latest trouncing, Mussolini lost more than 40,000 men, mostly captured. British casualties totalled 130 killed and 326 wounded. Continuing sixty miles west along the Libyan coast, O'Connor's newly designated XIII Corps reached the fortified port of Tobruk on the morning of 7 January. Another folly, the Italians were reluctant to relieve their fortress and its 72-year-old commander, General Petassi Manella. Neither the Italian Navy nor Air

Force intervened in helping their entrapped comrades, save for dropping leaflets encouraging them to stand firm.

Notwithstanding the belief by both the German and Italian high commands that Tobruk would be held for a considerable period – Italian propaganda bragging of 'long and obstinate opposition' – the fortress fell to Major General Iven Mackay's Australian 6th Division just 29 hours after the first troops pierced the outer perimeter. O'Connor commended the operation for its 'great dash by Australian infantry, and British tanks, supported by British and Australian artillery, British Machine Gun Units with the co-operation of the RAF.'[35] It netted him a further 25,000 prisoners, 208 artillery pieces (later to form the nucleus of the 'bush artillery') and 87 medium and light tanks. British losses were again low at 400 casualties. 'Seldom has a victory over such a large area been more swiftly won', the *Times* proclaimed.[36]

Reconnaissance reports of a new Italian withdrawal west prompted O'Connor to direct his 39 operational cruiser tanks inland 'across the unknown country in full cry' to intercept the retreating enemy columns. The Australians would continue along the coast road to Benghazi, Cyrenaica's principal port.[37] Contact with the Italians, now low on fuel and ammunition, was made near the small coastal town of Beda Fomm. Many Italians fought courageously, launching uncoordinated frontal attacks. The furious three-day battle ended on 7 February 1941. It spelt death for the Italian Tenth Army. Spoils were again colossal – another 25,000 prisoners, 112 medium tanks, 216 guns and 1,500 vehicles. British casualties were remarkably light: nine dead and 15 wounded. O'Connor, whose daring and unorthodox flanking moves across open desert would soon be emulated by a new foe, observed: 'I think this may be termed "a complete victory" as none of the enemy escaped.'[38]

British tank crews later returned to the battlefield to recover repairable enemy armour. The sight of partially cremated bodies horrified them.

> Men were hanging half-way out of the tanks with their legs blackened, and these dropped off when we pulled the bodies free. Heaps of gooey black stuff inside the tanks, and these heaps had been men.[39]

Arabs swarmed over the detritus of battle, 'scavenging amongst the wreckage' and selling eggs.[40] Italian troops, many in tears, dug graves along the roadside. 'It is incredible', General Henry Maitland 'Jumbo' Wilson wrote to the Duke of Connaught (son of Queen Victoria), 'that the Italian Army of Libya should have been wiped out in two months exactly from the date of the attack on Sidi Barrani.'[41] They were a 'cumbersome force', Brigadier C.N. Barclay concluded, a 'rank and file...apathetic towards to a war which they did not understand.'[42]

The immediate threat to Egypt had been smashed. O'Connor's army of 30,000 men had advanced more than 500 miles and utterly defeated an army five times its size. For the cost of 476 British dead and 1,225 wounded, XIII Corps had destroyed or captured 380 light and medium tanks, 845 artillery pieces and 130,000 Italian troops including 22 generals. O'Connor victoriously cabled Wavell (unencrypted for Mussolini's benefit) of the 'Fox killed in the open'.[43] Wavell, with unwitting irony, received the original moniker of the Western Desert 'Fox'.[44]

Halted at El Agheila, O'Connor's XIII Corps was preparing to march on Tripoli when a cable from London (on 12 February) notified Wavell that his 'major effort must now be to aid Greece and/or Turkey. This rules out any serious effort against Tripoli.'[45] The decision precipitated one of the most contentious issues of the desert war. Should O'Connor have been allowed to take Tripoli, the capital and main port of Libya? Given the poor state of Italian morale and strength, and the initially small commitment of German forces, such a drive might possibly have wound up the fighting in North African two years earlier than its eventual conclusion. 'We lost', General Sir Francis de Guingand regretted, 'an enormous opportunity to finish off North Africa.'[46]

O'Connor later blamed himself, asserting that it was 'quite inexcusable'. Instead it was Churchill, privy to Ultra intelligence divulging German preparations for a Balkan Blitzkrieg, who opted to send the cream of O'Connor's force to protect Greece – Britain's sole remaining continental ally.[47]

As we shall see, anything less than the utter destruction of an army tended in the overall course of the desert campaign to favour the defeated army. In General John C. Fuller's words, the desert war was a 'race-course' where

> each army in turn galloped forward until its momentum was exhausted and then was compelled to gallop back to avoid annihilation. The reason centred almost entirely in supply and,

like a piece of elastic, the line of supply of both armies could be stretched with comparative safety to between 300 and 400 miles from its base – Tripoli on the one hand and Alexandria on the other. But as these two main [supply] bases were 1,400 miles apart [the Axis at Tripoli, the British at Alexandria], to try and stretch them farther before immediate bases were established was to risk snapping the elastic.[48]

'Reasons of strategy, politics, and psychology': German intervention in North Africa

Mussolini's Greek fiasco compelled Hitler to move into a new theatre, not only to rescue his humiliated ally, but to protect his southern flank and safeguard vital raw materials from the Balkans. On 13 November 1940, the Führer issued orders to invade Greece. Plans were also drawn up to send assistance to North Africa following appeals by Generale Ugo Cavallero, shortly to become Chief of the Italian Supreme Command (*Comando Supremo*), and Mussolini, the latter now left with little choice but to swallow his pride.

From his Bavarian alpine retreat, the Berghof, Hitler announced in early January 1941 that a specially composed *Sperrverband* (blocking force) with an armoured regiment was to be shipped to Libya to stave off the British threat to Tripoli. Formally sanctioned in Führer Directive No. 22 (11 January 1941), the operation was viewed pragmatically as a political rather than a military intervention for 'reasons of strategy, politics, and psychology.'[49] Berlin's (small-scale) support was intended to avert internal collapse within Italy, Mussolini's possible downfall and the demise of the Axis partnership. In light of the forthcoming invasion of Russia, Hitler intended to commit just enough troops to bolster the defence of Tripoli and hold Tripolitania.[50] The objective, General Siegfried Westphal recalled, 'was to tie down as many British troops as possible and to cover the southern flank of Europe. We had never the intention to conquer Egypt or cross the Suez Canal.'[51]

The Axis formations chosen to defend Libya included the German 5th Light Division (Generalmajor Johannes Streich), the Italian 132nd Ariete Armoured Division and 102nd Trento Motorised Division. Generalmajor Hans Freiherr von Funck was the original commander of Germany's new African army until his pessimistic appraisal of the situation became known. As Hitler explained to an Italian diplomat, he just wasn't the type of leader to 'carry away his troops' – a leadership condition the Führer considered vital for this challenging new environment.[52] Instead 49-year-old Generalleutnant Erwin Rommel – a decorated First World War veteran who had made a name for himself during the victorious French campaign – was chosen to lead the *Deutsches Afrikakorps* (DAK).

'But the Germans came instead'

Italy's military was left reeling after the chain of defeats. With at most six divisions to defend Tripoli and only 100 aircraft, Graziani 'voluntarily' resigned. His successor was Generale d'Armata Italo Gariboldi. Mussolini 'reassured' his new Libyan commander with the knowledge that 'I could not occupy myself with Libya. Between it and Greece I had to choose the latter because Italians could resign themselves to be beaten by the English but not by Greeks.'[53] Rommel touched down at Tripoli's Castel Benito airfield the next day, accompanied by Oberst Rudolf Schmundt, Hitler's army adjutant. First impressions were far from favourable. Disconsolate Italian officers waited with bags packed for their evacuation home. 'We had been awaiting the British fatalistically – almost gladly', an army doctor made clear, at 'least the whole business would be over. But the Germans came instead.'[54]

Leutnant Heinz Heggenreiner, liaison officer to the Italian High Command in North Africa, received Rommel on 12 February. He 'briefly put me in the picture concerning the set-up of the Italian forces in Africa', Rommel recounted, 'and described some very unpleasant incidents which had occurred during the retreat... Italian troops had thrown away their weapons and ammunition and clambered onto overloaded vehicles in a wild attempt to get away to the west. This had led to some ugly scenes, and even to shooting. Morale was as low as it could be in all military circles in Tripoli.'[55] Perhaps as a consequence of his combat experience during the First World War, Rommel held little respect for his Axis ally. 'Many Italian officers had thought of war as little more than a pleasant adventure,' he wrote, 'and were, perforce, having to suffer a bitter disillusionment.'[56] Not surprisingly, Nazi propaganda minister Joseph Goebbels observed how 'Rommel gives the most denigrating judgement of the Italians. He thinks nothing of them.'[57]

South African-born Leutnant Heinz Werner Schmidt, who would serve as Rommel's aide-de-camp, found the first German troops 'tolerated rather than popular.'[58] Hans-Joachim Schraepler, equally, was less than inspired by Tripoli: 'a town of 105,000 inhabitants, 30,000 Italians, Libyans, the latter poorly dressed. In the streets many "soldiers", whites, blacks, Italians, sailors also, a few Germans in their new uniforms.... in the streets, of course, no discipline.'[59] Schraepler, who would serve as Rommel's adjutant, found the general to be an 'impressive and also impressing personality ...[with] great plans.'[60]

Gariboldi, whom Ciano later described as 'old and stupid', was, unsurprisingly, far more more conservative in his approach. He was also Rommel's nominal superior. Whereas Rommel looked hungrily to drive the British back, Gariboldi was happy to surround Tripoli in a defensive cordon. Rommel recorded the general's malaise: he 'looked very dubious about it all. He was extremely discouraged by the [recent] defeat.'[61] In total disregard of his orders, Rommel decided, 'in view of the tenseness of the situation and the sluggishness of the Italian command', to deviate from a reconnaissance. Instead, *he* would seize the initiative.[62] Relishing this new command, he confided to his wife, Lu (Lucia 'Lucie' Maria Mollin, to whom he wrote regularly) on 14 February that 'I'm very well... A lot to do.' [63]

The first German combat formations began to arrive by sea into Tripoli. Decoy tactics inflated their menace. *Kübelwagen*, the German equivalent of the famous US Jeep, for example, were disguised with a canvas superstructure and a dummy gun to resemble tanks. Rommel later wrote: 'Concealment of intentions is of the utmost importance...to [achieve] surprise... Deception measures of all kinds should be encouraged, if only to make the enemy commander uncertain... and cause to hesitate and hold back.'[64] To bluff enemy agents, the initial elements of the 5th Panzer Regiment were paraded multiple times through the mains streets, with 'a devil of a noise on the macadamised streets', before being ordered forward to Sirte.[65] Rommel took the salute. A long line of Italian tanks followed, the commanders posturing bold and daring. Cries of 'Viva Italia' arose. Addressing the crowd, Rommel expressed his confidence in the ability of his coalition army to stem the British tide. Several hours later the Axis tanks trundled out into the desert towards El Agheila.

'At 1800 hours, the Panzers rumble through the port along the *Via Balbia* towards the east,' Leutnant Joachim Schorm (5th Panzer Regiment) pencilled in his diary: 'All night long we are greeted by soldiers, settlers and natives.'[66]

'Not a war in a palm grove'

Africa held the promise of adventure, at least at first. Siegfried Westphal recalled how the 'number of volunteers for this theatre was understandably large, as the magic of the Orient has always attracted youth.'[67] Leutnant Ralph Ringler (104th Panzer Grenadier Regiment) welcomed news of his assignment. 'Like madmen we jumped and hugged each other... We became a separate caste in the barracks – "The Africans"...our young comrades envied us, the old ones were amused by our enthusiasm...in Africa there awaited great adventure.'[68] Hans Schmitz's first impressions were 'yellow and sandy...Palms and small trees...Solitary settlements, mud huts and mats, tents, caravan roads, dried-out riverbeds. Everything disappeared against the sandy horizon.'[69] A German officer in the 21st Panzer Division enthused: 'Fantasy has had a free rein – Africa – that's tropical nights, palm trees, sea breezes, native oases and tropical helmets. Also a little war, but how can we be anything but victorious?' Even the privations of thirst, heat and cold were to be braved in this 'wonderful of theatre of war', a captured letter championed: 'One might almost envy you [in] all these hardships.'[70]

The largely featureless Western Desert – a title bestowed by the British during the First World War to the desert region west of the Nile River – was an ancient battlefield where decaying ruins attested to earlier occupations by the Greeks, Romans, and Ottoman Turks. These latest combatants too discovered an arid expanse capped by natural geographical barriers at either end. The narrow point in Libya was at El Agheila on the border of Cyrenaica and Tripolitania (Libya's east and west provinces respectively); the eastern bottleneck, as we will see, lay six hundred miles to the east at El Alamein. The Germans were novices in this setting, the distances unprecedented. Rommel's 7th Panzer Division in France, for example, had traversed 268 miles to reach the English Channel in 1940. He now faced a march of 1,415 miles to reach the Egyptian city of Alexandria.

In stark contrast to a rumoured *corps d'élite,* Hitler's army in Africa was a hastily assembled formation devoid of experience, specialised acclimatisation or training. Measures before leaving Europe were little more than briefings by officers who had visited Africa and lectures on tropical medicine. Not surprisingly, the DAK faced myriad problems. While the pitiless desert heat may have been expected, the cold nights were an unexpected misery. 'Night and morning [were] really lousy cold,' Hauptman Wolfgang Everth complained. 'Even with three blankets one is frozen like a naked ski instructor. One's feet aren't warm until midday.'[71]

German troops were hurriedly outfitted for their new posting. The basic tropical uniform was cut in a style reminiscent of the Kaiser's colonial forces. 'What we were "fitted" out with defies description,' Major Hans von Luck (who served with Rommel in France in 1940) wrote after receiving his tropical uniform. 'One could see that Germany had no longer any colonies since 1918, and so had no idea of what was suitable for the tropics. We need only to have asked our allies, the Italians, but no, the commissariat had designed the tropical equipment strictly in the Prussian mode.'[72] The stiff, tight-fitting uniform linen material provided little protection against the summer heat or insulation against the penetrating cold. Further accoutrements included a linen belt, high lace-up boots and a pith helmet, which, supposedly, 'was essential wear in the tropics' and shirts 'impermeable to air'. As von Luck writes,

> Wounded men from North Africa, waiting there for reposting, told us how they, like many others, had carried on a lively trade with the Italians in order to exchange at least some of their equipment for the more appropriate Italian uniforms.[73]

British tropical uniforms made of pure wool were also found to be much more practical in the desert arena.

Shipped in haste, the first German vehicles unloaded at Tripoli's Spanish Quay still sported a dark grey European camouflage. Conceived to fight a war on the Continent, the Panzers suffered enormously in desert conditions. The average life of a tank engine, for example, was halved without appropriate air filters and operating in a low gear for extended periods over long distances. Frustration features in Leutnant Schorm's diary (6 April), shortly after setting off early in the morning:

> Every vehicle loses its way. When we reach the *Via Balbia* again – who will? – our Panzers, or at least their engines, will be ruined. According to instructions, the engines must be changed at 2,000 km. Their life is given by the firm at

2,500 km. They have already done 500 km in Germany. We have come 1,000 km along the *Via Balbia*. By the time we reach Derna, every Panzer will easily have passed the limit of 2,000 km. 600 km will have been carried out across the desert – in dust and heat, and that counts for more than treble [the normal strain].[74]

Though trucks could traverse much of the terrain, broken springs and shock absorbers engendered frequent breakdowns. Leutnant Dr Kurt Wolff Tank (5th Panze Regiment) watched as repair groups came to life at dusk, industriously repairing engines and cleaning carburettors.

Springs, track rollers and track links have to be seen to and fixed. Guns and machine guns have to be checked. You can hear the swearing of hard-working men, the clanging of hammers in the wet and cold night. As soon as the sun rises through the morning mist, the Regiment starts to roll forward.[75]

With spare parts not readily available, Rommel's formations would rely heavily upon captured enemy transport. 'If you want vehicles, then go out into the desert and get them', he directed.[76] 'Our destroyed vehicles are being replaced by excellent British cars,' Schraepler noticed, so much so that 'some German units will not be recognised as German, and one might think that there are English here. Besides, our men can barely be identified, covered by dirt and dust.'[77]

Diet was another problem for the German soldier. A DAK Feldwebel vented his frustration in an October 1941 diary entry: 'Isn't it perfect mockery what they offer us here for food? Here of all places where you need more to keep your health than elsewhere. It doesn't matter a damn if we go to the dogs: what matters is that Germany saves foreign exchange and will win the war.'[78] Schraepler dismissed the Italian catering as 'more than poor…dry mouldy bread, for dipping into edible oil, butter substitute, plus canned meat. That was our lunch.'[79] As Schmidt explained to General Paulus during his visit to Tobruk in May 1941: 'fruit and vegetables are unknown to the soldier. They miss their potatoes especially. The usual rations consist of sardines in oil, bulky tinned-meat sausages (Bierwurst)' and Italian tinned beef, stamped AM (for *Administrazione Militare,* Military Adminstration) – a staple derided as *Alter Mann* (Old Man) because of the letters embossed on the can.[80] Worse still, the Italian rations, rich in pulses (leguminous plants) and conserved meat with a high fat content, often led to jaundice.

Disease debilitated both sides. An Australian soldier poeticised the scourge, writing of a 'Land of filth, of flies and fleas; home to every known disease... So we may when then battle's won give Libya to the greedy Hun; For never could worse existence be, than to live in Libyan misery.'[81]

Rommel, for all his vitality, was stricken with jaundice and other chronic illnesses during his time in Africa. He was 'a sick man', Schmidt wrote.[82] In the period from March to June 1941 alone, the DAK lost 12,203 men – 3,512 as battlefield casualties, the rest through sickness. Rommel's adjutant recorded the extent of the problem as early as May 1941, noting 'scores of soldiers are sick. This number is increasing every day.'[83] Another officer complained, 'sometimes as many as sixty per cent of us suffer from dysentery-like diarrhoea at the same time. No one is spared. When you have it, you don't know whether you want to live or die.'[84]

No army was immune. Paolo Caccia-Dominioni wrote on 8 October 1942:

> Lieutenant Meleri of the 31st was among the patients of Field Hospital 165. Every so often dysentery reduced even the bravest of men to such an extent that they could not keep on their feet... In a field hospital at El Daba, ten miles away, Lieutenant-Colonel Crivelli was also lying seriously ill – not as a result of wounds sustained in action; that would have been too bad. Another wound now would have been his fourth... But no, the unfortunate Crivelli was laid low by a violent and humiliating attack of dysentery.[85]

Of the rampant illness, the *British Medical Journal* (1944) concluded that a 'frontline force with forty to fifty per cent of its strength affected by dysentery and diarrhoea can scarcely be called a vigorous army.'[86] Lieutenant Colonel R.K. Debenham elaborated on a hospital's case mix at El Alamein:

> At first sight one may imagine that a convoy from a battle consists exclusively of wounded men. This is not so. Out of

7,952 troops who arrived at the hospital during the heavy fighting of July [1942], only 2,237 were battle casualties... The remaining 5,665 consisted of cases medically sick (especially enteritis and malaria), also an assortment of skin conditions, superficial suppurative lesions, piles, sore feet, cases of anxiety neurosis, and the counterpart in less-educated troops – viz., self-inflicted wounds.[87]

The desert was an unforgiving setting where simple scratches, grazes or insect bites were easily infected. 'Desert sores', as they were known, were common ulcerated wounds that were especially slow to heal. To avoid abrasions on bare legs, German troops were forbidden (in theory) from wearing shorts in combat. A captured German diary entry quibbled, 'The new commander had forbidden the wearing of short trousers. So now you run around the whole day in longs and sweat like a pig. I don't know which is worse – the commander, the flies, or the rats.'[88] A German army mechanic remonstrated,

> Did I volunteer for Africa just to have my left leg slowly rot away through neglect... It's like this here. If you go down with anything, as for example I did with my leg, it's just one damn thing after another. A small wound on the forefinger of my left hand has already grown to a big septic wound as big as a penny piece. No ointment's any good, you can't get any soapy water to bathe it in. The water won't take the soap. The water here is just all fifth.[89]

British troops also suffered from the chaffing of their battledress soaked in sweat and coated with sand that could rub their skin raw. A survey of the British 11th Hussars in the summer of 1942 found 25 per cent of the regiment were afflicted by infected sores. Private Francis Paget (2/28th Infantry Battalion) found himself 'so covered [by lesions]...I couldn't dig or get in and out of a trench... When the shelling started, I could not bend my legs because of all the boils at the back of my knees.'[90] The 'desert sores' caused much discomfort and a serious loss of efficiency. Gervase Markham (124th Field Regiment, Royal Artillery) recalled the ignominy of being classified as 'undesertworthy'. 'I got this dysentery after a bit. I got boils on my face so had to have bandages all over my face and so looked an awful sight for some time. In fact, I had to be sent back and be treated at one time.'[91]

Helping to spread disease was the Bazaar fly, *Musca sorbens,* a bulkier, more vexatious relative of the common house fly that bred exclusively in (human) excreta. To Major Christopher Seton-Watson they were the 'curse of the desert', a pest 'responsible for three-quarters of the exasperation, short tempers and genuine hardship.'[92] 'Plagues of flies and the danger of infection,' a German report protested, 'are the inevitable results of any but the most scrupulous cleanliness… The menace of flies cannot be exaggerated, as they convey the most serious diseases with which the armies in the field will have to contend.'[93] They 'plague us in millions from the first hour in the morning,' an Italian officer griped.[94] 'They were horrid,' Martin Ranft (220th Artillery Regiment, 164th Light Afrika Division) recalled:

> We had those nets over our heads but even then with those nets they'd cling against the net, trying to get in your eyes – everywhere where they sensed there was moisture.[95]

Dr Alfons Selmayr (surgeon, 5th Panzer Regiment) wrote in disgust

> [how] dressings were only removed when the people were standing directly in front of me. But I frequently had to take the little beasts out of the wounds with tweezers, only to have them creep into our eyes and the corners of our mouths.[96]

Sergeant Fred Hunn (12th Lancers) shared a similar experience camped in a fly-blown *wadi* – the name given to a dry riverbed that only fills with water after heavy rainfall. 'If one made a mug of tea, within seconds the whole of the brew would become a mass of heaving insects… The only relief came when one was covered completely by a mosquito net.'[97] The fly problem and its effect on morale was even exploited as a tool of war. Australian infantry at Tobruk, for example, would carry their rubbish out on patrol and dump it close to enemy lines.

Challenged by the need to transport the necessities of life and war over ever-lengthening supply lines across a hostile environment, German troops learned the basics of desert warfare through trial and error. In one instance, Rommel flew in search of a missing armoured column, which he eventually located 15 to 20 miles further south than expected. He landed amongst the vehicles to blast their progress, only to learn of an earlier attempt to cross a salt marsh and detour around a large body of water, which, of course, was a mirage. 'People' similarly spotted from afar were often only camel thorn bushes.

'The desert face changed as the day advanced', a British Eighth Army driver explained. 'The appearance of an object in the morning was completely different from the same object at evening time. The hour before darkness was the most difficult... Everything took on odd shapes and appearances at that time.'[98] A shimmering heat haze likewise distorted what gunners viewed through their sights while shadows later in the day would exaggerate an object's size.

A much-despised curse blew in from the Sahara. Hans Schmitz was erecting a tent,

> when suddenly from the west the world and the sky...were filled with dense sand that quickly raced towards us. In a few seconds the previously sweltering hot wind was ice cold. The daylight became a sulphurous yellow... Immediately the air was full of dust, the daylight disappeared, and an eerier black-gold night prevailed... It was like before the creation of the world: one saw no beginning and no end.[99]

The fierce sandstorms, war correspondent Alan Moorehead wrote, 'blew indifferently upon Germans and British'.[100] To the British they were a *khamsin,* the Italians a *ghibli*. With visibility reduced to barely a few yards, all movement would halt. Vehicle maintenance ceased, weapons clogged and lungs choked. Flying was impossible. The storms could sometimes last for days, cloaking hundreds of square miles. 'Everything is suspended until it blows itself out', a British soldier recalled. 'Friend and foe alike retire to any shelter they can find and bury their heads in anything likely to stop the dust. If you succeed too well you are likely to die of suffocation, if you settle for more air you breathe in great lungfulls of the abrasive dust.'[101]

Schraepler, in his words, was as 'dirty as a pig', unable to use his eyes, his teeth gnashing.[102] Rommel described a wind often so 'strong that one could not drive at all... It was only with difficulty that we could breathe through a handkerchief held in front of the face and perspiration poured from our bodies in the unendurable heat.'[103] One Italian major, however, took advantage of a *ghibli*, 'which had risen up in one dense uniform cloud' to forget the war and pen a letter to his wife. 'A day therefore of unexpected, if not exactly comfortable, tranquillity, which I will turn to good use by sending you something better than the usual brief postcard…'[104]

Once a sandstorm abated, a Stuka pilot noted how Luftwaffe ground crews faced a 'task that was completely new and unfamiliar to them. Using their hands or empty ration tins, they began scooping incredible quantities of sand out of the innermost recesses of our machines. They had to make sure all moveable parts still actually moved, that all air intakes were free of sand and that the aircraft were operational again.'[105]

Clear air and a dearth of cover, conversely, made aerial attacks deadly. Joachim Schorm observed how warfare in 'Africa is quite different from the war in Europe… Here there are not the masses of men and material. Nobody and nothing can be concealed.'[106] Vehicles, accordingly, were dispersed over wide areas, to lessen the risk of becoming a target, and detract attention from dumps and headquarters. Troops would dig themselves in for protection, though penetrating the hard limestone desert floor often required the use of explosives or power tools. As an Australian army training bulletin taught, 'slit trenches will be dug on all but the shortest of halts. Even a shallow trench is better than nothing. Unwilling troops will quickly become keen to dig after their first raid.'[107] Experienced soldiers looked to where desert rats had dug their holes – a sign of softer ground. 'So long as we were just below ground level,' a New Zealand engineer explained, 'we were quite safe. If any trench, deep or shallow, had a hit then it was just too bad.'[108]

Nightfall brought a new problem, with men disorientated in caliginous night. Frustrated and lost, Lieutenant Charles Potts (British 8th Armoured Brigade) remembered 'after walking round in circles for hours one gives up hope of finding the way back, scoops a trench in the sand and sleeps in it, then one wakes up in the morning and finds the camp half a mile away.'[109] Ugo Tebaldini (61st Infantry Division Sirte) was in charge of an artillery battery: 'One night I misplaced a field gun. I finally found it after spending several hours searching for it, just in time to avoid being disciplined for it.'[110] Brigadier Charles Donald, a surgeon with the Eighth Army, discovered that 'to have pre-operative and post-operative tents at a distance, even 50 yards, from the theatre was tiresome and annoying, especially in a moonless period. It could be ridiculously easy to get lost in darkness "black as Egypt's night."'[111]

Rainfall, though rare, produced another test. Sudden winter storms could flood *wadis* and transform the neighbouring desert into a bog.[112] Hans von Luck recalled seeing a 'truck, with our field kitchen, which had failed to get out of the *wadi* fast enough' swept along by a sudden torrent for hundreds of yards. Once the water subsided, the sticky mud could challenge all movement. During the Axis retreat from the El Alamein position in 1942, a Panzer unit became stuck fast near Fuka, leaving no alternative but for their crews to abandon and destroy their precious armour. Simultaneously, it prevented the British in their pursuit of Axis troops hastily retreating west.

Drinking water was always scarce: 'One's thirst becomes almost unquenchable', Rommel complained.[113] A German officer's diary captured outside Tobruk asked: 'Where would you find anyone in Germany who would drink water of this colour and taste? It looks like coffee and tastes something like sulphur. But that is all to the good, otherwise it would stimulate one's thirst.'[114]

British censors commonly read of the shortage of water in soldiers' mail. Havildar Nila Kanten (5th Indian Brigade) cursed, 'why the hell are we fighting here!? Godforsaken place, no water, nothing.'[115] Tainted by chlorine, British troops frequently found their water contaminated with petrol, oil or the internal coating (paraffin wax, benzene or bitumen) lining containers, which tended to flake off and further foul the contents. Worse still, wells could be deliberately tainted with animal carcasses and rendered undrinkable.

Petrol was sometimes more abundant than water for British troops, who used the volatile fuel to cook with, even to wash clothes and equipment, though at a cost. 'The third time you washed your shirt in the petrol, the shirt disintegrated and disappeared entirely', a medical officer experienced.[116] British tin fuel containers, poorly constructed and known as 'flimsies', lost some thirty per cent of their contents between base and consumer. General Sir Claude Auchinleck acknowledged 'the deplorable wastage due to the rough desert going'.[117] Because of this, a special effort was made 'to salve as many as possible of the very efficient German petrol and water containers' before the Allies resorted to copying the *Wehrmacht-Einheitskanister*, a sturdy pressed-steel container we know as the 'Jerrycan'.[118]

Predictably, the appeal of the Orient soon waned. The immense open spaces and monotonous landscape, totally unlike anything in

Western Europe, proved psychologically challenging for many. Susan Travers, the only woman to serve in the French Foreign Legion, found the desert to be 'a severe shock to our system…the vast empty landscape that stretched to the horizon imposed its own psychological strain. Just finding one's way around was exhausting.'[119] To his dismay, Schraepler discovered a land 'definitely very much bleaker than I ever imagined.'[120] A German dispatch rider's first impression of North Africa after landing in October 1942 was 'frightful'.[121] Unteroffizier Kurt Martin (5th Panzer Regiment) marked his fourth day in the desert as 'terribly boring…all the time sandstorms and wind… We reach the stage where every movement is an effort.'[122] Not surprisingly then, Westphal observed a number of men suffering from 'severe attacks of homesickness'.[123]

British censors noted in July 1941 how the desert pushed men to almost the limit of 'physical and mental endurance', a state one individual described as 'desert lunacy'.[124] Undermining morale, Major John Devine (an Australian medical officer inside Tobruk) noted, were the unfamiliar privations, a 'monotony of the landscape, the food and the dust'. One British soldier's journal tells how

> for months now we've been cut off from nearly every aspect of civilised life, and every day has been cast in the same monotonous mould. The desert, omnipresent, so saturates consciousness that it makes the mind as sterile as itself. It's only now you realise how much you normally live through the senses. Here there's nothing for them. Nothing in the landscape to rest or distract the eye; nothing to hear, but roaring truck-engines; and nothing to smell but carbon exhaust-fumes and the reek of petrol.[125]

Both sides were equally tormented. 'To see the desert sprinkled with tanks, soldiers, tents, and lorries,' Major Alf Flatow (45th Royal Tank Regiment) bemoaned, 'was to see a hot Hades of flies, and sand and discomfort.' 'It was a wretched business,' Max Reisch, a DAK driver recalled, 'fighting the desert, the heat, the floods, other human beings, not to mention your own frayed nerves.'[126] But one had to be careful from expressing negative thoughts to family members back in Germany, Schraepler discovered:

the court martial has now sentenced to death a man, who in
a letter to his father, vehemently criticised the war... Who of
us, gripped by the heat of the climate, the sirocco, artillery
fire such as the members of the court martial have not seen,
has not expressed his feelings on this kind of war which is
not a war in a palm grove, in a letter, to feel better?[127]

'An ugly route with panic spreading like a bush fire'

The desert war unfolded quickly, 'so quickly,' Hans von Ravenstein, former
commander of the 21st Panzer Division, recalled, that both 'opponents were
amazingly ignorant of each other.'[128] Flawed intelligence featured in both
armies. German knowledge of the British was scant, a problem compounded
by the Italians' reluctance to share information and advice. Their maps, for
one, were panned for being so inaccurate and incomplete 'that they were
used only for lack of something better.'[129] As it stood, only a single captured
map was on hand to guide Rommel against the British forces in Cyrenaica,
leaving him unaware of the departure of the 7th Armoured Division, and
its less than capable replacement, the 2nd Armoured Division, plus the
transfer of Australian 6th Division to Greece.

British intelligence in Cairo, conversely, erred on 23 February in the
belief that 'there are no indications that the enemy intends to advance from
Tripolitania.'[130] Despite Ultra intelligence decrypts to the contrary, Wavell
did not foresee an enemy counterattack until the end of April 1941 at the
earliest. But, as he later admitted, this was the ideal moment for Rommel
to make his first move. Wavell's command was stretched thin by the need
to syphon off troops to Greece and undermined by O'Connor's absence
through illness. He entrusted the defence of Cyrenaica to Lieutenant
General Sir Philip Neame VC, a relative novice to both the desert and to
armoured warfare.[131] Although Wavell actually knew little of Neame, he was
impressed by his firm friendship with O'Connor, whom Wavell respected.

Neame's newly established Cyrenaica command comprised the
inexperienced, under-equipped and partially trained 9th Australian
Division plus Major General Michael Gambier-Parry's poorly equipped
2nd Armoured Division. The march from Egypt had taken its toll on
the division's armour, Cruiser tanks past their engine lives and beset
with mechanical troubles, plus captured Italian medium and light tanks.

This 'holding force' was expected to finish its training before engaging in any major operation.[132]

The first shots were exchanged on 24 February 1941 when a probing German patrol ambushed British armoured cars from the King's Dragoon Guards and a troop of anti-tank guns from 16th Australian Anti-Tank Company near the coastal town of El Agheila. Much to Gariboldi's horror, Rommel then pushed his motorised forces forward and seized Sirte, a 'shabby little Arab village of mud huts, clustered on the banks of a foul-smelling stream', with only limited resistance.[133] Grasping the initiative, Rommel again pushed east in earnest, driving the British front lines back some 700 kilometres from Tripoli. 'The advance of the English troops was stopped! A great success', Schraepler proudly penned.[134]

Wavell flew from Greece on 16 March to assess the situation – one that 'gave me increasing cause for anxiety' – unfolding in Libya.[135] He found Neame 'pessimistic and asking for all kinds of [unavailable] reinforcements'.[136] To his alarm, Neame's tactical dispositions were 'just crazy', for example, positioning the immobile Australian 20th Brigade (9th Division) on the open plain between El Agheila and Benghazi at the mercy of enemy armour with both flanks exposed.[137] General Leslie Morshead, the newly appointed commander of the Australian 9th Division, was grappling with the challenge of turning his composite formation of volunteers into a cohesive fighting unit, one that would fire its first shots against troops flushed with success from victories across Western Europe. Morshead also faced Neame's bias and vitriol over his troops' conduct at this crucial time: 'Your Division will never be a useful instrument of war unless and until you can enforce discipline on a mob', he wrote, 'prone to instances of drunkenness.'[138]

'Anxious and depressed', Wavell returned to Greece to oversee the British expeditionary force, his primary task at this time.[139] At the end of March he sent Neame his only available reinforcements – the 3rd Indian Motor Brigade. He also hoped to send at least part of an Indian Division from East Africa once the campaign against the Italians had ended.

Despite evidence to the contrary, both Wavell and Air Marshal Arthur Tedder, C-in-C Allied Air Forces in the Mediterranean, believed that Rommel posed no serious threat to Egypt. Rather it was assumed that his actions were a part of a major, well-timed diversion preceding a new Balkans offensive. Wavell rejected intelligence warnings to the contrary as 'far from conclusive'.[140] He was no doubt reassured by an intelligence report tabled on 24 March 1941 that foresaw an enemy advance impossible before the first week in April, and then only via the coastal roads.[141] A follow-up report on 30 March similarly concluded that no evidence existed of a large scale Axis operation in the near future.[142]

Rommel meanwhile flew to Berlin on 18 March, leaving orders for an operation against El Agheila to kick off a week later. Meeting with Hitler, he received the prestigious Oak Leaves to his *Ritterkreuz* (Knight's Cross) for his actions during the French campaign. He afterwards explained to the Führer how the British were withdrawing and setting up a new Agedabia – Marsa el Brega defensive line. This was the ideal moment, he enthused, to strike. His request for additional reinforcements, however, was refused with the warning not to strike a 'decisive blow' until adequate forces became available.[143] German intervention in Libya was, after all, a defensive sideshow against a much broader strategic backdrop. Furthermore, he was ordered not to undertake further offensive operations until the arrival of the 15th Panzer Division in May.

Back in Libya, Rommel rallied his so-called 'Afrikaners' forward to occupy El Agheila, which they reached on 24 March. Unfortunately, as Schraepler noted, the 'English had escaped'.[144]

From the other side of the hill, Private James Witte (160th Light Anti-Aircraft Battery, Royal Artillery) found the British withdrawal, essentially without a fight, an 'ugly route with panic spreading like a bush fire'.[145] Here was an indication that Wavell would not put up any serious resistance to defend Cyrenaica. It heartened the Axis and alarmed Churchill. The British premier duly cabled his C-in-C to enquire, 'I presume you are only waiting for the tortoise to stick his head out far enough before chopping it off.'[146]

Scaling the observation tower at El Agheila's ancient citadel, Rommel signalled his next objective – the small coastal village of Mersa el Brega. Troops and supplies were brought forward, giving him, by 30 March, some 9,300 German and 37,000 Italian troops and over 200 tanks. The British were forced to retire the next day after a fierce and heroic battle. Brigadier John Combe (11th Hussars) afterwards found Brigadier Gordon Rimington (commander of the 3rd Armoured Brigade) 'sitting in his staff car crying with his head in his hands.'[147]

Though Rommel had clearly exceeded his brief, success was his. 'Berated violently' by Gariboldi for contravening orders and neglecting his exposed lines of communication, he had no intention of 'allowing good opportunities to slip by unused.'[148] In the midst of a heated argument, a communiqué arrived from Berlin. Rommel disingenuously declared that it announced 'complete freedom of action'.[149] In actual fact, the signal underscored other major Axis commitments, warned of the delayed movement of the 15th Panzer Division, and prohibited further action unless it was established 'beyond any doubt that the enemy is withdrawing most of his mobile units from Cyrenaica.'[150]

Rommel now began a full-scale offensive. Discarding conventional wisdom, he divided his combined Italo-German force into four columns, which were to race across the protruding portion of the Cyrenaican coast, known to Allied soldiers as 'The Bulge', in chase of the retreating British. In the midst of the sudden Axis advance, Wavell added to the escalating confusion by issuing orders and counter-orders that frequently were received too late. He also recalled O'Connor (with Churchill's prodding) to replace Neame. Still in poor health, O'Connor was reluctant to succeed a personal friend and preferred to remain as his liaison officer. 'I cannot pretend I was happy', he later wrote, 'at the thought of taking over command in the middle of a battle, which was already lost.'[151] Both senior officers, however, continued to issue orders from the field, hampering an increasingly muddled situation.

As his Panzer regiment lumbered east, Leutnant Schorm observed 'scattered Arab camps'. He was unimpressed by these Bedouin 'rogues', who 'robbed wounded British soldiers down to their shirts and left them helpless in the cold. I am sure they would do the same to us too. At the roadside are masses of Italian lorries abandoned in their [earlier] flight.'[152]

Benghazi fell to German troops on 3 April. Schraepler noted 'the great joy of the inhabitants…expressing their joy by getting drunk. The soldiers were covered in flowers.'[153] British setbacks continued. On the night of 6 April, a detachment of troops from Oberstleutnant Gustav Ponath's 8th Machine Gun Battalion pulled over two British staff cars scurrying east in darkness towards Derna. Inside were Generals Neame, O'Connor and John Combe. Neame recalled his capture:

> I was awakened from a doze by armed Germans opening
> the doors of the car and shouting at us, "Auf! Auf!"… We
> were herded into the centre of a laager…and kept there in
> the bitter desert cold until dawn.[154]

To O'Connor it was 'a great shock… [being] miles behind our own front, and by sheer bad luck we drove into the one bit of desert in which the Germans had sent around a reconnaissance group and we went bang into the middle of them.'[155] Dismayed by the loss one of Britain finest desert generals, Wavell assigned Major General John Lavarack, his only available senior officer, to take charge of Cyrenaica Command. One of Lavarack's first decisions was to defend Tobruk. The fortress's reputation – even at this early point in the war – weighed heavily on his mind. On the grounds of prestige alone he demanded that if 'Tobruk could be regarded as even only possibly defensible, it should be held.'[156]

Mechili was Rommel's next objective. Gambier-Parry's 2nd Armoured Division had fallen back to the former Ottoman fortress, losing most of its tanks in the withdrawal through breakdowns and lack of fuel, where it joined the 3rd Indian Motor Brigade, 3rd Australian Anti-Tank Regiment and the 3rd Royal Horse Artillery (RHA) Anti-Tank Regiment. In his approach, Rolf Krengel (3rd Reconnaissance Battalion) was caught in a 'firefight' with Australian troops on 4 April. One of his fellow soldiers was killed 'by a bullet to the head', two more were wounded. Krengel received 'some tiny bits of shrapnel in my hand but nothing serious.'[157]

Rommel's original plan to storm Mechili on 6 April was delayed while Johannes Streich's tanks negotiated the stony desert terrain and refuelled. An argument erupted after the divisional commander refused to attack since many of his vehicles had broken down during the long march from Tripoli. Losing his temper, Rommel accused his general of cowardliness. Enraged, Streich tore the Knight's Cross from around his neck, shouting at Rommel for his remark to be withdrawn and threatening to throw the medal at his feet. A half-hearted apology followed.

As an aside, an Italian private in conversation with a German soldier, asked about the number of operational Panzers on hand. 'And he said, "Tell me the truth – how many working you have now still?" And he said, "This morning we report 7 but the truth is" he whispered in my ear, "we have 16" – but if Rommel knows that, he attacks immediately.'[158]

Impudent demands for Mechili to surrender were 'treated with contempt', Wavell later wrote.[159] After the remnants of the 3rd Armoured Brigade failed to arrive in support, orders were issued for the defending troops to retire to El Adem, south of Tobruk. Despite heavy artillery and machine-gun fire, elements of the 1st RHA, some Indian troops and Australian anti-tank gunners slipped through the Axis cordon. The remainder of the British defenders, including the headquarters of the 2nd Armoured Division, surrendered to Major General Pietro Zaglio (Italian 17th Pavia Infantry Division) on 8 April. Rommel was delighted by the 'coup' – a windfall of some 3,000 prisoners, including Major General M.D. Gambier-Parry, together with an invaluable stockpile of vehicles and equipment. Among the spoils were three British 4 x 4 AEC 'Dorchester' command trucks that were immediately pressed into service. The German general also spied a pair of British anti-gas goggles (officially Eyeshields, Anti-Gas, Mk I). 'Booty – permissible, I take it, even for a General', he remarked, placing them over the rim of his peaked officer's cap.[160]

Frank Sharp (Australian 3rd Anti-Tank Regiment), a decorated First World War veteran, and his son Keith were both captured at Mechili. In a magnanimous exchange, a German officer surprised Frank: 'I am sorry to be taking prisoner a man of your age.' Irreverently promising to buy his captor a beer after the war had been won, the pair would indeed meet after the war when the former enemy located Frank in Australia for the promised beverage.[161]

Rommel could boast how that the British 'troops were taken completely by surprise and probably were deceived as to our true strength.'[162] However, Mechili had come at a cost. Consolidating his forces had provided the window of opportunity needed for retreating British forces along the coast to withdraw into Tobruk. At one point Axis forward troops were only 48 miles south of the port of Derna, while most of the retreating Australian troops from 20th and 26th Brigades (9th Division) were still perilously one hundred miles west of Tobruk, devoid of armour, artillery and anti-tank guns. Their transport, much of it captured from the Italians, was practically unserviceable. A northerly thrust to the coast road at this point by Rommel may well have been disastrous.

*****

Albert Handscombe, a wireless operator in the Tower Hamlets Rifles, was sitting in a truck beside the driver outside Derna when a German tank appeared. Suddenly, and without warning, his vehicle was rocked by a 'tremendous crash... I got myself together and looked across the road to see if I could do anything for my pal, but he was beyond recognition. The cab was demolished... I could see troops withdrawing all round me. I fell in with other chaps from all regiments. So we made for the nearest town, which was Tobruk.'[163]

Having retaken Cyrenaica – an achievement as impressive and even more rapid than O'Connor's recent conquest – Rommel was also headed for Tobruk.

Chapter Two

Thwarted by Rats

Old Jerry soon besieged us and began to treat us rough,
He dropped a kindly hint or two as to how soon we would cop it.
Advising us to turn it in, forget the war and hop it.

–Anon

Rommel now posed an even greater threat to Egypt. As his columns closed on Tobruk, Churchill, in conjunction with his chiefs of staff, cited its strategic location to convince Wavell of the wisdom in keeping it. After meeting with Anthony Eden, the Middle East C-in-Cs, Admiral Andrew Cunningham and Air Chief Marshal Longmore on the afternoon of 6 April in Cairo, Wavell agreed to hold Tobruk for two months. This was ample time for armoured reinforcements to arrive from Egypt to mount a new counter-offensive. Retaining Tobruk would also keep the enemy at bay and frustrate Luftwaffe bombers from targeting the British fleet at Alexandria. Churchill, who was already questioning Wavell's appropriateness as C-in-C, pressed him – Tobruk was 'a place to be held to the death without thought of retirement.'[1]

'A poor place to defend, with an extended perimeter'

9 April 1941. The final runners in the colloquially named 'Benghazi Handicap' or 'Tobruk Derby' withdrew into Tobruk under cover of a *khamsin*. Here they would finally stand and fight – news that was especially welcomed by the Australian infantry. Unaware of the circumstances behind their withdrawal, as an army chaplain noted, 'many of the men were inclined to criticise in frank and lurid language the action of the higher command.'[2] Frustrated by the flight east, Sergeant F.H. Legg (2/48th Battalion) arrived:

[in a] pretty poor state. For eight days and nights we'd been out in the desert on the move (chiefly in the wrong direction) and always on the verge of action but always denied the opportunity of having a go. We'd experienced our first taste of bombing and shelling. We'd had our first casualties, but most of us hadn't struck a blow.[3]

Axis forces, in the meantime, were closing. Unteroffizier Kurt Martin was in the vanguard.

The advance continues. We are on the enemy's heels. Suddenly, our engine fails. Every attempt to get it going again is in vain. We just have to stay where we are. For the first time, we realise how much stuff is moving forward. More and more troops pass us.[4]

Within his new headquarters, Morshead instructed his senior officers to stand their ground: 'There'll be no Dunkirk here. If we should have to get out, we shall fight our way out. There is to be no surrender and no retreat.'[5]

But could Tobruk, which only months earlier had fallen to Mackay's Australian 6th Division, withstand Rommel? Wavell relayed his concern to both the Australian and British High Commands: 'Tobruk is not a good defensive position. [Its] Long line of communication behind is hardly protected at all and [it] is unorganised.'[6] Major General John Kennedy, British Director of Military Operations, also found Churchill's assessment 'absolutely wrong', adding: 'We should not dictate strategy and tactics from London to a commander in the field... Holding Tobruk would be like letting go the anchor of a battleship in the midst of a naval battle.' A better course, he suggested, would be for the British to fall back, 'as we did originally with the Italians', wait for Rommel to become over-extended and then 'fall upon him'.[7]

Meanwhile, the atmosphere in Whitehall grew increasingly tense. Kennedy noted that General Sir John Dill, Chief of the Imperial General Staff (CIGS), a proponent of defending Tobruk, was 'so tired mentally that he could not concentrate on the papers for the Cabinet, and more than once he asked irrelevant questions as we discussed them.'[8] Sensing another military disaster, Australian Prime Minister Robert Menzies slated Wavell for grossly underestimating the capacity of German armoured divisions. He too challenged the decision, arguing that Tobruk was 'a poor place to defend, with an extended perimeter'.[9] Visiting London to discuss the defence of Singapore, Menzies was concerned over Australian divisions serving under Wavell's command, Britain's military leadership, even Churchill's fitness for leadership – a topic, as we shall see, which reappeared in June 1942.[10]

Surrounded by open desert, Tobruk was far from a natural or flawless citadel. Italian engineers had laboured to construct a lengthy outer defensive arc stretching for twenty-eight miles. Steep wadis bookended the eastern and western sides. The 'piecrust' perimeter comprised minefields, an anti-tank ditch and two concentric rows of concrete perimeter positions. The outer ring of posts, 600 to 800 yards apart, enclosed a second line of mutually supporting posts 500 yards behind. Sequentially numbered, each of the 128 defensive posts contained three circular pits for automatic and anti-tank weapons. Each post was self-contained with an all-round field of fire. Flush with the surrounding terrain, the posts were interconnected by subterranean passages with living and storage facilities.

A typical post was manned by fourteen troops with a captured Cannone da 47/32 mod. 1935 47mm anti-tank gun, three machine guns (two captured), a Boys anti-tank rifle and a Thompson sub-machine gun. Improved by digging alternate positions and communications trenches, few men could actually fight from the weapons pits. Although well protected against shellfire, the Australians were quick to condemn the posts as 'death traps'.[11] Captain Vernon Northwood (2/28th Infantry Battalion) was equally critical.

> We are now living in a concrete fortification built by the Italians in 1936… The whole of this dugout is below ground level. The passages would, I suppose, be about 50 yards long, with bays forming off-shoots and a central control post. All of these posts are modelled on the same pattern. Though they might be good shelters and some protection against shelling and divebombing, I don't like them. I certainly think 'dugoutitis' (if I may coin such a word) has bred in the Italian a preference for staying below rather than coming up to fight. We don't intend to be caught the same way.[12]

The new occupants were disgusted to find the underground shelters abandoned with the 'filth and squalor – mute, if unpleasant evidence, of the unhygienic habits of the recently departed Italian soldiery.'[13] Engineer field companies faced the grisly task of battlefield clearance. John Flak (2/4th Field Company) explored the posts.

> The grey concrete walls of a passageway of one was heavily sprayed with blackened blood; in the next post, the floor of a passage leading to a bunker was awash with a soup of putrefaction, in all probably human… As I prowled the passages linking one firing point to another, I became aware of a heavy offensive odour… On the bed lay an Italian soldier in an advanced stage of decomposition. He had no face. It appeared to have melted, but a hastily struck second match revealed a seething wall of maggots.[14]

Frank Perversi (2/32nd Battalion) was struck by the 'all-pervading characteristic smell of the long dead, and of dried excreta. Big rats with light coloured hair, like fur, were everywhere visible during daylight hours.'[15]

Strengthened with new minefields, the outer perimeter posts formed the *Red Line*. A second defensive zone – the *Blue Line* – was constructed over time some 4,000 yards inside the perimeter to provide defence in depth.[16] Inside the perimeter, the terrain steps down to the harbour in a series of terraces. The highest point was a small peak, known variously as Ras el Medauuar, Hill 209, or Fort Lloyd in the southwest corner.[17] A third and final defensive line – the *Green Line* – was eventually built roughly two miles from the harbour as a 'last resort' line of defence should evacuation by sea arise.

Morshead's garrison at this time numbered 35,307 men including non-combatant, RN and RAF personnel. The primary formation was the 9th Australian Division, supported by the 1st Royal Northumberland Fusiliers Machine Gun Battalion, the 1st, 104th, and 107th Regiments of the RHA, 39th and 40th Light Anti-Aircraft Batteries and the 51st Field Regiment. A scratch force of armour made up of the 3rd Armoured Brigade and the recently arrived 1st Royal Tank Regiment (RTR) numbered six Cruiser tanks, twenty obsolete light tanks and four Matilda tanks.[18]

Many of the raw Australian troops now received hurried instructions in the fundamentals of combat. Basic weapons training included how to throw a 'live' hand grenade and grasping its lethal radius. Accidents could be horrific. The *British Medical Journal* (August 1943) reported that 'a grenade exploding in the hand causes the most ghastly wounds… One or both hands are blown off or mutilated; the face is spattered and the sight of one or both eyes is destroyed. Life continues and the patient recovers, but without hands or sight.'[19]

Marksmanship was practised by taking pot shots at tin cans; instructions were given how to disable an enemy tank by using a heavy iron bar to jam the tracks.

Hurricane fighters of RAF No. 73 Squadron joined No. 6 Squadron (Hurricanes and Lysander tactical reconnaissance aircraft) at El Gubbi, one of four landing grounds within the fortress. As Rommel's noose tightened, the Hurricanes were invaluable in ground strafing approaching enemy transport. Watching on, war correspondent Jan Yindrich reported RAF fighters 'roaring down the truckloads of infantry, machine-gunning them from 50 feet and scattering the entire convoy.'[20]

'All sorts of rumours are flying'

8 April. Private Frank McGillvray (2/28th Battalion, 9th Division) spent the day unfurling barbed wire and building barricades. 'All sorts of rumours are flying,' he penned in his diary, 'too numerous and fantastic to write.'[21]

Rommel's coalition army reached Tobruk's southern perimeter two days later. It comprised the German 5th Light Division, advance elements of 15th Panzer Division, Italian 132nd Ariete armoured division and 102nd Trento and 27th Brescia motorised infantry divisions. The rapid desert march, however, had taken a heavy toll on the tanks. A report from the 5th Panzer Regiment specified the nature and extent of the damage: 'The cylinders and the pistons were worn up to six millimetres. Out of the eighty-three disabled tanks, the maintenance company swapped out the engines in fifty-eight vehicles.'[22]

Rommel, characteristically, was eager to strike his first blow. Aerial reconnaissance revealed a large force inside Tobruk and several ships in the harbour (disembarking the infantry of the Australian 18th Brigade). Perhaps Rommel sensed an opportunity similar to the 1940 French campaign, when he seized the Channel port of Saint-Valéry-en-Caux, netting 12,000 British and French prisoners – his greatest victory to date. 'I am convinced that the enemy is giving way before us', he wrote. 'We must pursue him with all our forces. Our objective, which is to be known to all troops, is the Suez Canal.'[23]

In the meantime, Jack Barber's platoon (2/17th Battalion) established itself at Post R13.

> We were far too tired to be superstitious about the number. And, tired as we were, we knew there were supposed to be important duties to perform before we could allow ourselves the luxury of sleep... There was a listening post to be manned and guards to be set, two hours on and four hours off, and we stood-to at dawn, ready if we were attacked, but the first hour of daylight passed without incident.[24]

Staring ahead into the unknown, Jack and his fellow infantrymen watched and waited. When and where would Rommel attack?

The men of the 2/28th Battalion observed an enemy column approaching along the Derna road. Quick to act, sappers demolished a bridge while the so-called 'bush artillery' made its debut. Schooled by bemused British artillerymen, the amateur Australian gunners brought their captured Italian 75-mm and 105-mm guns to bear. Lacking sights and crudely aimed by looking through the barrel and adjusting the fall through trial and error, the aberrant shelling nevertheless forced the leading vehicles to abruptly retire.[25]

Another bush battery later joined with the 25-pounders of the British 51st Field Regiment to repel another German column, in the process killing (posthumously promoted) Generalleutnant Heinrich von Prittwitz und Gaffron, the recently arrived commander of the 15th Panzer Division. Rommel also came close to becoming a casualty the next day. Stopping to talk with a group of soldiers taking up position, as Schmidt described, 'a salvo of enemy shells fell among us.'[26] A young Leutnant was killed, another officer lost an arm.

Along the southern perimeter, the 2/13th Battalion forced probing enemy infantry to retire. Desultory fire was exchanged along the western perimeter throughout the afternoon and into the night as Axis forces assembled outside the wire – the Italians alongside the western perimeter sector, the Germans in the south. With the fortress invested, Rommel urged Streich to 'attack Tobruk with everything we have… before Tommy has time to dig in.'[27]

'Scores of German graves, marked by crosses dated 11 April'

'And so, what does Tobruk mean to us? Oberleutnant Harald Kuhn (5th Panzer Regiment) asked. 'We will overrun it, just like we did Bengasi and Derna.'[28]

Rommel launched his first assault on Good Friday, 11 April. The German 8th Machine Gun Battalion joined Italian tanks and 25 Panzers and 10 Panzerjäger I tank destroyers that had survived the long march. Confidence was running high in the German camp with reports that the garrison would easily retire, its morale sapped by a lack of artillery and armour.

With the prize of Tobruk seemingly within their grasp, the Italo-German force rushed blindly forward towards a sector of the south-eastern perimeter manned by Brigadier John Murray's 20th Brigade. Unexpectedly strong resistance, particularly from the garrison's artillery, forced the infantry to ground. The chain of 'hidden' defensive emplacements was also an unwelcome surprise. The 'desert spread out in front of us, grey yellow and dead', Oberleutnant Kuhn observed, but 'there were countless eyes hidden there, along with firing batteries. How was that possible? Dust and dirt swirled around us and made it impossible to identify neighbouring vehicles.'[29] Furthermore, as Oberstleutnant Dr. Ing. Herbert Olbrich (5th Panzer Regiment) explained, the Panzers were 'unexpectedly held up by an impassable anti-tank trench'.[30]

Captured anti-tank guns operated by the 2/13th Battalion's mortar platoon engaged the enemy tanks as did Cruiser tanks of the 1st RTR. In the first skirmish Rommel lost seven tanks, Morshead two. Independent of their luckless armour, German infantry now moved forward. Major J.W. Balfe (2/17th Battalion) witnessed the one-sided engagement.

> About 700 of them advanced almost shoulder to shoulder. The RHA let them have it again, but, even though some of the shells fell right among them, they still came on. In later months our patrols in no-man's-land found scores of German graves, marked by crosses dated 11 April.[31]

35

Schraepler afterwards reflected on the bewildering pasting:

> The English artillery shot heavily on us, Rommel,
> [Oberstleutnant i.G.] von dem Borne and I were quite
> surprised about the resistance. Our strategy was not good in
> general, because I believe that the tanks were not aggressive
> enough. If they had attacked aggressively, Tobruk would
> have fallen... I am surprised that Rommel stayed calm.
> I know him well and would have expected otherwise. Many
> vehicles remained entrenched, simply accepting the strong
> artillery fire.[32]

Chronicled in the DAK war diary as a 'reconnaissance advance', the
first Axis push stood in stark contrast to Major General Iven Mackay's
meticulously planned assault three months earlier.

Enemy tanks unsuccessfully reconnoitred the perimeter later that
night in search of a suitable crossing point. Confidence in the DAK
remained unbroken; Schraepler imagined the memo he would write
announcing Tobruk's surrender.

The next day German snipers targeted garrison anti-tank guns
brought forward to meet the invaders. Clouds of dust several miles
distant, the tell-tale sign of massing enemy transport, were brutally
targeted by RHA gunners and RAF Blenheim bombers. No assault
eventuated and twelve approaching tanks were later repulsed by the
newly sited anti-tank guns. Kuhn's frustration grew: 'We need more
here than being cheeky and a sense of superiority. We are in need of
systematic reconnaissance and well-planned employment in view of
our modest means.'[33]

Beside bombs, propaganda leaflets were dropped on Tobruk urging
the garrison to surrender – 'it is useless to try and escape' – much to
the amusement of the troops, who pocketed them as prized souvenirs.
Such leaflets, Major John Devine observed, 'soon sold for £2 each,
and when last quoted were still rising, with buyers exceeding sellers.
It was even seriously suggested that the enemy be asked to speed up
production and drop more.'[34]

Tobruk was shrouded in clouds of swirling dust on the morning of
13 April. The garrison's artillery 'had a crack' at German motorcycles
and staff cars some 2,000 yards distant, registering several hits.[35]

Unperturbed, Axis tanks and infantry again approached the perimeter in the afternoon. Once again the garrison's artillery fire halted the progress of some three hundred vehicles reported south of the perimeter. The DAK war diary ascribed the failure of the 'reconnaissance raid' to the 'anti-tank ditch and wire'.[36]

Concerted mortar and machine gun fire preceded an attack that night, the largest so far, against the posts Major Balfe's company manned. Approximately thirty German soldiers successfully breached the barbed wire entanglements, bringing forward machine guns, mortars and light field guns. With small arms fire failing to dislodge the dug-in enemy, Lieutenant Austin Mackell (platoon commander in Post 33) took the initiative. With bayonets fixed, he led six men in a surprise flanking attack. 'We charged and yelled, but for a moment or two the Germans turned everything onto us. It's amazing', Mackell later described, 'that we weren't all hit. As we ran, we threw our grenades and when they burst the German fire stopped.'[37] Even though Corporal John 'Jack' Edmondson was mortally wounded in the neck and stomach, he continued to charge the panicked enemy. Bayoneting one German, he raced to help Mackell, who was wrestling an assailant on the desert floor. Another German soldier appeared brandishing a pistol. Edmondson bayonetted both, and 'at least one more', before collapsing. Helped back to Post 33, he died the following morning.[38] An Australian sergeant continues the narrative: 'Those enemy who escaped were driven back through the wire. But for this they would probably have surrounded our post and with their superior numbers made a wide gap in our defences. As it was they didn't make another push for several hours.'[39]

'The casualties were horrific'

14 April. Rommel remained optimistic. 'Today may well see the end of the Battle of Tobruk,' he advised 'Dearest Lu'.[40] His straightforward plan involved two battalions of thirty-eight tanks breaching the perimeter from the southeast. The 8th Machine Gun Battalion would shadow the armour. Once a foothold was established, the first wave of German tanks would drive towards the harbour; the second wave would 'pursue the enemy' while the Ariete division exploited the breakthrough.

Morshead's defensive plan was simple – his Red Line infantry were to avoid all contact with the approaching enemy tanks. Only once the tanks had passed would the perimeter posts engage oncoming infantry.

Airburst shells from German 8.8 cm Flak guns preceded the assault. It soon floundered. Concentrated artillery fire annihilated German machine-gunners riding on the tanks. Then at 0520 the first fifteen Panzers, some towing anti-aircraft or anti-tank guns, emerged through a perimeter breach close to Mackell's post. A German Leutnant recounted:

> We begin storming Tobruk. With the least possible noise, the battalions move off, with their cars completely blacked out. It is bitterly cold. Of course, the enemy recognises us because of the noise... Soon, artillery fire starts up on us, getting the range. The shells explode like fireworks. We travel 10 km, every nerve on edge.[41]

Wheeling east inside the perimeter, the German armour was targeted by the Australian 2/3rd Anti-Tank Regiment's gun, the RHA, and the 2-pounder guns of the promptly deployed 1st RTR Cruiser tanks.[42] As they had done in France and Poland, the heavier Panzer IIIs and IVs closed in tight formation, stopping to fire while the lighter tanks provided continuous cannon and machine-gun fire. British 25-pounder gunners firing over open sights soon destroyed five enemy tanks; Australian anti-tank gunners disabled another two. The perimeter infantry now emerged to engage the unarmoured enemy reinforcements advancing on foot. Numerous German dead were later found in hollows between the perimeter posts. Major Ernst-Otto Ballerstedt (115th Motorised Infantry Regiment) later reported:

> The Australians, who are the men our troops have had opposite them so far, are extraordinarily tough fighters. The German is more active in the attack but the enemy stakes his life in the defence and fights to the last with extreme cunning. Our men, usually easy-going and unsuspecting, fall easily into his traps, especially as a result of their experiences in...the Western Campaign. The Australian is unquestionably superior to the German soldier:

(i)   in the use of individual weapons, especially as snipers,
(ii) in the use of ground camouflage,
(iii) in his gift of observation, and the drawing of the correct conclusions from his observation,
(iv) in every means of taking us by surprise…

The enemy allows isolated individuals to come right up to his positions, then fires on them.

Enemy snipers have astounding results. They shoot at anything they recognise. Several NCOs of the battalion have been shot through the head with the first shot while making observation in the front line. Protruding sights in gun directors have been shot off.[43]

Leutnant Schorm's Panzer, number 625, was in the thick of the fighting.

We must, of course, regulate our speed with that of the infantry. Thus, the enemy has time to prepare resistance. As the darkness lifts, so the enemy strikes us harder... Our heavy Panzers fire for all they are worth…but the enemy, with his superior forces and all his tactical advantages on his own ground, blasts large gaps in our ranks... Some of our Panzers are already on fire…. English anti-tank units fall upon us with their machine guns firing into our midst. But we have no time... Above us, Italian fighters come into the fray. Two of them crash in our midst. The optical instruments are spoiled by the dust. Nevertheless, I get several unmistakable hits. A few anti-tank guns are silenced, several enemy tanks are burning. Just then we are hit, and the radio is smashed to bits. Now our communications are cut off. What is more, our ammunition is running out.[44]

Under a hail of fire from all sides, the Panzers veered east where they clashed with several Matildas – a tank held in high regard by the Germans after first encountering them in the 1940 French campaign. 'Retire!' Exasperated Panzer crews and accompanying infantry now hurried to flee from what Schorm termed a 'Witches' Cauldron'. 'Our attack is fading out. From every side, the enemy's superior forces fire at us', Schorm later recounted. Now in full retreat,

> the lane is in sight. Everything hastens towards it. English anti-tank guns shoot into the mass… We drive by instinct. The tank almost gets stuck in the two ditches, blocking the road; but manages to extricate itself with great difficulty. With their last reserves of power, the crew gets out of range and returns to camp.[45]

The withdrawing tanks ran chaotically into the path of an oncoming second wave. Several collisions occurred. 'Could Hell be any worse?', Oberleutnant Kuhn wondered.

> A large portion of our vehicles were on fire; a few were still moving about and firing, on fire themselves. It was a terrible, unforgettable picture!… It seemed to take forever until we fought our way back… Among the tanks that returned there was not a single one that did not bring considerable scars with it. Shocked, we determined how many of our comrades were missing. The casualties were horrific. A few tears left their traces in the grey, encrusted faces…the old vets from the First War claimed they had never experienced a blacker day. The younger ones believed them.[46]

The result of Rommel's largest attack to date was a total rout. An Australian sergeant summed it up from the defenders' perspective:

> About forty tanks went through and then we came up and engaged the German infantry and gunners who were trying to bring their guns through the gap. These were easy meat. We shot up their crews before they could get into action, and every time the infantry tried to get through the gap we drove them back with Bren guns and no infantry got past… the Jerries got their worst hiding they'd had to that time.[47]

While the German tanks were fighting their way out, an aerial armada of forty Junkers Ju 87 dive-bombers and Messerschmitt fighters appeared over the harbour to deliver the intended *coup de grâce*. Instead Tobruk's remaining Hurricane fighters shot down six aircraft; the ack-ack (anti-aircraft artillery) accounted for another four.

Marooned on the battlefield, the German machine gunners fought bravely until their ammunition was exhausted. Fighting had ceased by 0830. Gustav Ponath and 110 of his men were killed, a further 254 were taken prisoner. Stunned by the defeat, 'I was not the only one with tears in my eyes,' Oberfeldwebel Rudolph Liessmann (8th Machine Gun Battalion) wrote. And 'we did not need to be ashamed of it... Our march to Tobruk continued, but as prisoners of war.'[48]

Hoping to make contact with the isolated German machine-gunners, Rommel ordered the Ariete Division to move forward into the sector south of Ras el Medauuar. On the receiving end of the garrison's artillery, the Italians 'broke up in complete disorder, turned tail' and fled south in several directions.[49] The central role played by the British artillery (under Brigadier L.F. Thompson) was commended in a contemporary report as an 'outstanding feature' of Tobruck's defence.[50] A German prisoner agreed: 'If only we had artillery to reply to yours, but now it is just a question of holding on after every salvo from the Tommies.'[51] Even President Franklin D. Roosevelt received word of captured enemy soldiers 'badly shaken' by Tobruk's firepower.[52]

Having fought across Poland and Western Europe, Schorm reflected that this 'was the most severely fought battle of the whole war.'[53] Shattered, Olbrich tallied up his losses from within the 'Hell of Tobruk':

38 tanks went into battle
17 tanks destroyed by the enemy
2 officers are missing and 7 wounded
21 N.C.Os and men are missing
10 N.C.Os and men are wounded; this means a total loss of 50 per cent.[54]

The striking victory cost Morshead just twenty-six men killed and sixty-four wounded. Two cruiser tanks were destroyed and two Hurricanes were shot down. 'Bravo Tobruk!' Churchill cabled.[55]

Tobruk had survived its first real test. Robert Low of *Liberty* magazine examined a German tank, seemingly undamaged. The 'Aussie' sitting on the turret explained its demise:

If you walk around to the other side, you'll see a piece of angle iron stuck in the track. I just lay doggo in my little trench over there till she came right up close. Then I jumped up and ran toward her blind spot and jammed the iron bar between the wheels. Then I shouted to them to come out waving white handkerchiefs… But they didn't want to get out. So, I crawled around to the back and tossed a hand grenade in through the exhaust hatch.[56]

A brief respite in the fighting saw Jack Barber assigned to a burial detail. Returning to the scene of earlier carnage, he recalled

…picking up the bodies that were spread over a large area… This wasn't a pleasant task, as we recognised many of the men we were loading into the vehicle… It was also unpleasant bringing in the German dead. Apart from the uniforms they looked just like us. A lot of them had been killed by small arms fire, but the RHA accounted for quite a number.[57]

Protestations from Streich and Olbrich prevented a follow-up attack. Notwithstanding Tobruk's staunch resistance, reproaches and recriminations followed beyond the wire. 'Impatient and unsympathetic', a furious Rommel castigated his two senior officers for 'lacking resolution'.[58] Excusing himself from any culpability, Rommel criticised the 5th Light Division for having 'lost confidence in itself and being unwarrantedly pessimistic about' his plan. Moreover, it had 'not mastered the art of concentrating its strength at one point, forcing a break-through, rolling up and securing the flanks on either side, and then penetrating like lightning', before the enemy could react.[59] The Italian soldier's fighting qualities were also called into question. Schraepler derisively noted in his diary how the 'brave Italian soldiers just run away and cannot be held back once shots are fired.'[60] Finally, Rommel censured his allies for withholding intelligence about Tobruk's fixed defences, which 'stretched much farther in all directions, west, east and south, than we had imagined.'[61] Olbrich concurred, since his men 'had not the slightest idea of the well-designed and constructed defences nor of a single battery position nor of the awful number of anti-tank guns. Nor was it was known that he had heavy tanks.'[62]

Back in Germany, Generaloberst Franz Halder noted critically that Rommel's push towards Suez was an operation that could only be staged as a raid, with 'neither the troops nor the supply facilities' to hold it.[63]

'What Tommy must think of us!'

15 April. Major Hohman (5th Panzer Regiment): 'At 0700 hrs the [garrison] artillery started off again, and the bombers began playing their nasty game.'[64] This time Rommel would pitt the Italians against the western perimeter defences. Schorm grumbled, 'I wish they would drop it; otherwise we shall have to give them half our clothes and rations again.'[65]

Shortly after dawn a party of Italians appeared before the 2/48th Battalion, only to be rebuffed by Bren gun fire. Throughout the morning, the guns of the 51st Field Regiment drove off new enemy groups approaching the perimeter. The largest assault came at 1730 when a thousand Italian troops penetrated the outer wire and overran a perimeter post. Automatic fire from 2/24th Battalion however held the Italians to ground, while a company from the 2/23rd Battalion counterattacked. Within an hour the incursion had been blunted; the only Italians still inside the wire were the dead and 113 men taken prisoner.

In the wake of this latest defeat, Hohmann logged: 'what Tommy must think of us!'[66]

Rommel's misfortune continued at sea where RN destroyers sank an entire Italian convoy transporting much of the 15th Panzer Division. An additional blow came on the morning of 19 April when HM battleships *Warspite*, *Barham*, *Valiant* and *Gloucester* blasted Tripoli's harbour, sinking another five merchantmen. Besides the enormous task of supplying his troops, Rommel's army now occupied a vast geographical area, albeit one of scant return. No decisive battle had been fought and no strategically vital location had been taken. Stalled at Tobruk and unable to push ahead through the frontier, an increasingly intolerant German High Command – whose attention was fixed firmly on the forthcoming invasion of the Soviet Union – refused to send reinforcements.

'Like so many sheep'

16 April. Rommel misguidedly clung to the notion that Tobruk was being evacuated. He crowed in a letter home that his small force had achieved a 'tremendous amount' with the fortress expected to fall 'shortly'.[67] A renewed attempt to capture Ras el Medauuar was undertaken by

elements of the Ariete and Trento Divisions plus several German companies. Forewarned by Cairo intelligence analysts, the garrison was prepared for the 'half-hearted' attack. British artillery again threw the attackers into confusion, scattering infantry and armour.

Australian Bren gun carriers worked around the Italian flank, delivering to the 2/48th Battalion 'the ludicrous sight of a battalion of infantry being herded like so many sheep through a gap in the wire into our hands.'[68] A 'few 'spiteful rounds' from disapproving German tanks so infuriated an Italian colonel (62nd Trento Regiment) marching into captivity, that he helped draft a surrender leaflet to his compatriots urging them to follow his example: 'Yesterday thousands of your countrymen were taken prisoner at Tobruk. It is quite useless to make any further sacrifices of this kind.'[69]

The Australian 2/48th Battalion's 'bag' for the day stood at 803 prisoners, including twenty-five Italian and one German officer. Under interrogation the Italians revealed their plans to capture the hill, confident that once their tanks were through the wire the defending infantry would surrender.

Axis armour and infantry were again flung against the perimeter near Ras el Medauuar on 17 April. Lieutenant Don Bryant (2/48th Battalion) watched the enemy armour press forward

> ...on through the shelling and forced their way down part of the wire. One Italian 'light' blew up on the battlefield, and two more were knocked out by our anti-tank rifles before they got very far. The rest continued on and we couldn't stop them.[70]

Unable to suppress the perimeter posts, the enemy tanks withdrew in due course; their accompanying infantry unable to advance. In another corner of the fortress, Stanley Christopherson (Sherwood Rangers Yeomanry) watched as enemy shells fell on the harbour.

> Their ranging was very accurate and they almost scored a hit on a minesweeper, destroyer and gunboat in the harbour. Some of the shells came unpleasantly near our shore. The destroyer and the gunboat dashed out of the harbour and started a bombardment, after which we got no more shelling. Certainly an exciting day.[71]

Aerial attacks on the town and harbour were commonplace with 787 raids logged in the first three months of the siege. 'Over Tobruk the sky is seldom silent. The sound of our motors continually terrifies the Tommies', a German war correspondent enthused.[72]

Major Devine watched the ungainly Ju 87s hammer the town:

> With puffs of [ack-ack] smoke all around them, the bombers fly serenely on their course, the sun glittering on their metal wings, the glassed-in noses standing out clearly. Over their target they break formation, and down they come one at a time in deep, flopping dives which, at quite low altitudes, flatten out with the simultaneous release of little clusters of bombs... Now and then a plane, obviously hit, starts to smoke and lose height: the anti-aircraft fire has claimed another victim.[73]

The terror of being dive-bombed featured in a soldier's letter home:

> 2 bombs landed in the middle of my section line but by the grace of God only the first (and smaller) exploded. The second weighed a ton but happily was a dud. Two dugouts were ten feet away from the first but fortunately the inmates were elsewhere – every scrap of their clothing was torn to shreds – blasted away but no one was hurt. I was cowering in a hole about 50 yards away listening to the fiendish whistle of the bombs falling – that is the worst of the lot and fear does not diminish in each succeeding raid.[74]

Yet as Morshead later narrated, 'dive-bombing attacks were remarkable for the relatively small number of casualties caused, the small amount of material damage and their inaccuracy against a point target. But they can have a considerable moral effect on troops in the target area.'[75] His assessment was corroborated by a captured German officer who cited the ineffectiveness of the Stukas as a key reason for the Axis fiasco at Tobruk.[76]

In a separate corner of the sky, Oberleutnant Hans-Joachim Marseille claimed his first aerial victory, a Hurricane fighter shot down over Tobruk on 23 April. Marseille would earn the epithet 'The Star of Africa' as one of the Luftwaffe's most successful fighter pilots. Fellow ace, Werner Schröer, depicted Marseille as something of a maverick:

> The most amazing and ingenious combat pilot I ever saw... He thought nothing of jumping into a fight outnumbered ten to one, often alone, with us trying to catch up to him. He violated every cardinal rule of fighter combat. High speed, attack from altitude, climb to escape, and attack again converting the altitude into speed, always with a wingman for protection, were doctrine. He abandoned all the rules.[77]

Literally a deadly hit-or-miss affair, Stuka pilot Helmut Mahlke attacked a ship berthed in Tobruk's harbour.

> I had ordered the attack to be made in a steep dive... A veritable wall of Flak came up to meet us; not just from the Tobruk defences, but from the target vessel as well. Even by Tobruk's standards, it was an impressive display – and we were in the middle of it! Swarms of red fireflies were flashing past my cockpit windows... In this much flak I'm never going to make it down another 500 metres, I said to myself, but before it gets me I can at least let go a few live ones... I therefore pressed the bomb release button prematurely – at a height of 700 metres – but continued to dive, expecting to hear that big bang and meet my end at any moment. But nothing happened! I recovered at low level and then raced out to sea... But our target had also more than its fair share of luck as well. It had taken only one hit – from one of my small 50 kg underwing bombs.[78]

To frustrate Axis air raids over the harbour area, Brigadier J.N. Slater (4th Anti-Aircraft Brigade), in command of 24 heavy and 60 light anti-aircraft guns, introduced an umbrella barrage. An immediate success, six of the thirteen intruding aircraft on 23 April were shot down. Axis pilots however were quick to modify their approach, diving through, around or under before dropping their bombs. Thickening the barrage with additional weapons at different altitudes also improved its effectiveness. By the end of the month, Slater's gunners had brought down 37 enemy aircraft, 16 more probables and another 43 damaged. As the target of increasing enemy attention, the steadfast gunners also suffered, with nearly fifty casualties on 27 April alone.[79]

One particular anti-aircraft crew earned renown for working the forward six-inch gun on the sunken HMS *Ladybird*. With only the fore part of the vessel remaining above water, where the gun was mounted, the crew worked tirelessly. As Devine writes,

> Despite constant bombardment, the crew of the gun refused to be relieved. Nobody could understand why until one day somebody discovered that the crew had been able, by diving, to bring up whiskey from the captain's cable. They did not care if the sky was full of Jerry planes or all the guns in the world were shelling them.[80]

John Flak investigated a Ju 87 downed by the garrison's ack-ack:

> The pilot and rear gunner sat in their seats, up to their middles in water, now yellow green from spilled hydraulic fluid. Fire swept the Stuka above the water level, and the crew burned. Later, the bodies of the Germans were brought ashore. We, who had been so recently bombed by them, looked at the dead men laid out on the rocks. The pilot had apparently been hit by anti-aircraft fire; both hands now roasted to the bone clutched a blackened chest.[81]

Outside the wire, Schraepler privately admitted defeat. His diary entry of 19 April reads:

> Here, we seem to be staying, or rather are forced to stay, as Tobruk, the hole, has not yet fallen…with existing forces we will not succeed… One has, of course, to bear in mind that the troops since Tripoli have been permanently in the desert and having to stand through all these hardships, which one cannot imagine in Germany, so that the troops have strong nerves no longer.[82]

Major Hohmann bemoaned the RAF: 'No German troops have ever received so much strafing from the air as we have.'[83] Roaming British aircraft also peppered Rommel's captured command vehicle outside Bardia. In yet another brush with death, Rommel's driver and dispatch rider were both killed. Climbing behind the wheel, Rommel drove back to Tobruk where, to his relief, he finally received plans detailing the former Italian defences. With this understanding, he began planning another assault, this time by the newly arrived 15th Panzer Division. He also instigated 'feverish training' since it had 'become only too evident' that his troops' training in positional warfare was inferior to that of the enemy.[84]

The break in fighting afforded Morshead time to reorganise and prepare for Rommel's next onslaught. Learning from the so-called 'Easter Battles', additional minefields were laid around the perimeter posts and in the Ras el Medauuar area – correctly assumed to be the next target. Fourteen new Matilda tanks were safely delivered by the RN despite the Luftwaffe's best efforts to sever Morshead's maritime lifeline. A miscellany of destroyers, minesweepers, gunboats, sloops and transports on the 'Spud Run' from Alexandria regularly plied 'Bomb Alley', the dangerous waters from Sollum to Tobruk to provision, arm and relieve the garrison through its back door. In the period from 11 April to 9 December 1941, 34,113 troops, 34,000 tons of stores, 72 tanks and 92 artillery pieces were landed while another 32,667 relieved troops, 7,516 wounded and 7,097 prisoners of war were evacuated.

Ships would arrive at night, Midshipman Frank Wade explained, 'because the Germans had a long range gun, dubbed Bardia Bill, which commanded the port during daylight hours. Trips were planned so that arrival was around midnight, to avoid air attack and shelling.' The harbour became a hive of activity as troops and cargo were unloaded and wounded solders embarked.[85]

While Tobruk was rightly termed 'a running sore' for Rommel, the siege was 'equally painful' to the British.[86] Admiral Andrew Cunningham calculated that one sailor was lost for every 50 tons of supplies, one ship for every 1,000 tons. In all, 26 naval vessels and five merchant ships were sunk; another four warships and four merchant ships were badly damaged. En route to Alexandria, SS *Chakdina* was a victim of an Italian air attack on the afternoon of 5 December. On this occasion, the armed merchantman had sailed as an unmarked hospital ship, carrying 380 wounded Allied troops and 100 captured Axis servicemen, including

Generalmajor Johann von Ravenstein.[87] Attacked by an S.79 torpedo bomber, the *Chakdina* sank within minutes. Some 400 men drowned. Captain Frank Gregory-Smith was on the bridge of the RN destroyer HMS *Eridge* (L68) when his ship reached survivors in the water.

> We still did not know if they were the victims of a submarine or aircraft but some were already swimming towards the ship from both bows, their cries for help assuming an animal like quality which was horrible to hear. Away in the distance an unseen voice was maintaining a constant, unnerving howl which rose and fell like a hound baying at the moon; nearer the ship, a little group clinging to the same spar was wailing in unison in a manner resembling a pack of beagles yelping around the carcass of their kill; beyond them, another swimmer was emitting a series of grunts which started as normal cries but dissolved into long, drawn out grasps as if his breath was being punched out of his body. Occasionally, a German prisoner of war's voice mingled with the others.[88]

'Make no-man's land our land'

Aggressive patrolling was a key feature of the Tobruk's dogged resistance from the very beginning of the siege – 'I determined we should make no-man's land our land', Morshead later affirmed, to 'besiege the besiegers.'[89] In response to a newspaper article claiming 'Tobruk can take it', Morshead shot back: 'We're not here to take it. We're here to give it.'[90]

Relieved to have returned safely from his first nerve-wracking patrol outside the perimeter wire on 13 April, Private Frank McGillivray wrote:

> I felt a little scared and quite a bit excited during the stunt but nevertheless I think I kept as cool as anyone. I was a little shaky afterwards though, when I arrived safely back to the dugout. Some valuable information as well as sundry water and petrol cans were obtained.[91]

Fortified by 'an occasional tot of rum', the nocturnal patrols were an unrelenting nuisance to the enemy.[92] As the eyes and ears of Tobruk, the usual strength of a patrol was an officer, two NCOs and twelve infantrymen. Patrolling, Morshead continued, caused 'considerable casualties...mines were either disarmed or shifted onto enemy tracks, or brought back for our own use and above all, the enemy [was] kept in a constant state of fear and trepidation, so that he was awake by night and slept by day.'[93] Also a valuable source of intelligence, the patrols helped push Axis troops back behind a no-man's-land buffer between one and four miles deep.[94]

One raid by 2/48th Battalion on 22 April, supported by three 7th RTR Matilda tanks, surprised an enemy formation from the rear. The unnerved Italians, Lieutenant D.G. Kimber recorded, 'shot wildly. Then the carriers came up on our left and drove straight into the Italian positions with every gun going.'[95] The Australians returned with sixteen Italian officers and 354 men plus a number of weapons and vehicles. Casualties were light on this occasion with two killed and seven wounded. A separate raid by 2/23rd Battalion against an enemy anti-aircraft battery and field artillery position the same day was far more costly. A bloody four-hour fight ensued with one man killed, twenty-three missing (mostly dead) and twenty-two wounded. Eighty-seven prisoners were taken and a similar number wounded or killed.

Rommel paid respect to the patrolling infantry as 'the best of soldiers, with their cold-blooded ability to carry out reconnaissance raids night after night.'[96] He personally investigated a report of 'feverish' activity by the Australians at Hill 201 on one occasion, only to discover a scene of silence. The mystery was solved as he cautiously peered over a rise. On the ground lay hundreds of feathered Bersaglieri helmets discarded by the Italian Fabris Battalion, which had been 'collected' during the night.[97]

Indian troops (18th King Edward VII's Own Cavalry) instilled fear by carrying their *Kukri* on patrols, a distinctive type of machete that scared the Italians 'stiff'.[98] Stealthily skulking through the darkness, the Indians would kill and appropriate weapons. In desperation, the Italians began chaining their machine guns to posts. Lieutenant Colonel H.O.W. Fowler wrote of one raid on the night 25/26 July.

> No prisoners nor actual identifications were brought back... The men saw red at the first attack and after that appeared oblivious of everything except killing the enemy. Jemadar Amar Singh, on being questioned as to why no identifications were brought back, explained that they were

under continuous fire; his men were thoroughly roused and in the darkness and excitement of the moment the only consideration was to KILL, KILL, KILL.[99]

Stress from these incursions, a psychological wrestle played out by both sides, was enormous. 'The Germans were very wary of [our] patrols', infantryman Neville Williams recollected.[100] In a grisly instance of retaliation, a patrol in September found the bodies of dead Italian soldiers wired with booby traps and surrounded by land mines. One corpse was purposely placed in such an 'unnatural position so as to invite investigation' by the unwary.[101] A German officer moaned in a letter home that his men were in a 'desperate state of nerves and lack of sleep because of the wretched Australians.'[102] In words echoing this sentiment, an Australian soldier whose patrol had been ambushed three weeks earlier, penned: 'The corporal of our squad…has not yet straightened up but gets about with a perpetual stoop and anxious glances enemywards; it jolted his nerve badly. Another member of the squad has been in hospital and I admit I felt jittery for a couple of days.'[103]

'Sometimes [however] it was a gentlemanly war', a German NCO recollected. 'While laying land mines outside the perimeter, a voice in the darkness said, "What are you doing here?" To our surprise one of our soldiers answered, "We are laying mines." The British answered calmly, "That's exactly what we are doing." Both sides went on laying mines, not shooting at each other.'[104]

Chivalrous acts were not uncommon, nor were unofficial understandings. The diary entry of a 'Rat' (6 June 1941) detailed:

> We throw everything at each other from daylight until about 10.30, when it starts to get hot and then both the Germans and ourselves appear to have a mutual agreement, that it is getting too hot and not a shot is fired until about 6 o'clock in the evening, then we go flat out again until about 9 o'clock, when it gets dark.[105]

A padre inside Tobruk recalled another noble 'agreement'.

> One of our men was seriously wounded in a forward post. His companion got a sheet of white paper, daubed a Red

Cross on it with the man's blood, held it up, raised the man and carried him on his shoulder to a place further back. The enemy didn't fire.[106]

'An area dedicated to men striving to kill one another'

The North African campaign is often termed as a 'clean' and chivalrous war, one 'without hate'. While the level of violence did not match the magnitude of brutality on the Eastern Front, it is unreasonable to believe that armies locked in a bitter contest to destroy each other would not be driven by malice. The desert was an 'area dedicated to men striving to kill one another', British Intelligence officer Geoffrey Cox wrote, 'enhanced only by the great arc of the sky in the morning and the stillness of noon and multitudinous stars that stared down at night.'[107] US correspondent Quentin Reynolds wrote of the acrimony in the desert.

> [The British] dislike very much being killed by Italians. They hate the Germans with a healthy, honest hatred – but they despise the Italians... They are more treacherous than the Germans. Often they will raise their hands and wait until the British come up to nab them. Then they will hurl grenades, and stick their hands up again.[108]

New Zealand Lieutenant Colonel H. Murray Reid told of the bitterness among his men after being bombed.

> It was pitiful to see the silent figures lying about, and to realise that they had been good men, in the prime of life, twenty minutes before. It made us boil, and many an oath was sworn to avenge their deaths at the first opportunity.[109]

Conscious of the shame it would bring, an Eighth Army driver described an incident when German troops shaved a Sikh soldier's head and sent him back to his lines. The soldier allegedly committed suicide.

Hatred and prejudice among Italian troops stemmed in part from the fascist vision of racial purity within a colonial mentality. Many detested the British for cooperating with the Jews and for their use of 'soldiers of every colour' – the conduct of employing racially inferior troops counter to their racial standing.[110] Italian soldiers beat, even murdered, non-white prisoners on their own accord. In an incident on 28 May 1942 near Bir Hacheim (also Bir Hakeim), a white British gunner taken prisoner witnessed an Italian guard execute five Indian soldiers on the grounds of their race.[111] Mussolini later chastised the treatment of prisoners during a PoW camp inspection the following month.

Bent on revenge from the Nazi occupation of their homeland, Polish soldiers of the Carpathian Brigade (under General Stanislaw Kopánski) arrived in Tobruk in August 1941. They were seen as merciless fighters. 'What a deep-seated, burning, bitter hatred they have', Captain Sean Fielding (Green Howards) noted.[112] They 'livened up the place at once', a war correspondent commented, revelling in any opportunity to strike back.[113] A British officer viewed their hostility: 'If they see an Italian working party of fifty, they ignore it; but one German shaking out his blanket brings "three rounds gun-fire".'[114] The Poles, in an Australian soldier's opinion, were the 'most ferocious and callous soldiers we had ever met. They literally butchered any Germans they came across.'[115] Richard Weston (24th Anti-Tank Company) recalled how 'we could hear them laughing, joking and singing patriotic songs [on patrol]… When they caught a German they tied his hands, put a grenade in his pocket and screamed laughing when he was blown in half.'[116]

The 2nd Battalion of the Free Czech National Army, which arrived at Tobruk on 21 October, also fought with a vengeance. Geoffrey Cox visited the Czech soldiers, positioned on the perimeter beside a barren wadi. Betrayed by the 1938 Munich Agreement, they 'knew well that they were the lucky ones. They had a chance now to fight, away from the Gestapo terror which darkened the lives of the men and women trapped now within the borders of the Third Reich.'[117]

'Things are in a mess'

Tobruk's heroic stand won praise in the world's press and provided Churchill with a measure of hope. 'Tobruk – the fortress of Tobruk – which flanks any German advance, we hold strongly', he announced to the House of Commons.[118] Conversely, Tobruk had earned Rommel few friends in Berlin. Franz Halder was particularly unimpressed. 'It is worrying me,' he logged in a damning war diary entry (23 April).

> I have a feeling that things are in a mess… Rommel is in no way up to his operational task. All day long he rushes about between his widely scattered units and stages reconnaissance raids in which he fritters away his forces. No one has a clear picture of their disposition and striking power… The piecemeal thrusts of weak armoured forces have been costly…his motor vehicles are in poor condition and many of the tank engines need replacing. Air transport cannot meet Rommel's senseless demands… After giving thought to the matter, I decline flying down myself… Perhaps it is better to dispatch Generalmajor [Friedrich] Paulus…perhaps the only man with enough personal influence to head off this soldier gone stark mad.[119]

As an emissary of the German Army High Command, Paulus arrived at Rommel's headquarters on 27 April. Having studied the situation, he immediately cancelled an attack scheduled for 30 April, only to sanction it two days later after Rommel deceitfully declared that sufficient ammunition was on hand. Gariboldi also agreed to the revised plan, now short of any grandiose talk of taking Suez. Should Tobruk fall, Rommel's remit was to secure Cyrenaica along a defensive line extending from Siwa northward to Sollum.

'A day of great anxiety'

29 April. Australian Signalman Harold Wilson turned to his diary: 'An enemy attack was expected at any time.'[120] Elsewhere in Tobruk Frank McGillivray took solace in the fact that the 'defences are all well manned and so far all German attempts to break through have been repulsed.'[121] Australian Lieutenant Ron Yates mused whether his adversary was his equal? 'I am beginning to lose faith in the German fighter. I think he is overestimated. They win because there is always so many of them, but with numbers equal they are not in the race.'[122]

Stanley Christopherson woke to a 'rather a hectic day' with the codeword received for the Yeomanry's guns to be prepared. Already the perimeter had come in 'for some very formidable dive-bombing and machine-gunning.'[123]

With his previous tank under repair, Leutnant Schorm received a new Panzer III, number 634. A pre-battle glass of Chianti was shared. Expectations again ran high: 'I intend to take Tobruk. My fourth attack on the town.'[124]

In his final attempt to seize Tobruk in 1941, Rommel hurled elements of his five divisions against Ras el Medauuar. He now had 81 available Panzers, double the number that fought on 14 April. This time the Axis hammer fell on the sector defended by the 26th Australian Infantry Brigade, under Brigadier R.W. Tovell. A preliminary softening-up by dive-bombing and heavy artillery preceded the advance of German assault troops. Mines were deloused and a gap blown through the perimeter wire. Bloody, chaotic fighting broke out with seven posts falling. Major Hohmann recorded the 'conspicuous courage' displayed by Obergefreiter Schaefer, who leapt into Post R1 armed with hand grenades, taking several prisoners.

German tanks charged through the breach before blundering onto a minefield. Schorm's tank reeled. A 'frightful crash in front and to the right. Artillery shell hit? No? It must be a mine.'[125] Within minutes seventeen Panzers were disabled, mostly with broken track links (by midday all but five were recovered). Much to his frustration, Schorm now faced repeated counter-thrusts by British tanks and strong, well-directed artillery fire. The 51st Field Regiment claimed a number of hits. Since Morshead was unsure whether the attack was a feint and was preparing to counter other threats, no mobile anti-tank guns or tanks were on hand to finish off the immobilised Panzers sitting helplessly on the battlefield.

Remorselessly shelled, the Germans were unable to coordinate infantry and armour. The Panzers assisted with the reduction of the perimeter posts still holding out. Eleven had fallen by midday. An Australian officer 'winkled out of our pit' and his men were taken prisoner, 'dumbfounded, incredulous and shocked' by the large number of 'Jerries' killed on the battlefield.[126]

German troops ferried into their hard-won foothold fell into disarray under an unrelenting RHA barrage. Morshead later counterattacked with three Cruiser and five Matilda tanks. A lopsided tank battle developed. 'Jerry tanks seemed to attack us from all sides', a Matilda commander later wrote. 'One cruiser was disabled... We were all hit many times, but our heavier armour saved us and we kept the Jerry tanks off' until poor light prevented vehicle identification.[127]

Schorm was confused: 'Which is friend, which is foe? Shots are being fired all over the place, often on one's own troops and on tanks which are on their way back. Suddenly – a wireless message! The British are attacking [the] gap with infantry.'[128]

Frank Hurley, official photographer with the Australian Imperial Force, was curious to see the German prisoners taken. 'They were in a grimy state', he logged, 'with faces encrusted with dust from which their eyes peered sullenly... I was told that fifty-four or fifty-seven lorry loads more had been dispatched from the battlefront...but they had never reached the internment cage – nobody asks any questions what has become of them. There is a preference here to bury dead Germans instead of taking prisoners.'[129]

2 May. Tobruk was blanketed in another sandstorm. Rommel focussed his troops on widening the bridgehead – a dent in the perimeter (with a frontage of some 4,900 yards and a depth of 3,300 yards) known as 'The Salient'. He now occupied six square miles, out of the 220-square-mile fortress, including the important high ground of Ras el Medauuar. Acquiring the toehold, however, had been a costly exercise. Generalmajor Hans-Karl Freiherr von Esebeck (15th Panzer Division) reported many units with '50 percent casualties, some even more'.[130] Rommel's losses stood at 1,398 German and 500 Italian troops, plus 46 tanks destroyed; the reversal ascribed to 'infantry and anti-tank fire coming from numerous undetected bunkers and from saturation artillery fire.'[131]

Private Harry Frazer (2/24th Battalion) took a moment to write home: 'Things are pretty hot up here believe me, but I'm hoping for the best... We have been in action, some of it pretty fierce, and just at present are in rather a tight spot, but we are hoping for relief soon now. Sleep is a thing that one has to grab when he can now, as we are continuously on the lookout for the enemy who has been very active all this week; on top of it all Mother I'm homesick.'[132]

Schorm also took time to reflect: 'Our opponents are Englishmen and Australians. No trained attacking troops, but fellows with nerves and toughness, tireless, taking punishment with obstinacy, wonderful on the defence.'[133] German First World War veterans likened the fighting to that earlier conflict; 'what we experienced in Poland and on the Western Front was only a promenade by comparison.'[134]

Although Paulus believed the attack was an important success, he directed no further action to be undertaken unless Tobruk was evacuated. Rommel was now thrown onto the defensive. A German battalion commander protested:

> Our people know nothing about the construction of defences. We have scarcely any exercise in this phase of warfare in our peacetime training. The junior commander does not realise that positional warfare is sixty per cent with the spade, thirty per cent with the field glasses, and only ten per cent with the gun.[135]

Morshead counterattacked the Salient flanks on the night of 2 May, achieving only modest gains, with 134 casualties suffered under intense fire. In the tough slugging match that followed, only 1,000 yards of territory had been retaken by the end of June. Stretched to capacity, Tobruk was simply not strong enough to break out on its own.

Schorm looked across no-man's land with envy. 'The men want to attack. Want to get into Tobruk. There, there's loot to be had.'[136] But as a fellow 'Afrikaner' reasoned, 'Hour by hour our advance becomes more difficult. The British lay mines, construct obstacles and positions which we shall have to take again.'[137] Dejected, a German soldier turned to his diary; his prospect of leave grim, his anger building:

> The latest news is not the war in Russia, but that two men from the battalion can go on leave every fortnight. I've worked it out that under this scheme we need five and a half years. Marvellous, isn't it?... Here we sit like birds in the wilderness, so they give us food for owls. I do not want to start a mutiny here, but there is no doubt that they could do better for us... I admire the iron resolution with which the British fight on in this isolated spot. It was in their power to abandon it by sea long ago.[138]

For the men manning the frontline Salient trenches and dugouts, daylight was spent in hiding before emerging after dark to patrol and develop the defences. Frank Perversi recalled the danger of being seen during daylight:

> To stand or even to kneel vertically in daylight was akin to committing suicide. Crawling on all fours was the only way to get along... One of the 'no hopers'... too lazy and too stupid to be told, tried to 'crawl along' on his feet and hands with his backside in the air. He was lucky. A bullet passed neatly through both buttocks without hitting bone.[139]

'Most of the boys are a bundle of nerves', a 'front-liner' later wrote. 'Anyone who reckons he's not scared is a blasted liar.'[140] The unremitting strain began to tell with at least 234 cases of self-inflicted wound (SIW) and 'shell-shock' – reported in the Australian division during May. In one week alone, thirty cases of SIW were reported. A dedicated 'war neurosis clinic' with seventy beds was established – of the 204 admissions, 61 per cent were serving in fighting units. Croswell Bowen, a volunteer ambulance driver in American Field Service, observed a number of men with burns taken to the Tobruk hospital. He discussed their injuries, a symptom of a broader malady, with a British medical officer: 'There's just been a Middle East order issued which forbids troops from spraying their dugouts with petrol [to kill fleas]... The order also states that anyone reporting sick with a burn received in this manner will be placed on a charge of having a self-inflicted wound. Frankly, I have never seen morale in the Western Desert as low as it is now.'[141]

The 'Rats of Tobruk'

London's *Times* presented Tobruk as 'a perpetual menace and an irritant on the flank of the Italo-German forces' – like the beribboned banderillas which 'stuck into the bull in the early stages of a bullfight, eventually can lay the animal low with exhaustion.'[142] Exasperating Rommel, who was compelled to hold 'back four Italian divisions and three German battalions from crossing the frontier', Tobruk fell under the sights of Nazi propaganda.[143] Announcing himself as Lord Haw Haw, the turncoat Irish American William Joyce (founder of the pro-Nazi British National Socialist League) broadcast daily tirades on Radio Berlin to undermine morale.[144] Failing miserably, Haw Haw's sneering became an unintended form of light relief, a 'bright interlude' that, if anything, accentuated the importance of holding the fortress. Scoffing at the garrison, 'caught like rats in a trap', Haw Haw's 'Rats of Tobruk' epithet immediately became a badge of honour for the garrison, a caustic term held in similar regard to Britain's 'Old Contemptibles' during the First World War.[145] An unofficial medal featuring the likeness of a rat was even struck from the metal of a downed German aircraft.

Bowing to political pressure, much to General Auchinleck's disapproval, the majority of the debilitated Australian 'Rats' were replaced by the British 70th Division (under Major General Ronald Scobie), the Polish brigade and Czech contingent in the period from August to October 1941.[146]

The 246-day siege – the longest in British history aside from the eighteenth century investing of Gibraltar by France and Spain – catapulted Tobruk onto newspaper headlines around the world. Like the Battle of Britain, it was a bright note for Churchill at a perilous time in the war for Britain. As Wavell prepared to relieve the fortress, Rommel was equally preparing through the summer months to (finally) take it.

Chapter Three

'Tobruk is relieved, but not as relieved as I am'

We'll leave the Godforsaken place
Without one backward look
We've called it lots of other names
This place they call Tobruk
                    –Warrant Officer W.B. Perkins
                    (2/7th Field Company, RAE)

Rommel's failure to storm Tobruk buoyed the British and raised eyebrows in Berlin. Franz Halder's situation reports in early May judgmentally recorded 'a campaign with very scanty forces on a widely extended front' and the loss of fifty-three officers and 1,187 men at Tobruk – 'Very high!'[1]

Rommel naturally deflected any criticism. With a propensity to condemn others for his own failures he ascribed the casualties to the nature of the conflict – a change from movement to 'positional warfare'.[2] Rather than admitting culpability for rushing in assault troops at night without sufficient reconnaissance, he denigrated their 'lack of training'.[3] He also distanced himself from logistical sufficiency. When quizzed by Halder whether he could maintain his ever-extending supply lines, he curtly countered: 'That's quite immaterial to me. That's your pigeon.'[4] 'The [North African] quartermaster occupied a difficult position,' Generalmajor Friedrich von Mellenthin explained, 'for not until 1941-42, when reverses were suffered in this field, did Rommel give more attention to the supply situation.'[5]

Thanks to British cryptographers at Bletchley Park, Churchill was privy to Paulus' intercepted report detailing Rommel's overly taxed lines of communication, non-existent reserves and exhausted troops. These insights fuelled the premier's pressure on Wavell to counterattack, since 'Those Hun people are far less dangerous once they lose the initiative.'[6] British intelligence also warned that the bulk of the 15th Panzer Division (whose 8th Panzer Regiment was a veteran of the French campaign) would reach Tobruk at the beginning of May.

Though 'dangerously weak' in tanks at home, Churchill was jolted into action by Wavell's reports of inadequate tank strength in the desert and the enemy build-up. Discussions behind closed doors in Whitehall pondered the loss of the Suez Canal, 'frustration of the enormous forces we have built up in Egypt [and] the closing of all prospects of American co-operation through the Red Sea.'[7] Disregarding 'admiralty reluctance', Churchill directed a fast convoy – dubbed Operation Tiger – to sail directly through the Mediterranean during a moonlit period, shaving three weeks off the lengthy passage round the Cape.[8] Fraught with the danger of Axis sea and air attack, the convoy docked at Alexandria on 12 May, disembarking Churchill's 'Tiger cubs' – a mixed bag of 238 tanks: 21 light tanks, 15 Mk IV Cruiser tanks, 67 Mk VI Cruiser tanks and 135 Matildas.[9] These were the tanks Wavell needed to take the offensive, though significant time in army workshops was needed to bring them up to a 'desert-worthy' standard. In the interim, Wavell assured Churchill that he was 'anxious to act as quickly as possible before [the] enemy can be reinforced.'[10] He entrusted Brigadier William 'Strafer' Gott to undertake a limited offensive, which he codenamed Brevity, to drive the Axis from the frontier and push forward towards Tobruk. Success would be the precursor for a much larger operation, then in the planning stages.

Launched on 15 May, Brevity took the enemy by surprise. Gott attacked in three groups – a coastal column (2nd Rifle Brigade and 8th Field Regiment, RA); a centre column (22nd Guards Brigade and 4th RTR); and a desert column (7th Armoured Brigade Group). Early success saw Halfaya Pass, Sollum and Fort Capuzzo change hands before Oberst Maximillian von Herff counterattacked. 'Very many British were killed. They handled themselves like a new battalion that had only recently arrived', the DAK War Diary declared.[11] Herff later praised the Italian *Bersaglieri* defending Halfaya for their 'lionlike courage until the last man against stronger enemy forces. The greatest part of them died faithful to the flag.'[12]

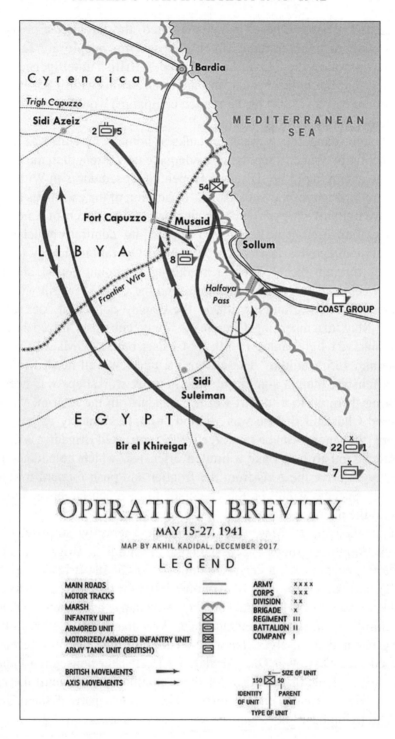

OPERATION BREVITY
MAY 15-27, 1941
MAP BY AKHIL KADIDAL, DECEMBER 2017

LEGEND

MAIN ROADS	ARMY — x x x x
MOTOR TRACKS	CORPS — x x x
MARSH	DIVISION — x x
INFANTRY UNIT	BRIGADE — x
ARMORED UNIT	REGIMENT — III
MOTORIZED/ARMORED INFANTRY UNIT	BATTALION — II
ARMY TANK UNIT (BRITISH)	COMPANY — I

BRITISH MOVEMENTS
AXIS MOVEMENTS

x — SIZE OF UNIT

150 ⊠ 50

IDENTITY   PARENT
OF UNIT   UNIT

TYPE OF UNIT

Rommel reacted by strengthening his grip around Tobruk and dispatching Oberstleutnant Hans Cramer's 1st battalion, 8th Panzer Regiment, to reinforce Herff. The threat posed by the enemy armour prompted an uneasy Gott to withdraw the Guards Brigade, leaving Halfaya Pass as his only prize. Wavell panned the operation for failing, 'in object', to clear the enemy from the 'Sollum-Bardia areas'.[13] Churchill saw otherwise, commending his C-in-C: 'Results of action seem to us satisfactory... You have taken the offensive, have advanced 30 miles, have captured Halfaya and Sollum, have taken 500 German prisoners and inflicted heavy losses in men and AFVs upon the enemy.'[14] Small losses on the German side amounted to 12 killed, 61 wounded and 185 missing. Three Panzers were knocked out and several hit with minor damage. Italian losses stood at 395 men with 347 taken prisoner.

Brevity cost Gott at least 206 casualties, the loss of five Matilda tanks and another thirteen damaged. The fighting underscored the 'utmost value' of the Sollum and Halfaya Passes, the only sites where the desert escarpment could be crossed.[15] Rommel counterattacked (Operation *Skorpion*) to retake Halfaya on the morning of 27 May. Wavell was taken by surprise. With the Coldstream Guards in danger of being surrounded, Gott authorised a withdrawal. The British, as Rommel put it, 'were soon driven out and fled in panic to the east, leaving considerable booty and material of all kinds.'[16] Scanning the battlefield, Herff counted nine 25-pounders, nine tanks and forty prisoners. Rommel's losses were 'comparatively insignificant'.[17]

Axis troops now set to work consolidating a new and formidable defensive line, centred on Halfaya Pass, with dug-in 8.8-cm and 5.0-cm anti-tank guns. Turrets from knocked-out Matilda tanks were retrieved and set in concrete emplacements flush with the coastal plain – an 'intelligent employment of enemy material' that especially pleased Rommel.[18]

'They are tearing my tanks to bits'

Wavell's comprehensive Middle East command was now saddled with the conflicting demands of a pro-Axis revolt in Iraq, a German airborne assault on Crete, and possible German intervention in the Levant.[19] Churchill, who was busy warding off criticism over Crete (which fell on

1 June), prodded Wavell to invade Vichy Syria and Lebanon (Operation Exporter, 8 June to 14 July 1941) and, above all, bring his 'Tiger Cubs' into action. Wavell had earlier notified Churchill that the 'weaning of the Cubs was proceeding satisfactorily', though with the caveat that 'even tigers have teething troubles'.[20] Armoured strength would be a 'deciding factor', Wavell informed Dill (CIGS) on 28 May, though considerable time in the workshops was needed to rectify an array of defects – including manufacturing problems with the suspension arms, which snapped 'like carrots', an inadequate cooling system and water pumps prone to leaking – on the machines Churchill needed to relieve Tobruk and inflict a crushing defeat.[21]

Churchill's 'terrible anxiety and even anger' for action in North Africa was finally tempered by Wavell's confirmation of the new offensive, codenamed Battleaxe.[22] But as Churchill later pointed out, 'there was a dark side'. A cautious Wavell relayed 'some disquieting features' revealed in recent operations.

> Our armoured cars are too lightly armoured… Our Infantry tanks are really too slow for a battle in the desert and have been suffering considerable casualties from the fire of the powerful enemy anti-tank guns. Our cruisers have little advantage in power or speed over German medium tanks. Technical breakdowns are still too numerous. We shall not be able to accept battle with perfect confidence in spite of numerical inferiority, as we could with the Italians.[23]

Battleaxe's ambitious aim was to 'defeat the enemy troops in the Western Desert and drive them back west of Tobruk'.[24] Plans were drawn up for British XIII Corps to stage a three-part operation: (i) Matilda tanks from the 4th Armoured Brigade, attached to the 11th Indian Brigade, would assault and re-capture Halfaya Pass; (ii) the remainder of the 4th Armoured Brigade and the 22nd Guards Brigade would overrun Fort Capuzzo and Sidi Aziez; and (iii) the newly equipped 7th Armoured Division would swing past on the left flank to join up with and relieve Tobruk. The combined force of some 25,000 men and some 190 tanks would be led by Lieutenant General Sir Noel Beresford-Peirse, who had earlier led the 4th Indian Division against the Italians at Sidi Barrani.

But as the British would discover, the 'means and methods that had done so well against the Italians' would not be good enough against the Germans.[25]

German intelligence correctly predicted the date of the British offensive: 15 June. This allowed Rommel to position the 5th Light Division in readiness between Tobruk and Bardia. Fighting began with the 33rd Flak regiment, under the command of the remarkable German cleric, Hauptmann d.R. the Reverend Wilhelm Bach, wreaking havoc at Halfaya, or 'Hellfire Pass' as the British called it.[26] The first kill, a cruiser tank, was scored at 2,000 metres. The German gunners then waited for the heavily armoured Matildas to lumber to within 300 metres (eliminating the problem of dust obscuring their sights) before opening fire.[27] 'Within a minute all but one of the 13 Matildas were in flames', Lieutenant Colonel Walter O'Carroll, 4th RTR Commander, wrote.[28] Over the air he heard Major C.G. Miles cry, 'They are tearing my tanks to bits', shortly before his death.[29]

Switching to high explosive shells, the Axis gunners forced the accompanying infantry to ground. Rommel later acknowledged the efforts of Major Leopoldo Pardi's artillery battalion and its 'distinguished service...thus showing that Italian troops could give a good account of themselves' when well led.[30]

German Flak guns along the coast brought the thrust by the 7th Armoured Division to a standstill. British tank losses were catastrophic. Out of nearly 100 Matildas (4th Armoured Brigade) that had set off, only 37 were still runners plus a further 11 repaired overnight. Immobile steel hulks littered the desert; the reign of the so-called 'Queen of the Desert' had ended. The 7th Armoured Brigade had also lost 30 of its new Crusader tanks and was down to 28 Cruisers. Only in the centre of the fighting had headway been made with Fort Capuzzo changing ownership again and a counterattack beaten off. Axis troops at Halfaya were left sandwiched between the 22nd Guards Brigade and the 11th Infantry Brigade.

The second day of fighting began at first light with the 15th Panzer Division again attacking Capuzzo. It suffered heavily from emplaced Matildas and 25-pounders and withdrew at midday. A violent tank skirmish developed between the 5th Light Division and the British 7th Armoured Brigade. Wilhelm Wendt (5th Panzer Regiment) struggled to identify targets, the 'contours of the enemy vehicles were obscured to such an extent by the flickering heat that you could no longer tell what type of vehicle you had in front of you.'[31]

British tanks engaging Panzers would find them retreating behind a screen of anti-tank guns. German doctrine, as the British were learning, assigned the task of destroying enemy tanks to anti-tank guns; tanks were best employed against troops and thin-skinned vehicles. This tactic was only appreciated in time by the British, who lost most of their precious armour to cleverly emplaced anti-tank guns, chiefly to the deadly 8.8-cm anti-aircraft gun in its ground attack role, and the 5.0-cm (*Panzerabwehrkanone* or *Pak*) Pak 38 anti-tank gun.

Brigadier C.E. Lucas Phillips later wrote, 'The infantry who so often criticised our armour, even the most senior infantry commanders, quite failed to see…that tanks, whether British or German, could no more advance in the face of resolutely manned anti-tank guns than the cavalry in their father's day could advance in the face of quick-firing field artillery. The guns had to be eliminated first.'[32]

16 June ended with both regiments of the 7th Armoured Brigade having withdrawn back across the frontier with only 17 Matildas and 21 Cruisers still running. Rommel's tanks began their advance before dawn the following day, again engaging the 7th Armoured Brigade. Capuzzo fell. Leutnant Frede (5th Panzer Regiment) was in a battalion commander's Panzer III, which sported a dummy wooden gun barrel (on the morning of 17 June) when nine Matildas were reported approaching. One of the British tanks had broken down and its crew were picked up by another Matilda. Frede's driver assumed in view of the British tankers 'sitting there like sardines in a can' that the tank wouldn't fire. Tempted to take it 'with a wooden gun', he rammed the British tank, causing it to halt. The British crew emerged, 'somewhat battered'. A senior sergeant saluted, since it was 'fair that we had not engaged his overloaded tank with our main gun.' As Frede explained, 'We were a bit ashamed... No one worked up the gumption to tell him the truth.'[33]

Disarray within the British HQ reached Rommel via an intercepted message requesting guidance.

It sounded suspiciously as though the British commander no longer felt himself capable of handling the situation. It being now obvious that in their present bewildered state the

British would not start anything for the time being, I decided
to pull the net tight by going on to Halfaya.[34]

The threat to the British flanks by an estimated 200 enemy tanks and the
danger of encirclement prompted a withdrawal. 'Our stroke had failed',
Churchill later admitted.[35]

Captain Peter Vaux (4th RTR) was ordered to prevent broken-down
tanks falling into enemy hands. After smashing wirelesses and removing
the breech blocks, he placed an anti-tank mine inside each tank vehicle.
Petrol was poured in and ignited with a Very flare cartridge. 'Most
satisfactory', Vaux reported, 'they all burnt and blew their turrets off.'[36]
German recovery crews, however, did salvage a number of Matildas,
which received a conspicuous black and white *Balkenkreuz* (bar cross)
symbol to avoid mistaken ownership, before returning to battle their
erstwhile owners.

After three days of fighting, Wavell's Battleaxe lay broken. The battle,
which marked the first occasion in the war when a sizeable German
force had fought on the defensive, finished in abject failure. Beresford-
Peirse lost 122 men killed, 588 wounded and a further 259 missing. The
RAF lost thirty-three fighters and three bombers. British tank losses
included 64 Matildas and 27 Cruisers to either enemy fire or mechanical
breakdown.

Rommel tallied his armoured losses at 25 Panzers destroyed, 443
men killed or wounded and 235 missing. Italian losses are unclear
with some 350 men taken prisoner and released during the British
withdrawal. 'The joy of the "Afrika" troops over this latest victory
is tremendous', he wrote home on 23 June. 'Now the enemy can
come, he'll get an even bigger beating.'[37] Victory was celebrated by
an invitation to his senior officers to share a glass of champagne –
'we emptied four bottles', Schraepler recorded. The 'beautiful
spectacle' of a Hurricane being shot provided the victors evening
'entertainment'.[38]

News of this latest defeat struck Churchill as a 'most bitter blow'.
Wavell apologised for his failure and the 'loss of so many Tiger cubs...
I was over-optimistic,' adding the 7th Armoured Division required
further training and that Exporter should have been deferred.[39] Leaving
London, the prime minister retreated to this country home at Chartwell,
where he wandered 'disconsolately for some hours'.[40]

'No British commander has been asked to assume greater responsibilities': Auchinleck

Rommel's success against *Battleaxe* was entirely overshadowed by Barbarossa. On 22 June 1941, three-quarters of the German army, 153 divisions, plus Axis satellite troops from Romania, Hungary, Croatia, Finland and pro-Nazi Slovakia, poured across the Soviet frontier. Mussolini also offered his support in a show of Axis solidarity.[41] A string of victories followed. Within weeks the largest military operation in history had pushed deep into Russia and seized Smolensk, some 200 miles from the Russian capital. Eleven days earlier Hitler had assuredly drafted Directive No. 32 which outlined operations after crushing Stalin's Red Army. The Wehrmacht would then be free to turn its attention to Tobruk, and beyond:

> It is important that Tobruk should be eliminated and conditions thereby established for the continuation of the German-Italian attack on the Suez Canal.[42]

Churchill was delighted by news of *Barbarossa* – he now had a new ally. In the hours preceding Barbarossa, he dispatched two telegrams. The first notified Wavell of his dismissal, the second advised the viceroy of India, Lord Linlithgow, by protocol, that Auchinleck would take up a new responsibility as Wavell's replacement.

It was a debatable appointment. General John Dill considered Auchinleck best suited to a role overseeing the expansion of the Indian army in light of foreseeable hostilities against Japan. New to the Middle East and inexperienced in desert warfare, Auchinleck was also largely unfamiliar with the British Army from whose ranks he would draw his subordinate officers. Unable to convince Churchill otherwise, Dill welcomed Auchinleck as C-in-C Middle East, though with the coda in his telegram that 'no British commander has been asked to assume greater responsibilities.'[43]

Churchill, who was critical of Auchinleck during the 1940 Norway campaign for being 'too much inclined to play for safety and certainty, neither of which exists in war', wasted no time in ruthlessly pressing 'the Auk' to 'renew the offensive'.[44] While he agreed in principle, Auchinleck (who assumed command on 5 July) was prepared for

Churchill's impatience and remained firm: 'No further offensive Western Desert should be contemplated until base is secure' – the nod to security in reference to Syria, Iraq and Cyprus.[45] A 'sharp disappointment' in the premier's unsympathetic eyes, it hinted at the 'serious divergencies of views and values' between the two men and a future collision.[46]

Churchill's communique of 6 July spelt out the clear need for a desert victory in the short term – as soon as possible, should a Russian collapse occur. 'I could not help feeling at this time a stiffness in General Auchinleck's attitude', Churchill recalled.[47] To resolve the strategic impasse, Auchinleck was summoned to Britain on July 29 to voice his grievances before the War Cabinet. He explained that his planned offensive – now named Crusader, the largest British desert operation yet launched – could not proceed before 1 November. Numerical strength in tanks was one thing, he argued, but training at all levels was indispensable. The forum concluded with Churchill 'unconvinced' though he 'yielded to the November date for the offensive'.[48]

North Africa, for the moment, disappeared from the front pages of the news as the world focussed on titanic events unfolding in the East. 'For the moment we are only stepchildren', Rommel noted.[49] However, *Barbarossa* was no replay of the Wehrmacht's earlier triumph in the West. By the end of August 1941 it was clear that the offensive had fallen short of expectations; by October, OKW was forced to postpone its Middle East ambitions. Any thought of discontinuing the siege at Tobruk, though, was undesirable, primarily from a propaganda perspective.

In the meantime, both sides concentrated on building up their armies.

Rommel's 'Midsummer Night's Dream'

14 September 1941. In a period of relative quiet, Rommel and Generalmajor Johann von Ravenstein mounted a reconnaissance raid, dubbed *Sommernachtstraum,* into Egypt. As the 21st Panzer Division battle group punched through a gap in a German minefield, a good-humoured Rommel, perched on the roof of his *Mammut* (what he called his British armoured command vehicle captured at Mechili) like a 'U-boat commander on his bridge', shouted, 'We're off to Egypt.'[50] Surging across the frontier south of Sidi Omar, the German generals planned to engage enemy forces and plunder supposed British forward supply dumps.

Generalleutnant Philipp Müller-Gebhard (DAK) was 'stunned to find General Rommel waiting for us at the rendezvous – he had driven on ahead of us all.'[51] This was, however, not an unusual circumstance, for, as Generalleutnant Alfred Gause recalled,

> [Rommel was a keen hunter] His close affinity with nature had sharpened his sense for terrain appreciation and his orientation ability to a remarkable degree. Frequently he would drive day and night through the trackless desert without maps, using only a compass only rarely to check the direction.[52]

But no game awaited the huntsman on this occasion; captured tinned fruit and Scotch whisky proved to be a pipedream. The sole reward was a British truck, seized by a mobile column, holding a swag of documents including codes and orderly room papers leading to the – erroneous – suspicion that British operations would not interfere with his next plan to reduce Tobruk, timed for 20 November.[53]

Formed-up into a defensive leaguer and refuelling, the Germans were hit hard by British 25-pounders, which the Germans labelled 'Ratsch-booms', and a costly bombardment by RAF fighters and South African Air Force bombers. Rommel and his driver sprinted from their vehicle and flung themselves on the ground as a stick of bombs exploded. Good fortune was again on Rommel's side – his driver was severely wounded while the general limped away with a steel splinter having ripped a heel off his boots. Rommel was later behind the wheel of the lone vehicle, after a nerve-wracking night-time puncture repair, driving at a 'furious pace' across no-man's land to reach the frontier.[54]

Chance smiled again on the general during a daring British commando raid (Operation *Flipper*) – to 'get Rommel' – on the night of 17-18 November at a private villa behind enemy lines wrongly believed to be his headquarters.[55] The attack, mainly by members of No. 11 (Scottish) Commando, proved disastrous, with the leader of the raid, Lieutenant Colonel Geoffrey Keyes, killed and twenty-eight men captured. Heinz Werner Schmidt commended the commando's 'fearless exploit', posthumously recognised with the Victoria Cross.

Rommel, who was in Rome at the time, requested that Keyes be buried with full military honours beside the four German troops killed.[56]

Keyes' final letter home read, 'if the thing is not a success, whether I get bagged or not, it will raise our stock a bit and help the cause.'[57]

'Everybody was full of the exhiliration which marks an offensive'

16 November 1941. 'There is battle in the air; I swear there is. It lies thick on the palate', Captain Sean Fielding scribed in his diary.[58]

> Everywhere there are eager faces; convoy commanders sitting up aloft their trucks like sunburned gods – their sun-compasses pointing a black sliver of shadow towards the Boche; dispatch riders bumping incredibly through the sandy, rutted tracks; officers in groups, their maps on knees…lorried infantry waiting, waiting, waiting; guns, their dust covers off…[59]

Canadian war correspondent Matthew Halton also noted the air of optimism in the Eighth Army's approach march.

> Everybody was full of the exhiliration which marks an offensive. The desert that day was an unforgettable sight. Nearly 10,000 machines – tanks, armoured cars, gun-portées with the 25-pounders and anti-tank guns bouncing wildly behind them, machine-gun carriers and trucks of all kinds, each vehicle engulfed in its individual cloud of sand – were roaring into the great desert quadrilateral which was to be our arena.[60]

Lieutenant General Sir Alan Cunningham (younger brother of Admiral Andrew Cunningham), whom Auchinleck appointed to lead Operation *Crusader*, gathered an audience of war correspondents for a pre-offensive briefing.[61] Alexander Clifford was present.

> In pitch-darkness, we stumbled through the camp, picking our way among slit-trenches and tent ropes, to his undergound headquarters scooped out of the sand-hills.

There we sat round a plain bare trestle table and drank whiskey-sodas while he told us what was going to happen. Zero hour, he told us, would be before dawn on Tuesday.[62]

Closely monitoring the situation, Churchill fired off a characteristic entreaty: 'Now is the time to strike the hardest blow yet struck for final victory, home and freedom. The Desert Army may add a page to history which will rank with Blenheim and Waterloo.'[63]

However, all was not well behind the scenes. Cunningham was already showing the strain of his new command. A novice to the desert and unfamiliar in directing armour, he was smoking heavily and afflicted with a related eye condition. Although Cunningham had trounced the Italians in East African, the two theatres were vastly dissimilar. In his memoirs, Brigadier Sir Bernard Fergusson (Middle East staff officer) contended, 'There could have been no more complete contrast to the swiftly moving war of the Desert, and the mental adjustment required of Cunningham would have been difficult for anybody. It was tantamount to saying: "If you can drive a bulldozer, you can drive a racing-car."'[64]

Cunningham's newly created Eighth Army was organised into two primary formations: the XIII Corps (formerly the WDF), under Lieutenant General Alfred Reade Godwin-Austen: 2nd New Zealand Division, the 4th Indian Division and the 1st Army Tank Brigade; and the newly formed XXX Corps (under Lieutenant General Willoughby Norrie): 7th Armoured Division, 1st South African Division and 22nd Guards Brigade. General Ronald Scobie's (Morshead's successor) Tobruk garrison encompassed the 70th Division, 32nd Army Tank Brigade and the Polish Independent Carpathian Rifle Brigade.

XXX Corp was given the task of destroying the enemy armour and protecting the left flank of the largely unarmoured XIII Corps, which was to advance to Bardia while the bulk of the armour continued northwest to link up with the 70th Division breaking out of from Tobruk. Deception would mislead the enemy into believing the offensive was scheduled for early December.

Rommel's reorganised and renamed Panzergruppe Afrika – now virtually an army command – contained the DAK, Italian Twenty First Corps, and Italian 55th Savona Division. A new formation, Division z.b.V (zur besondere Verfügung – 'for special use') Afrika was formed from various independent regiments and battalions besieging Tobruk.

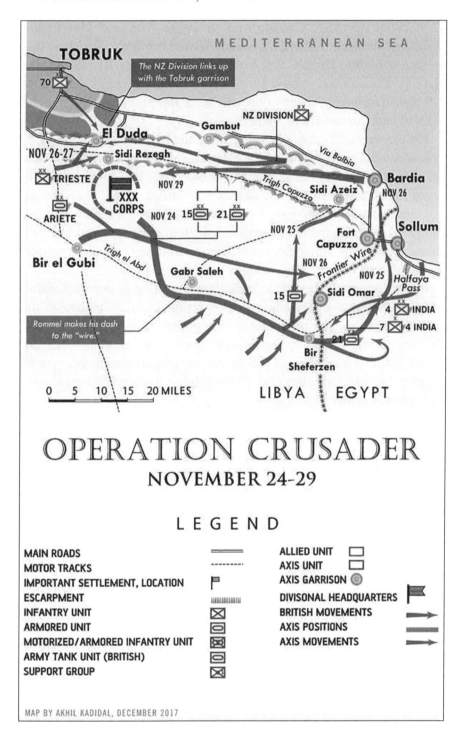

In terms of numbers, German armour in the 15th and 21st Panzer Divisions (the latter enlarged from the former 5th Light Division) was no match for the British. Only forty-four new Mark III and sixteen Mark IV Panzers had survived the Mediterranean crossing – a total of 249 tanks (including seventy obsolete Mark IIs) plus an additional 137 M13/40 tanks in the Ariete Division.

British armour, conversely, had grown, and now included 300 Mk VI Crusader tanks, sixty new infantry Mark III Valentine tanks and 300 new M3 Stuart light tanks. Tank crews welcomed the speed and reliability of the new American Stuart, despite its limited range, thin armour and diminutive 37-mm gun. Crusader crews, correspondingly, were hampered by its outmoded 2-pounder gun, thin armour and mechanical unreliability.[65] The Valentine, while more reliable and heavily armoured, also carried the same 2-pounder gun.

Major General Neil Ritchie lamented the hitting power of Britain's 'outgunned' tanks, conceding, 'there is no doubt in the campaign the gun is everything and the tank, in my opinion, should be built round the gun, not the reverse.'[66] The Cruiser tanks, in his opinion, were 'not robust enough... to withstand the rigours of campaigning in this type of country. The M3 American tank...as a fighting machine is certainly not up to the Germans.'[67]

'After 2¾ years of war', Richard Casey (Australian representative of the British War Cabinet as Minister of State in the Middle East) noted, 'We are still not making a tank that is any good.'[68]

But were Panzers superior to the British tanks at this time, or was Rommel's early success due more to his adroit handling of armour? Unlike the various types of tanks used by Britain in the desert in 1941, their German counterparts used parts standardised across several models. Powered by reliable, purpose-built Maybach engines, the early British and American designs, by necessity, were built around existing truck and aircraft powerplants. We have already looked at the various types of British tank in North Africa in 1941. Germany, by comparison, initially shipped three classes of tank, categorised by their armament. There were two light tanks: the 5.4-ton Panzer I was armed with two 7.92-mm machine guns; the heavier 8.9-ton Panzer II was armed with a 2-cm cannon. The Panzer III was a reliable and versatile 20-ton 'medium' tank with a 5-cm gun, and the larger 25-ton Panzer IV, with its 75-mm gun, was classed as a 'heavy' tank. At the outset of the campaign, nearly fifty per cent of

Rommel's armour was either obsolete or useless. A contemporary German report on the Panzer I, which comprised a quarter of the DAK's armoured strength, dismissed it as totally unsuitable for desert operations. Although the heavier Panzer III and IV enjoyed a similar thickness of armoured protection to their British counterparts, the use of face-hardened armour provided a metallurgical edge in deflecting the kinetic energy of solid shot projectiles. Later vehicles also had face-hardened armour bolted on to afford even more protection. British and Italian designs, by comparison, used less-effective homogeneous armour plating.

Britain's outdated 2-pounder gun was supplied at this time with non-explosive, solid-shot ammunition, incapable of penetrating enemy armour beyond 500 yards. The projectiles were of limited utility against soft-skinned vehicles, anti-tank guns and personnel. Not until the arrival of US-manufactured tanks were British tankers able to reply with high-explosive ammunition. The heavier German tanks, conversely, were able to fire both armour-piercing and high-explosive ammunition. German armour-piercing ammunition above 37-mm in calibre came in both high-explosive and delay-fuse options. These projectiles often caused irreparable mechanical damage and horrendous crew injury, unlike solid-shot ammunition, which frequently wounded the occupants but rarely knocked out a tank through fire or unrepairable damage.

Flawed doctrine also undermined British performance on the battlefield. It was standard practice at the time for British tanks, except when partially hidden, to fire on the move. A 1938 British report provides some idea of the poor accuracy – a twenty-one per cent chance that a 2-pounder gun while moving at ten miles per hour would hit a large target at 650 yards. Axis tank crews, alternatively, were taught to fire when stationary, irrespective of available cover.

The British 3.7-inch (94-mm) anti-aircraft gun had, perhaps, the potential to tip the scales against Rommel's Panzers. Primarily retained in its archetypal role through British Army conservatism, as well as the inherent problems of weight, optics and the strain on the mounting and recuperating gear when fired at low angles, it nevertheless proved to be a formidable weapon when it was finally used against enemy armour.

German intelligence possessed a comprehensive understanding of every British tank in service up until June 1941 (when the Cruiser Mark VI was introduced) from earlier combat in France. Anti-tank crews as a result appreciated the critical range at which to engage enemy armour. It was not until several Panzers were captured at Tobruk in April 1941 that British intelligence was able to gauge the thickness of their adversary's armour. And it was not until May that range tables were issued for the 2-pounder gun against the heavier enemy tanks.

We should remember that more tanks in the desert succumbed to mechanical breakdowns and damage than to enemy fire. Whereas the Germans excelled at battlefield recovery and repair, the British lacked appropriate recovery equipment in the early stages and were more often compelled to abandon damaged yet repairable tanks.

'Everywhere in the desert everyone's tangled up in hopeless confusion'

17 November 1941. Major Robert Crisp (3rd RTR) moved forward in darkness in his Stuart tank (which the British reverentially nicknamed 'Honey') towards the jumping-off point, 'nose to tail, the desert filled with the low-geared roaring of the radials and the creaking protestations of hundreds of springs and bogie wheels.'[69]

Although telltale British radio silence alerted German eavesdroppers, heavy rain prevented aerial reconaissance. The waterlogged Axis landing grounds presented an inviting target to RAF fighters and bombers, with many aircraft destroyed. Rommel (who was in Athens) and Generale d'Armata Ettore Bastico (who succeeded Gariboldi on 19 July) were both taken by surprise. Presumed to be a reconnaissance in force, the advance of XXX Corps continued uninterrupted for 48 hours. Meeting little opposition, Cunningham was nevertheless unable to deliver his planned counterblow.

The advance of the 22nd Armoured Brigade stalled at an Italian defensive line at Bir el Gubi on the morning of 19 November. There Italian gunners took a fearsome toll on the British tanks, which lacked accompanying infantry support. A later counterattack by 100 tanks of the Ariete Division forced the British to withdraw, contrary to the belief that the Italians were incapable of 'putting up a decent fight'.[70] In the first successful Italian tank battle of the campaign, the British lost close to 50 tanks, the Italians 35.

To the north, the 7th Armoured Brigade reached Sidi Reweigh – only ten miles from Tobruk – and overran the airfield, wrecking nineteen

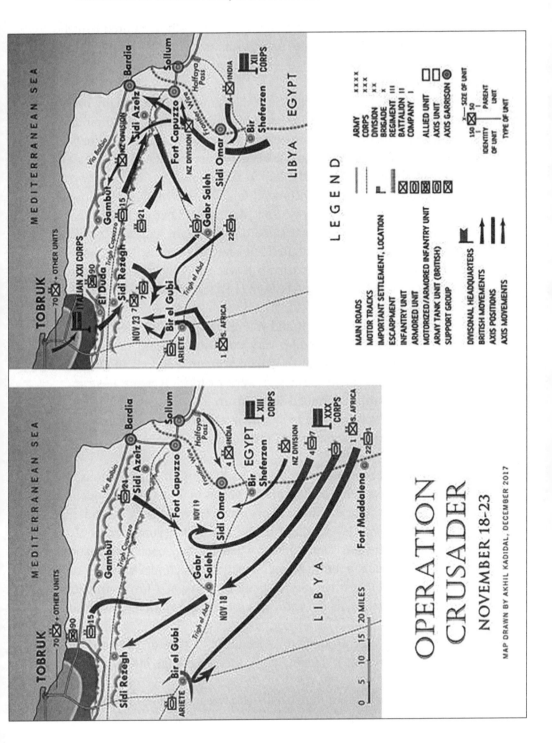

OPERATION CRUSADER
NOVEMBER 18-23

MAP DRAWN BY AKHIL KADIDAL, DECEMBER 2017

aircraft. Rommel authorised an attack against the 4th Armoured Brigade near Gabr Saleh. The two sides later withdrew at dusk – Cunningham lost another 24 tanks against three German tanks knocked out and a further three damaged.

Fielding toured the battlefield on 20 November, finding 'many Italian tanks and some of ours. All very badly shot up and some with their dead still in them. The oddest details remain in one's mind. The commander of one Wop tank, lying dead beside his machine, had his fingers crossed; and he had absurdly small feet cased in new boots.'[71]

Not until that evening did Rommel finally acknowledge that a major British offensive was underway. Von Mellenthin later conceded that a 'great opportunity' was missed since 'Cunningham had been obliging enough to scatter the 7th Armoured Division all over the desert, and we had failed to exploit his generosity.'[72] It was a day of heavy fighting, as Lieutenant Colonel David Lloyd Owen (LRDG) recounts:

> The enemy fought back and retook Sidi Rezegh from us. There then followed some very confused fighting in that area and some of the most gallant armoured actions of the whole campaign in the desert were fought. Over the next days the battle continued indecisively but the garrison in Tobruk were beginning to tear their way out and join hands with the leading elements of the Eighth Army.[73]

In place of set piece movements by mutually supporting formations, the battle blurred into a fierce contest of tank versus tank. A DAK serviceman scrawled in his diary: 'From every direction artillery thundered. Where is the front? Everywhere in the desert everyone's tangled up in hopeless confusion. The front is wherever two enemy formations meet.'[74] From such a bewildering situation, Auchinleck could only inform Churchill that it is 'very difficult to arrive at a firm estimate of the enemy tank losses, as the battle has moved and is moving with such great speed.'[75]

British war correspondent Alexander Clifford watched the 7th Armoured Division's 'Honey' tanks literally charge into combat:

> They met and intermingled and there was utter, indescribable confusion. There was noise – the quick, jarring crack of

78

tank guns firing, the pulsing clamour of the tank treads, the grinding of the gears. There was dust – a hundred separate cyclones of whirling choking yellow dust. There was smoke – the thin bitter smoke of explosives and the exhaust smoke from a couple of hundred raving engines. There was flame – the quick stabbing flash of guns firing, the red-black blaze of a tank set on fire...there was no pattern or design of coherence about it all.[76]

Fellow correspondent Canadian Matthew Walton was struck by the turmoil before him:

We learned the meaning of the phrase, 'the fog of war'. We were engulfed in a swirling, nightmarish melée of dust, smoke and shellfire. At one moment we were on the edge of a battle, half an hour later we were caught up in its vortex. The enemy behind us and around us, we were behind and around the enemy. Tanks, trucks and aircraft were burning here and there. Men, vehicles and guns moved in all directions for no apparent reason and the furious cannonade never ceased. One hundred square miles of desert was a flaming, smoking confusion by day and night.[77]

Crisp wondered how many troops were 'killed by their own sides' bullets, shells and bombs. Identification in the confused, swift-moving desert war was always difficult, and was made more so by the paucity of information available about the movements of either force.'[78]

R.D. Lawrence, a Stuart gunner in 7th Armoured Brigade, survived his tank being knocked out, though the shell's penetration killed the driver and commander instantly.

The projectile entered with a dreadful bang through the driver's protection port. It smashed Harold's head to a pulp, pierced through the thin metal basket that formed the floor of the turret, ricocheted against the curved wall of the cupola and entered John's chest. The tank kept on going and was subjected to more enemy fire... John Ferguson was dead, his blood flooding into the turret... Steve helped me to push John out of the turret opening, whereupon machine-gun bullets sprayed the corpse and the tank.[79]

Peter Roach (1st RTR) confronted the 'dread of the tank brewing up [catching fire] when hit, so that if you were not wounded you had to move very fast to avoid incineration. We had all seen and smelt the burnt-out tank and seen the charred remains of a crew.'[80] Machine gunner Noel 'Wig' Gardner (2nd New Zealand Division), too, recalled the horror of watching an anti-tank strike.

> It was never a sight that I became inured to. Seeing a tank hit by a shell and explode was quite shattering, especially when the high-octane petrol went up in flames. Many were fried in a trice…the smell of burnt men is not nice, it made many of us quite sick.[81]

Cyril Joly (7th Armoured Division) inspected an abandoned Italian M13 one evening in last light, only to recoil in revulsion.

> The interior of the tank was blackened and scorched with flame and, peering upwards, as if waiting for salvation, was all that remained of the head of the tank commander, the black recesses of the empty eye-sockets staring malevolently upwards, the white teeth, bared by the lips, which had been burnt away grinning hideously at me. Trembling with the shock of the surprise, I threw myself into my turret and moved the tank hurriedly away.[82]

Back on the battlefield, Brigadier John 'Jock' Campbell fearlessly led a body of troops into the fighting near Sidi Rezegh ridge. He was seen

> riding in an open armoured car, and as he stood there, hanging on to its windscreen, a huge well-built man with the English officer's stiff good looks, he shouted, 'There they come, let them have it.' … The men loved this Elizabethan figure. He was the reality of all the pirate yarns and tales of high adventure, and in the extremes of fear and courage of the battle he had only courage. He went laughing into the fighting.[83]

Wounded on 22 November, Campbell continued to direct fire, even acting as an anti-tank gun loader at point blank range, where he inflicted 'heavy losses'. His courageous leadership won a VC.[84]

In a separate clash, a troop of four 2-pounder anti-tank guns mounted portée[85] under the command of Second Lieutenant Ward Gunn (J Battery RHA) opened fired on sixty oncoming Panzers. Three of the four guns were quickly knocked out, the crew of the fourth lay dead. Ignoring the danger of exploding ammunition on the burning vehicle under enemy fire, Gunn took over the remaining weapon, firing between 40 and 50 rounds. His 'shooting was so accurate at a range of about 800 yards that at least two enemy tanks were hit and set on fire and others were damaged before he fell dead, having been shot through the forehead.'[86] Gunn was posthumously awarded the VC for gallantry in preventing the German tanks overrunning his position.[87]

Pinned down by heavy enemy fire from several directions, Rifleman John Beeley (The King's Royal Rifle Corps) singlehandedly stormed an enemy post containing an anti-tank gun and heavy machine gun. Sweeping fire from his Bren gun silenced an enemy anti-tank crew twenty yards away. Hit at least four times, Beeley collapsed dead. His gallantry was rewarded with a posthumous VC.[88]

Inside Tobruk, Captain Philip John 'Pip' Gardner (4th RTR) was ordered on 23 November to rescue two immobilised armoured cars of the King's Dragoon Guards, out of action and under heavy attack. Covering fire from a tank allowed Gardner to hitch a tow rope to one car and rescue an officer whose legs had been blown off. Exasperatingly, the rope broke. Gardiner returned to the car and, despite being wounded in the neck, arm and leg, he retrieved the wounded man and transferred him to a tank, which carried him safely through heavy shell fire to British lines. For courage shown in saving his fellow officer, Gardner was awarded the VC.[89]

It was a day, Major General Gerald Verney's (7th Armoured Division) later wrote, of 'hard, confused and scattered fighting'.[90]

Above the desert, Australian fighter pilot Clive 'Killer' Caldwell was 'busy as hell' in his P-40 Tomahawk. In one engagement he shot down German ace Hauptman Wolfgang Lippert (Gruppencommandeur of II/ JG27); 'I was able to put [in] a very satisfying burst with all guns.'[91] Lippert bailed out from his stricken Messerschmitt Bf-109, hitting the tailplane and breaking both legs. Captured and taken to a Cairo hospital,

Lippert developed gangrene and died of an embolism on 3 December during surgery. He was buried with full military honours.

On the ground, Rommel launched a concentrated counterattack to smash the 7th Armoured Division and annihilate the 1st and 5th South African Infantry Brigades. Gunner Cyril Herbert Glass (3rd Field Regiment, Transvaal Horse Artillery) remembered the enemy artillery opening up

> with everything he had… His shelling was terrific, but the most demoralising fire was from his mortars, which had a crack like a whip and the shrapnel kept low and we were well within range of them. One mortar shell killed two of our gun-team and another threw the empty ammunition boxes several feet in the air.[92]

Captain D. Matthews (5th South African Infantry Brigade) watched the flashes of German tracer in fading light, 'There was a streak of light as each shell was fired. One of our armoured cars, which was to my left and slightly ahead of me, received a direct hit from a German tank shell and a friend of mine lost his leg at the hip.'[93]

Separately, Cyril Joly viewed the demise of a Panzer III.

> Ammunition and fuel were burning fiercely… I wondered what had happened to the crew and whether any had escaped or would escape. Their chances of survival were getting smaller each moment… when the German tank finally blew up. The flames and black smoke seemed to hesitate for a moment. Then, at the base of the turret, there suddenly appeared what seemed to be a ball of fire… I stared as with uncanny deliberation this ball rose, slowly expanding as it lifted the turret and shattered the sides of the tank… The whole desert was lit with the brilliant light, so that each tank was plainly visible, still moving steadily away from the fire.[94]

Despite losing seventy tanks, the highest single daily loss during Operation *Crusader*, the Axis could claim to have won the battle of Sidi Rezegh. Rommel, von Mellenthin observed, was in a 'jubilant mood'.

He had, however, 'overestimated his success', believing that now was the time to begin a general pursuit.[95] A signal to Berlin summarised a bold plan to break off battle and turn the tide by swinging the 21st Panzer Division deep into the British rear to destroy the 7th Armoured Division. Rommel's 'dash to the wire', as it became known, terrified Cunningham, who wanted to withdraw immediately into Egypt, nearly stampeding 'Eighth Army into a headlong flight'.[96] Scattered British armoured units had already lost 530 tanks in the four days from 18 November. Flying to Eighth Army Headquarters, a steely-nerved Auchinleck met with his perturbed senior commander on 22 November, giving orders to 'continue to press the offensive'.[97] A letter followed urging Cunningham to 'Hold on, bite deeper and deeper, and hang on till he is finished.'[98]

Fighting continued in earnest. Capitano Sergio Falletti (27th Infantry Regiment, Pavia Division) was killed by machine-gun fire while calling artillery and mortar fire during a British attack. For helping constrain the British Tobruk garrison, Falletti was posthumously awarded the *Medaglia D'Oro al Valor Militare* (Gold Medal of Military Valour). His posthumous citation noted, 'Although mortally wounded by machine gun fire, he didn't hesitate in calling in artillery and 81-mm mortar fire on his strong point, now occupied in part by the enemy.'[99]

In yet another Middle East leadership revision, 'the Auk' returned to Cairo on 26 November whereupon he drafted a letter relieving Cunningham of his command.[100] Major General Neil Ritchie (his deputy chief of staff) would assume the position with the rank of lieutenant general. Inexperienced both in desert warfare and as a senior field commander, Ritchie was a questionable, albeit temporary, choice to lead the Eighth Army and continue the offensive. Auchinleck, however, had little choice, and no time for another commander to be dispatched from Britain; he later conceded that Ritchie was 'pitch-forked into a command at a desperate moment, knowing little or nothing of his subordinate officers or troops and told to retrieve an apparently lost battle'.[101]

'He was straight-forward and absolutely honest', Lieutenant General Sir Arthur Smith, his immediate superior, later recalled. 'If one could criticise him, he was a little slow – but caution is often better than being too slick.'[102] As an unknown to the desert army, Ritchie's appointment, General Godwin-Austen related, elicited 'no general reaction'.[103] Although Ritchie's last field command was leading a battalion in the First

World War, to the 'Auk', he was a 'thrusting general', at a time when Allied and Axis forces were chaotically intertwined, with information from the front frequently late and inaccurate.[104] But then as General Sir Frank Messervy (then commanding officer of the 4th Indian Division) wrote, Ritchie was 'put into a position which at the time was beyond his capacity. Although he had leadership and powers of command, he was thrown into a very difficult position before he had time to develop methods of command.'[105]

Rommel, Generalleutnant Ludwig Crüwell (DAK commander) and staff spent the night of 24/25 November hopelessly lost on the Egyptian side of the frontier, sandwiched uneasily between British positions. Their escape the following morning was sheer luck.

In an extraordinary frontline encounter, German troops overran a British dressing station – literally a lean-to behind a three-ton truck – swamped with wounded. Scottish surgeon Major Ian Aird (Royal Army Medical Corps) was operating when a German stretcher arrived carrying a seriously wounded soldier – Oberstleutnant Fritz Stephan (Olbrich's successor as commander of the 5th Panzer Regiment). A German doctor requested a pressure dressing to stabilise the bleeding before Stephan's evacuation to Germany. Aird replied that he required immediate surgery or would die. In a strange twist, the German physician inquired whether he was 'Aird of Edinburgh'?[106] Astonished, Aird replied that he was. His German opposite number then explained his interest in Aird's intestinal surgical procedures.[107]

Aird performed a thoracotomy on Stephan to stem the bleeding, watched, as he later learned, by Rommel. Tragically, Stephan died shortly afterwards.

Hours later the dressing station returned to British hands, such was the fluid nature of the desert arena. Both sides understood that surgeons, being close to the front lines, were not to be troubled and left free to continue their work, often treating wounded from both sides simultaneously.

Alan Moorehead wrote of similar empathy on the battle ground:

> The Germans were not unkind to our wounded. They took their rations but gave them hot tea, covered some with blankets, bandaged one or two sufficiently to give them a 50-50 chance of living till the next day. Many were left lying on the wet sand through the night. Marvellously, a

> British squadron leader, with both legs gone, survived till
> we picked him up in the morning. He described how the
> Nazis were round him all night salvaging their gear.[108]

25 November. Axis woes continued at sea where Ultra intelligence
had forewarned the RAF and RN when convoys were sailing from Italy.
The loss of replacement vehicles, reinforcements, fuel and ammunition
for Panzergruppe Afrika was proving so calamitous that even Rommel
was having to reassess his position. In November alone, 14 out of
22 merchantmen attempting to reach Libya were sent to the bottom. On
land, Axis forces had achieved little with heavy losses. The 21st Panzer
Division fruitlessly manouevred south of Halfaya Pass without making
enemy contact while the Ariete Division was stopped from reaching the
frontier by the British 4th Armoured Brigade. The 5th Panzer Regiment
lost half of its tanks against the 7th Indian Brigade, buttressed by the 1st
and 25th Field Regiments. British air attacks also inflicted casualties on
Axis formations throughout the day.

Southeast of Tobruk at El Duda, Captain James Jackman (Royal
Northumberland Fusiliers) was leading a machine gun company in
support of Matilda tanks from the 32nd Tank Brigade. 'Standing up in
the front of his truck, with calm determination', Jackman 'led his trucks
across the front between the [British] tanks and the [enemy anti-tank]
guns – there was no other road – to get them into action on the left flank.'
Lacking radio communication, he calmly directed his crews to target the
gun positions by flag until killed by a mortar round. His inspirational
leadership was recognised by a posthumous VC.[109]

'This evening we are to withdraw'

'It is almost midnight', Fielding wrote by torchlight. 'This has been a
horrible 36 hours. I feel a little sick with fatigue, dust and sand and
cordite fumes.'[110]

'Wreckage of battle strews the battlefield,' Moorehead wrote,

> ...with burnt-out tanks, a few crashed aircraft and all
> the forlorn, pathetic wreckage of dead-men's clothing –
> bedding, mess tins, letters and papers. There is a litter

of rifles which has been flung away, piles of British and German shell cases, tens of thousands of petrol tins, German water containers, broken tank tracks spilled along the sand like great lizards, up-ended trucks, biscuit and bully tins; and among all this the intermingled graveyards of British and German dead. These men were buried at the height of their battles beside their tanks. Most have a cross or some symbol like an empty cartridge belt placed by a comrade. As we pass, a half-demolished tank takes fire again. It fills the western sky with black smoke, its shells blowing off in mad, roaring volleys, its petrol sending up wave after wave of flame.[111]

'The news to-day is so far scanty, but good', Auchinleck informed London on 26 November.[112] Tobruk was now within sight of New Zealand troops while Sidi Rezegh had been retaken. Auchinleck could also report that Rommel's 'raid to divert our attention from Tobruk...has failed signally.'[113] The 19th New Zealand Brigade, von Mellenthin narrated, 'smashed through our lines of investment' before briefly linking up with the fortress garrison. It was then isolated again in a brutal see-sawing contest.[114] The savagery of the fighting is contained in the New Zealand *Official History*:

The enemy forces comprised a number of Germans and troops of 9 Bersaglieri Regiment (Italian)... There was an enormous number of dead and wounded all over the battlefield. A significant feature was the sight of many men who had been hit by solid shot anti-tank guns, fired at point blank range. These projectiles had torn large portions of flesh from the bodies of the unfortunate victims and it would be hard to imagine a more unpleasant sight or a more heavily contested battlefield. The Bersaglieri Regt fought with much greater determination than is usually found among Italian troops and the numbers of their dead and the positions in which they lay showed that they had kept their guns in action to the last.[115]

Reluctant to accept the seriousness of his situation, Rommel attempted to press on. German forces though were too weak to relieve Bardia and an attempt to seize Ed Duda on 4 December broke down. Investing Tobruk could not continue and Axis forces fell back to a new defensive line running southwest of the fortress where Rommel hoped to hold the Eighth Army. Axis transport was again taxed. The Germans attached to the 25th Bologna Division and the Italian officers escaped in vehicles, leaving the rank and file to walk. Many preferred to surrender.

A German serviceman turned to his diary (5 December), scrawling,

> This evening we are to withdraw. The position is said to be serious but not hopeless, but everyone has his own thoughts. I have felt this in my bones. All through the night British aircraft have flown over our position and dropped bombs. Imprisonment in British hands is said to be good. Who knows where is best to be? Down with all warmongers.[116]

Brigadier Bernard Ferguson was inside Tobruk when news of Japan's attack on Pearl Harbor broke, followed three days later by the devastating loss of the RN capital ships *Prince of Wales* and *Repulse* off Malaya. Another low point in the war for Britain, he remembered:

> For all that these events were happening so far away, for all that we realised that America was now on our side, for all that our own immediate battle was over, our morale slumped to a low level. The snakes in this war game seemed so much more numerous just then than the ladders.[117]

Hitler was thrilled by the news of Japanese hostilities. In a stunning miscalculation, he turned to Walter Hewell, his liaison officer, declaring, 'We cannot lose the war at all. We have an ally who has not been defeated in three thousand years.'[118] On 8 December 1941 the Führer suspended the Wehrmacht's ill-fated march on Moscow and declared war on the US: the spectre of defeat creeping a step closer.

Back in Libya, both sides were locked in desperate fighting. Schraepler confided in a letter home how the 'English fight remarkably well. Their artillery is especially effective. It threatens us from all sides.' For the German command, it was 'a very difficult and hard time...as we have not become stronger by the continuing fighting, now three weeks.'[119] Rommel vented his frustration during an acrimonious meeting with

Ettore Bastico – blaming his situation on Italian ineptitude and even threatening to retire all the way to Tunisia where he would give his forces over to the Vichy French and face internment.

11 December. Axis forces finally evacuated their hard-won footing, eight months to the day after his first assault on Tobruk. Faced with little alternative, Rommel also abandoned his frontier positions, leaving the fighting parson, Hauptmann Bach, surrounded at Halfaya plus an ad hoc division marooned at Bardia.

Sean Fielding noted the alacrity of the Axis withdrawal.

> We constantly came upon overturned Italian lorries, most of them burned out with their dead lying grotesquely in heaps beside them… Very rarely had the retreating Italians had time to bury their dead; occasionally they had laid a chap out and crossed his hands over his chest, but not often.[120]

From within Tobruk, Lieutenant General Sir Ronald Scobie announced: 'Tobruk is relieved, but not as relieved as I am.'[121] 'The first round has gone to us,' a British military spokesman declared.[122]

With the raising of the siege, Brigadier Bernard Ferguson was assigned the responsibility of managing a prisoner of war cage, housing some 6,000 Italian and 300 German prisoners. 'It took at least two days to get a routine established', he wrote, 'and during that period when milling, hungry men were trying to rush our embryo system, considerations about the Geneva convention had to walk the plank. I am not in the least ashamed to confess that early on we used our rifle butts quite a lot.'[123]

Throughout 18-20 December, the Italian 1st Carabinieri Paratroopers battalion repeatedly fought off the 4th Indian Division before reaching friendly lines, having suffered 35 men dead and 251 wounded and captured.[124]

BBC Correspondent, Richard Dimbleby, gave an upbeat account of the Axis withdrawal (20 December).

> The enemy front in Libya is broken… The Germans of Hitler's African army are running as fast as the Italians were running a year ago. Behind the Axis tanks, armoured cars, lorry-borne infantry, motor-cyclists and foot-sloggers as

they go piling back to the west along the roads to Cyrenaica, are the advance Allied forces, hot on their heels, pursuing them every inch of the way.[125]

This time, however, there would be no Beda Fomm. 'Throughout their retirement the enemy were never run off their feet', Verney made clear. 'They always managed to retain their rearguards strong enough to hit back hard.'[126]

Rommel adroitly manoeuvred the DAK, whose morale remained high, and Italian armour west – unlike earlier panic-stricken routs across the same desertscape – past Mechili towards Msus (sixty miles southeast of Benghazi). The Italian infantry hurried west along the coast road before the British armour could strike.

Schmidt was 'driving in wild haste' when attacked by RAF bombers. Emerging from a funk hole, he found his car's upholstery 'ripped to shreds'. 'I called out to my driver...but got no reply. A soldier touched me on the arm and pointed under the car. The driver's torn body lay there. A few minutes earlier we had been talking of his wife and family and of leave... There would be no reunion.'[127]

Axis troops evacuated Benghazi on 24 December. Before leaving, Schmidt helped himself to 'undreamed of delicacies' in a supply depot, savouring 'Italian tinned fruit, beer and chocolate' before stocks were torched.[128] Parties of Arabs, seemingly pleased to witness the Axis route, took pot shots at the fleeing army.

Jewish shopkeepers provided British troops with food and other goods while thousands of young Arabs came forward to join security forces. Libyans previously serving as soldiers and police likewise deserted and some 30,000 men joined the Libyan Arab Force – stark evidence of Mussolini's failed colonial policy.[129] Brutal measures were employed to stem the insurrection with thousands of Arabs, Jews and Berbers executed. Lieutenant Colonel Vladimir Peniakoff witnessed Arabs suspected of helping the British hanged with a 'steel hook inserted in the jaw' and left to die of shock.'[130] At one *campi di concentramento,* south of Tripoli, which opened in February 1942, some 600 of the 3,000 prisoners died from disease, malnutrition or exposure.

Few today remember the 100,000 native Muslims interned by the Italians in camps across Libya. Also forgotten are the racial attacks and reprisals against Libyan Jews and the 5,000 sent to concentration and forced labour camps within and outside Libya. Several hundred were even deported to camps in Austria and Germany including Bergen-Belsen.[131]

Rommel, meanwhile, had safeguarded the bulk of his forces and delayed his enemy's advance. What is more, the tables were now turning in his favour. The Italian navy slipped through the RN blockade to deliver much needed fuel and armour. Shepherded by no less than four Italian battleships, four cruisers, thirteen destroyers and six submarines, the German merchantman *Ankara* landed 21 Panzers at Benghazi on 19 December. Rommel's clout further increased with another 23 tanks disembarked at Tripoli. Newly reinforced, the DAK fended off an attempted envelopment, and even sallied forward to bloody the enemy's nose. On 28 December, Ludwig Crüwell mauled Brigadier John Scott-Cockburn's 22nd Armoured Brigade, destroying thirty-seven tanks. In an aggressive reprise two days later, the Germans knocked out a further twenty-three tanks before withdrawing in worsening cold weather to El Agheila – the starting position of Rommel's first offensive.

Although the pendulum of war had swung in Auchinleck's favour, the Eighth Army had failed to smash its foe. It was now the British who were beginning to feel the pinch of lengthening supply lines, slowing progress and individual units scattered across miles of difficult terrain. With rations, ammunition and other supplies dwindling, Crusader petered out. It had been a costly battle for both sides. Auchinleck (up to mid-January 1942) lost 2,900 men killed, 7,300 wounded and 7,500 missing – some fifteen per cent of his force. Rommel had lost thirty-two per cent of Axis manpower – German casualties stood at 1,136 killed, 3,483 wounded in action and 10,141 missing; Italian casualties were 1,036 killed, 2,122 wounded and 18,554 missing. Axis armoured losses are estimated at 220 Panzers (eighty-five per cent of the total) and 120 Italian tanks (eighty per cent of the total).

'My Commanders are ill – all those who aren't dead or wounded', Rommel despondently wrote on 20 December.[132] Misfortune had decimated his command: Generalmajor Walter Neumann-Silkow, commander of the 15th Panzer Division, died on 9 December after shrapnel smashed his lower jaw and slashed his neck near El Gubi; Generalmajor Hans von Ravenstein, second in command to Rommel, was taken prisoner by New Zealand troops at Sidi Rezegh on 28 November;

and Generalmajor Max Sümmermann, commander of the 90th Light Infantry Division, was killed during an air raid on 10 December (his last words – 'I have a son in Russia'). Rommel had earlier lost his adjutant, Schraepler, after an unfortunate vehicle accident involving his *Mammut* on 9 December.

Next to fall were the sequestered Axis formations still holding out near the frontier. Generalmajor Artur Schmitt's Bardia garrison (comprised of 2,120 Germans, mostly rear echelon staff, and 5,655 Italians) was besieged by the 2nd South African Infantry, the 1st Army Tank Brigade, the Polish Brigade and 2nd New Zealand Infantry Division artillery prior to an assault on 30 December.[133] Dummy M3 tanks 'driven' by the New Zealand Cavalry moved forward towards the northern perimeter at dawn – the sound of their engines provided by revving motorcycles and trucks minus their exhaust systems. The deception worked, drawing enemy fire for ninety minutes while South African infantry infiltrated the perimeter in the south-east.

Lieutenant Colonel John Geddes Page (Kaffrarian Rifles) and his battalion were caught crossing open territory by Schmitt's determined defenders:

> Having shortly been through a dust storm, our automatic weapons were jammed, as were most of our rifles. I was carrying a captured Mauser rifle, and, having got off the round I had in the breech, could not get the bolt action to work, it having completely jammed. About two minutes after the fire opened I received a severe wound in the chest, and two men within a few yards of me were killed.[134]

Schmitt's desperate appeal for reinforcements – an airborne battalion from Crete and additional anti-tank guns – was rejected due to poor weather and the distances to be covered. One of Rommel's final messages lauded his general's stand, though the inference was clear. Bardia would fall with the garrison inflicting as many casualties on the British as possible. With further resistance futile after losing ammunition and provision dumps to the enemy, a *parlementaire* was sent to on the morning of 2 January 1942 to negotiate an unconditional surrender. Two enemy officers, one a German and the other an Italian who spoke English, approached in a car bearing a white flag. Both gave the imperial salute. Major General Isaac de Villiers' ultimatum to surrender or be 'blown to hell' was followed by a reading of the surrender terms at his headquarters. Schmitt was the first German general to be captured by British Commonwealth forces. South African casualties stood at 139 killed and 295 wounded.

Correspondingly crippled by a supply shortage, Generale Fedele de Giorgis surrendered his three isolated Axis strongholds, including Bach and his embattled men at Halfaya on 17 January 1942. Polish artillerymen, in a spiteful riposte, lobbed shells into a group of surrendered Germans, their rifles and other equipment. Several were killed and a dozen or so wounded. The general state of the prisoners, especially the Italians, was pathetic, appearing, as General Norrie described, like 'underfed animals in a fourth-class zoo.'[135]

'Should have been caught like a rat in a trap'

Operation Crusader had failed to deliver a clear-cut victory, much to the frustration of several senior British commanders. Harking back to February 1941 and the decision not to march on Tripoli, General Bernard Freyberg felt that Rommel 'should have been caught like a rat in a trap', blaming faulty doctrine within British Army Command.[136] Auchinleck drew a similar lesson:

> We have got to face the fact that unless we can achieve superiority on the battlefield by better co-operation between arms, and more original leadership…we may have to forego any idea of mounting a strategical offensive, because our armoured forces are incapable of meeting the enemy in the open, even when superior to him in numbers.[137]

The collective failure of Brevity, Battleaxe and Crusader underscored the shortcomings of the British Army at the time. In a letter to Auchinleck on 30 December, Ritchie admitted to 'having some misgivings myself about our tactics and the general employment of our armed forces.'[138] Wrestling a Gordian knot, Ritchie was unable to unravel it before one of the worst British defeats of the war.

*****

31 December 1941. Hauptmann Wolfgang Evereth gathered his reconnaissance troops together in the evening to review their first year in the desert. He recalled the fallen, the wounded and the missing; a vow of loyalty to the Führer concluded his talk. 'At midnight', he recorded, 'the bells rang out on the wireless and the German anthem resounded. The whole horizon was full of Verey lights [flares]. Every troop sent off every colour, as if there was no war at all. Tracer ammunition blazed into the dark sky and the artillery fired for five minutes. After midnight all was quiet and still again.'[139]

Chapter Four

Counterstroke – Rommel's Reconquest of Cyrenaica

The desert, mighty, void of hope, immense,
Disturbed from tortured sleep by sounds of war,
Her barren bosom throbs with life once more.
Across her brow come men and guns to wrest
From foemen's grasp another sterile stretch.
                                    –Signalman G. Harker

This beginning of 1942 opened with both sides licking their wounds before landing the next blow. With Allied fortunes ebbing in the Far East, Auchinleck's command was stripped of the 18th British, 17th Indian, 6th and 7th Australian Divisions and 7th British Armoured Brigade to fight against the Japanese. Many formations that had fought in Crusader were refitting in Egypt, leaving largely inexperienced units to defend Cyrenaica, including the 1st Armoured Division (General Frank Messervy). Despite 'an apparent inferiority in leadership', Auchinleck opted to retain Ritchie, a 'trusted friend and subordinate', as his Eighth Army commander.[1] The Auk – aside from overseeing the defence of Iraq, Persia, Syria and a potential undertaking in Turkey – began rebuilding the Eighth Army. Writing to Ritchie, he agreed that his tanks were 'outgunned', 'too complicated' or too 'delicate' – but also probed whether 'superiority in numbers' would be an equaliser?[2]

Ritchie, busy readying for a renewed offensive, refused to prepare a new defensive system at Gazala should Rommel make the first move. General Headquarters (GHQ), as Messervy revealed, simply 'wouldn't believe there were large German tank reinforcements – which infuriated the forward troops who had actually seen them. That was why we were on the wrong foot when he advanced.'[3] Auchinleck likewise dismissed the Axis in Libya as tired, disorganised and short of senior officers and matériel. Hidden microphones had exposed the misgivings of captured Generals von Ravenstein and Schmitt over recent heavy losses and their dissatisfaction with Rommel's leadership. 'I am convinced the enemy is hard-pressed more than we dared think', the Auk posed to Churchill, while pushing for Acrobat – a follow-up operation to Crusader, to capture Tripoli and push as far as the Tunisian border. Churchill, then in Washington finetuning a 'Germany-first' strategy, was 'very pleased' with the Auk's memo, replying: 'I am sure you are quite right to push on.'[4]

For all of GHQ's musings, Rommel held the upper hand. Convoys safeguarded by U-boats and the recently arrived Luftflotte 2 had replenished Panzerarmee Afrika (soon to become Panzergruppe Afrika on 30 January 1942). An unmatched 150,389 tons of matériel and 86,031 tons of fuel were landed, while the Italians received their new Semovente da 75/18 self-propelled guns.[5]

Signals intelligence presented by von Mellenthin on 12 January shed light on Ritchie's dispositions and the chance to deliver 'an effective counterstroke'.[6] Decoded reports dashed off by the American military attaché in Cairo, Colonel Bonner F. Fellers, were another windfall. His commentary on British movements, according to Berlin, provided 'all we needed to know, immediately, about virtually every enemy action.'[7] As Dr Wilhelm F. Flicke (former cipher officer) wrote, Fellers 'ranged all over the battle area, saw and heard everything, knew all preparations, every intention, every moment of the British forces, and he transmitted it all to the United States.'[8] From reading what he called the 'Good Source', Rommel knew that he had front-line superiority in armour.[9] As the master of hiding his intentions and deceiving the enemy, he notified neither his German nor Italian superiors of his plans, thus blindsiding Ultra. The intelligence stakes, this time, were firmly in his favour.

A week later (20 January) Rommel was in Germany to receive the coveted Oak Leaves and Swords grade to his Knight's Cross for actions to date in North Africa. That evening he arranged for a few derelict huts and the hulk of an abandoned ship at Mersa el Brega to be set alight, duping the British into thinking he was withdrawing further west. Just hours later he opened a new offensive.

21 January 1942. German military police circulated Rommel's Order of the Day:

> German and Italian Soldiers!
> You have difficult fighting against vastly superior enemy forces behind you. Despite that your fighting morale remains unbroken. At present we are numerically stronger than the enemy to our front. Therefore, the field army is moving out today to destroy that enemy. I expect that every soldier will give his all during these decisive days.[10]

Two columns rolled forward – elements of the 90th Light Africa Division and the 21st Panzer Division along the Via Balbia in the north, the DAK (15th Panzer Division) south through the desert. They caught the Eighth Army napping. Richie fatefully downplayed the manoeuvre as a mere reconnaissance that would retire the following day. With aerial scouting and wireless intercepts indicating a British withdrawal, Rommel issued orders for the 1st Armoured Division to be encircled. Although a considerable number of British tanks and guns were destroyed, the soft terrain hindered German progress, allowing the bulk of the receding formations to slip through their cordon. These units, von Mellenthin noted, 'had no battle experience and… were completely demoralised by the onslaught of 15th Panzer… [They] fled madly over the desert in one of the most extraordinary routs of the war.'[11]

Back from Europe, Rommel returned to the helm, personally leading a combat formation into battle. Applauded as 'swift, audacious and flexible', he infiltrated enemy supply columns, throwing them into turmoil and capturing numerous vehicles.[12]

Amid this early success, Schmidt recounts how a young officer expressed concern about the lack of fuel, only to be told by an impatient Rommel to 'go and get it from the British.'[13]

Providence was again on Rommel's side, as Westphal recounts.

> Flying in the [Fiesler Fi 156 *Storch*] Stork, we came down to land by a group of vehicles which we supposed to belong to the DAK staff when suddenly furious light anti-aircraft fire broke out. Our escape [from the British] was a miracle and was fortunately overlooked by a squadron of [RAF] Hurricanes which were returning to base just above our heads.[14]

Against the 'unexpected strength' of the enemy surge, the Eighth Army withdrew from Agedabia and Beda Fomm. Auchinleck tried to mollify an anxious Churchill by admitting that Rommel had pushed further than expected, though he hoped to turn the situation around 'to our ultimate advantage.'[15] The desert horse racing motif restarted with the runners in the 'Second Benghazi Handicap' or 'Gazala Gallop' again in full flight. An Allied war correspondent reported on the confused fighting, 'spread over a wide area of desert…each enemy column supported by a group of tanks which are operating in close co-operation with the enemy guns, of which there are a considerable number.'[16]

The 15th Panzer Division continued its push, overrunning the British airfield at Msus and bagging twelve transport aircraft. Its tally of armoured vehicles also grew. By 26 January the DAK had captured 123 tanks and armoured cars, 56 field and self-propelled guns, and 217 trucks. Auchinleck disclosed the extent of the losses to General Arthur Smith a day later, writing off the 1st Armoured Division as a formation that 'can no longer be counted on as a fighting force. Its losses are said to be forty guns… [and] about a hundred or more tanks, and there is much doubt as to whether it was able to inflict any appreciable loss on the enemy.'[17]

Hauptman Wolfgang Everth and his men savoured their spoils:

> Slowly we ourselves became Tommies; our vehicles, petrol, rations and clothing were all English. I was somewhat international too – Italian shoes, French trousers, German coat and hat, English linen, stockings, gloves and blankets… The captured vehicles were painted with German crosses, so as to achieve at least some difference.[18]

Rommel, as usual, was eager to take advantage of the situation regardless of Cavallero's call for restraint. He ordered the DAK to manoeuvre towards Mechili in a ruse hoodwinking Ritchie, who had consolidated his tank force there. Pushing ahead through heavy rain, Rommel surprised British forces in Benghazi from the northeast. The city fell again, bringing 1,300 trucks into Rommel's hands. Victory, however, was not absolute. Through a 'blend of audacity, coolness, and skill deservedly blessed by fortune', some 4,100 men and officers of the 7th Indian Brigade succeeded in breaking out.[19]

Westphal observed, with some irony, 'the same Arabs [in Benghazi] who a few weeks previously had fired without cause after the retreating Germans now greeted them enthusiastically, waving the Green flag of the Prophet and throwing us plundered German rations.'[20] Rommel's success, quite naturally, surprised both sides. The native Senussi, 'the unhappy, bewildered inhabitants of Cyrenaica... changed their masters for the fourth time in little more than a year.'[21]

'At present the initiative rests with the enemy'

A British war correspondent summed up the situation: 'There is no denying that the loss of Benghazi will hamper our operations in this area... At present the initiative rests with the enemy... Rommel has emerged with a shade of odds in his favour.'[22] Even Churchill addressed the House of Commons on 27 January, paying tribute to Rommel as a 'daring and skilful opponent, and may I say across the havoc of war, a great general... Naturally, one does not say that we have not had a chance.'[23] A subsequent British intelligence review (23 February 1942) revealed the scale of his repute and how 'Axis propaganda has gone to considerable lengths to build up the legend of Rommel and the Afrika Korps... The picture of tough Germans under the waving palms of Libya has been built up. Strong, sun-tanned bodies, facing Churchill's unwilling colonial troops. The focal point of this picture is the romanticised figure of Rommel himself.'[24] And as the *British Medical Journal* (4 April 1942) detailed, morale, 'built by whatever means, is considered by the German leaders to be at least as important as weapons. This is all the more impressive when we consider how important they have proved weapons to be.'[25]

Disturbingly, James Chutter (senior chaplain with the South African 2nd Division) observed that Rommel was a 'general whose name, rightly or wrongly, was more of an admired household word among the Eighth Army than any held by our own.'[26]

Croswell Bowen (AFS) noticed the unease among British troops, unsure of their enemy's next move, tired of being on the receiving end.

> The soldiers seem discouraged and verging on a slight jitteriness. They don't know where and how Jerry will attack

next. I have heard at least a dozen British soldiers say, 'Why can't we do the attackin' for a change.'[27]

Auchinleck later urged his officers not to be taken in by the cult of personality surrounding their plucky adversary. He warned of 'a very real danger that our friend Rommel is becoming a kind of magician or bogey-man to our troops, who are talking far too much about him. He is by no means a superman... I wish you to dispel by all possible means the idea that Rommel represents something more than an ordinary German general.'[28]

Amid Rommel's ascendancy, Auchinleck recorded a growing inferiority complex among British tankers, 'owing to their failure to compete with the enemy tanks which they consider (and rightly so) superior to their own in certain aspects.'[29] Overwhelmed by an astute foe, his tactics and technology, the answer, he believed, lay in better training, equipment and leadership.

Recognition of Rommel's battlefield mastery also came from Berlin with his promotion to Generaloberst – the youngest officer to have attained such rank.

By 4 February, the British had been driven halfway back along the Cyrenaican 'Bulge' to a position 35 miles west of Tobruk. Rommel could now boast, 'We have got Cyrenaica back. It went like greased lightning.'[30] Summing up the flight, Lieutenant General Sir Francis Tuker slammed the 'dispersion of effort' and failure to concentrate forces: 'the 1st Armoured was attacked without a shot being fired by the 4th Indian Division, and 4th Indian Division was attacked without a shot being fired by 1st Armoured Division.'[31] Rommel's Panzerarmee though, as von Mellenthin recalled, was just 'too weak to do more than follow up, and on 6 February our advance came to a halt before the [British] Gazala position.'[32]

'No firm direction from the top'

Dissension over Britain's senior leadership in the desert echoed through the upper echelons of Middle East command and along the corridors of Whitehall. General Sir Alan Brooke (later Lord Alanbrooke), now CIGS, had written to Auchinleck on the day Rommel launched his offensive, worried 'that you have not got a first-class armoured force officer on your staff'.[33] 'News bad on all sides', Brooke noted privately on 30 January.

> The Benghazi business is bad and nothing less than bad generalship on the part of Auchinleck. He has been overconfident and has believed everything his overoptimistic [Director of Military Intelligence, Brigadier John] Shearer has told him.[34]

Auchinleck in turn was burdened by Ritchie's suitability as commander with disapproval rife in senor circles. Brigadier George 'Ricky' Richards (23rd Armoured Brigade), for one, was critical of 'no firm direction from the top... I found myself being switched about from one formation to another with very little or sometimes no warning.' Auchinleck's deputy chief of staff, then acting Major General Eric 'Chink' Dorman-Smith, blasted the 'usual slap-happy optimism' within Ritchie's headquarters where the 'immobility of minds equalled [the] immobility of formations.'[35] After interviewing divisional commanders, Dorman-Smith reported Ritchie to be a patronising commander, overly assured and limited in his ability to lead. He was not, Godwin-Austen affirmed, 'sufficiently quick-witted or imaginative enough for the command.'[36]

Morshead suspected that Ritchie suffered 'from an inferiority complex', being a 'terribly bad picker' of subordinates.[37] Brooke called for his dismissal. Auchinleck, however, was reluctant to remove his trusted commander in the present situation: 'He has gripped the situation, knows what to do and has the drive and ability to do it.'[38]

Announcing that he could no longer serve under Ritchie, Godwin-Austen offered his resignation after the fall of Benghazi. His replacement was Lieutenant General William Gott, who, as we saw, led the mobile forces outside Tobruk in 1941 and, as we shall learn, would become a hapless influence on Ritchie's decision-making in approaching months. 'We lost the wrong man,' Tuker later wrote. 'This serious and widely-advertised change of command was to lead', in his opinion, 'as inevitably as day follows night, to a British disaster only paralleled in World War II by that in Malaya.'[39]

The leadership quandary was further complicated by Auchinleck's jaundiced view towards many of his divisional and brigade commanders.

He cabled the War Office in March 1942 to complain of their poor 'standard of leadership', a shortcoming due to an 'almost complete absence [of] systematic and continuous instruction in simple principles in peace time. Staff training did not fill and is not filling this gap.'[40] Auchinleck's performance was also called into question. In yet another debatable appointment, the C-in-C exchanged his experienced chief of staff Arthur Smith with Lieutenant General Tom Corbett, whom he had known in India. Unsuited to the demanding role, Corbett would prove incapable of asserting himself and managing the complex Middle East General Headquarters. A 'furious' prime minister at one point even deliberated whether to replace Auchinleck with the Governor of Malta, Lord Gort.[41]

'Satisfied that enemy attack on this position should be repulsed'

The desert, for the moment, was quiet. British troops consolidated their positions along the so-called 'Gazala Line', which extended south from the coast at Gazala to Bir Hacheim, a remote oasis featuring a former Ottoman fortress. Auchinleck confidently advised Churchill:

> We now have [a] strong defensive position 36 miles square well-mined and organised in depth…designed to meet enemy break through to rear areas with armoured forces in [an] attempt to disorganise our system of command and supply. Am satisfied that enemy attack on this position should be repulsed with loss and it is too extensive to be enveloped or ignored. Real value of this position is that it provides security for Tobruk and therefore [it] forms admirable base for future offensive.[42]

The 'Line', however, was far from ideal. Rather than a continuous defensive belt, it comprised a number of independent 'keeps', or defensive 'boxes', enclosed by extensive minefields. Each box was garrisoned by a brigade from Gott's XIII Corps. Over a million land mines were laid, 'of a scale and complexity never yet seen in war', von Mellenthin afterwards wrote.[43] The rear of the line was defended by strongholds at Knightsbridge, El Adem and Tobruk, though crucially, as we will see, the latter's defences had been heavily stripped since the 1941 siege. Tactically unsound, these static positions squandered men and arms in mutually non-supporting positions without transport. They were also, misguidedly, intended as pivots of manoeuvre for British tanks, held in reserve.

The expansive desert minefields caused tragic and unintended casualties on all sides. Croswell Bowen was driving to the hospital in Tobruk when he passed a party of sappers working in a minefield. Unexpectedly,

> one of the mines goes up, hurling a Sapper into the air. He lands on his feet, but they are not really his feet for his feet and shoes have been blown off at the ankles. For an endless moment or two he danced around on the bloody stubs, then falls gracefully like a ballet dancer.[44]

Returning from the hospital at Tobruk, Andrew Geer (AFS) watched another inadvertent minefield fatality (a danger in the desert that continues to this day).

> A small herd of camels driven by two Arabs walking and one riding came along the desert paralleling the road. The camels walked into a mine field. Violent explosions killed two of the animals. The other swung about in a frenzied melee and trampled on more of the buried explosives. A hindquarter of a camel hurtled through the air, striking the hood of one of the ambulances. The field was littered with the torn and bleeding remains of the herd. The Arab who was riding the camel was never found.[45]

During a quiet period in the fighting, Major Stanley Aylett, a field surgeon in the Royal Army Medical Corps, took a moment to survey the battleground:

> All around are the relics of defeated armies. There are guns and lorries, tanks and armoured cars, all now a mass of twisted and deformed metal. Here and there are little collections of crosses to show the cost that this area of sand

has extracted. Some have inscriptions in English, some in German and others in Italian. Wherever you look there are shell cases, empty tins and discarded rifles and hand grenades, tin hats often riddled with bullet holes, clothing, gas masks, bandoliers, all in one awful confusion.[46]

Also traversing the now-quiet battlefield, Dr Alfons Selmayr (battalion surgeon, 5th Panzer Regiment) stopped to inspect a knocked-out Panzer: 'There was still a driver, carbonized and half decomposed at his driver's station. A horrifying picture. We had to leave him in his steel grave.'[47]

'In front of us a big tank battle was hotting up'

Both sides trained and replenished their forces in preparation for the next clash. Ritchie's Eighth Army was the larger force with almost 100,000 men divided into two corps: XXX Corps contained the bulk of the 1st and 7th Armoured Division armour and the 4th Indian Division; XIII Corps was comprised mainly of infantry including the 50th (Northumbrian) Division, 1st and 2nd South African Divisions. Held in reserve was the HQ 5th Indian Division, 10th Indian Brigade and part of the 10th Indian Division. His armour, a total of 849 tanks, included 167 new US-manufactured M3 Grant/Lee tanks.[48] An unusual design, the Grant was armed with a limited-traverse, hull-mounted M2 75-mm gun, firing both high-explosive and armour-piercing ammunition, plus a 37-mm gun in a turret. British troops also took delivery of the new 6-pounder anti-tank gun – a weapon on par with the German 5-cm Pak 38. Finally, the Desert Air Force had 320 aircraft, of all types, though less than 200 were operational around Tobruk and the frontier.

Rommel, too, had received newer model tanks: a Panzer III with a long-barrelled 5-cm main gun and a Panzer IV with a longer-barrelled 7.5-cm main gun. His Panzerarmee Afrika now numbered 90,000 men with 561 tanks (228 Italian) and 542 aircraft.

Churchill's impatience to take the offensive again intensified. Reminiscent of earlier – and future – exchanges, Auchinleck advised that the Eighth Army strike once it was fully prepared. He forwarded a seven-page appreciation to London on 27 February, outlining that his anticipated numerical superiority in armour, a prerequisite for any new offensive, would not happen before 1 June, when the Eighth Army would field four armoured brigades. Moreover, action in May was ruled out 'owing to intense heat causing great expenditure of water' for vehicle radiators. It closed: 'to launch [a] major offensive before then would be to risk defeat and possibly endanger [the] safety of Egypt.'[49] Churchill saw red. This was a seminal point in the war for the premier who urgently needed a victory to offset British fiascos in the Far East, the threat to India and the security of Tobruk. 'Winston's conviction', his doctor Charles McMoran Wilson (later Lord Moran) noted, was 'that his life as Prime Minister could be saved only by a victory in the field.'[50] It accounted for his biting exchanges with his C-in-C, who had already refused travel to London to discuss the Middle East situation in person. Auchinleck was directed to attack; once again, it was Rommel who dealt the first blow.

Word had spread within the Eighth Army 'that if the Boche were going to attack he would do so between 25th and 28th May.'[51] Cyril Joly, now in command of one of the new Grant tanks, readied for combat.

> We dispersed to our various tasks, thankful to have something to do to keep our minds off the impending battle… We ate our supper in solemn silence… Afterwards we went to bed – in my case to lie awake for some time…wondering at our chances, trying to remember whether I had forgotten to see to any vital detail and finally, and rather belatedly, regretting that I had not written home more often.[52]

On the afternoon of 26 May Rommel launched *Venezia*, an operation, he wrote in a letter home, that would 'bring the war to an end this year.'[53] Rommel set off in the midst of a fierce sandstorm, steering some 10,000 vehicles, including practically every Axis tank, in a bold outflanking manoeuvre at the southern end of the Gazala Line. It set in motion a sequence of engagements General Tuker condemned as 'one of the worst fought battles in the history of the British Army.'[54]

Rommel's plan directed the Ariete Division's tanks to neutralise the southernmost Bir Hakeim box; the 15th and 21st Panzer Divisions would continue further south, skirting around the Gazala line to strike British armour and isolate the infantry; and a Kampfgruppe of the 90th Light Infantry Division (renamed 90th Afrika Division on 26 July 1942) would advance to El Adem south of Tobruk, cut supply lines and attempt to hold British troops at Tobruk. Deception would assist with aircraft engines mounted on trucks to simulate dust clouds raised by a big armoured force. The remainder of the Italian formations would undertake a frontal assault in the north to pin down British forces near the coast. It was a plan not without risk, Alfred Gause explained:

> Determination and flexibility of command had to compensate for what was lacking in material. He could not afford to attempt to break through the heavily mined British positions, because he lacked the necessary tanks and ammunition for this purpose. His decision to outflank the positions in the south was a grave risk, particularly since all supplies also had to be moved forward around the British flank. Defeat in this battle might have involved the loss of Africa.[55]

Reports of German tanks south of Bir Hacheim prompted Major Gerry Birkin (South Notts Hussars) and his brother, Captain Ivor, to investigate. Engaged by the onrushing Panzers, an armour-piercing shell struck Gerry Birkin's armoured car, passing 'clear through the middle of him' and decapitating two radio operators. A third man suffered a broken leg when he had jumped into a slit trench and was run over by the shattered vehicle. The driver, Bobby Feakins, recoiled: 'I have to admit that I was in a bit of shock – headless bodies…just nothing but blood and flesh, bits of body all over the place.'[56] Peering inside, Sergeant Harold Harper was similarly revolted by the sight of the dead major and the 'two lads, their hands still holding their mouthpieces, although their heads were lying on the floor.'[57]

Recently flown to Africa, this was Leutnant Karl Susenberger's (21st Panzer Division) baptism of fire.

> In front of us a big tank battle was hotting up and the English artillery shells were landing only 200 metres away from us… I saw a Tommy sitting in a hole, his head to one side, around him was a swarm of flies. I wondered if he was alive and jumped from the vehicle. When I got up to him I realised he was dead. He was dead. He was buried on the spot, his hidey-hole became his grave.[58]

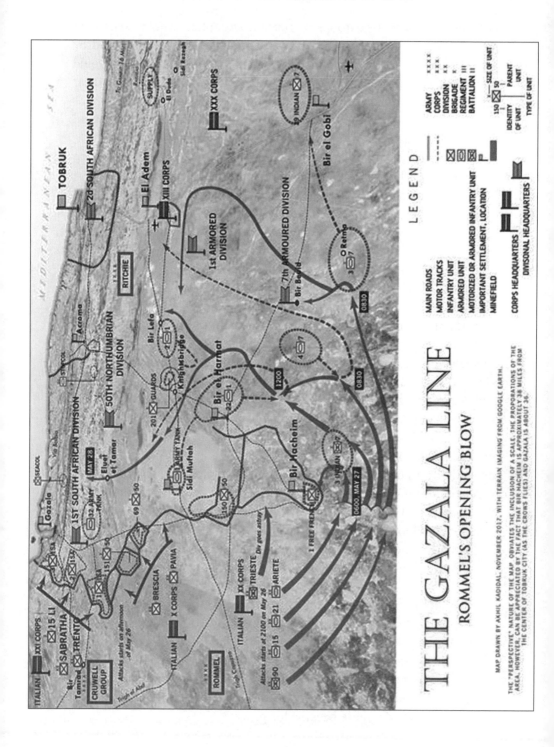

THE GAZALA LINE

ROMMEL'S OPENING BLOW

MAP DRAWN BY AKHIL KADIDAL, NOVEMBER 2017, WITH TERRAIN IMAGING FROM GOOGLE EARTH.

THE "PERSPECTIVE" NATURE OF THE MAP OBVIATES THE INCLUSION OF A SCALE. THE PROPORTIONS OF THE AREA, HOWEVER, CAN BE APPRECIATED BY THE FACT THAT BIR HACHEIM IS APPROXIMATELY 38 MILES FROM THE CENTER OF TOBRUK CITY (AS THE CROWS FLIES) AND GAZALA IS ABOUT 36.

LEGEND

MAIN ROADS
MOTOR TRACKS
INFANTRY UNIT
ARMORED UNIT
MOTORIZED OR ARMORED INFANTRY UNIT
IMPORTANT SETTLEMENT, LOCATION
MINEFIELD

CORPS HEADQUARTERS
DIVISIONAL HEADQUARTERS

ARMY   XXXX
CORPS   XXX
DIVISION   XX
BRIGADE   X
REGIMENT   III
BATTALION   II

SIZE OF UNIT

IDENTITY   PARENT
OF UNIT   UNIT

TYPE OF UNIT

Brigadier Anthony A. Filose, commander of the 3rd Indian Motor Brigade, radioed 7th Armoured Division that he was facing a 'whole bloody German armoured division.'[59] Indian gunner A.S. Naravane recalled, 'We were all so preoccupied with carrying out our duties and observing the enemy's relentless advance that we had no time to think of fear.'[60] The final Indian War Diary entry at 0845 ominously read: 'Positions completely overrun with enemy tanks in the box.'[61]

Inside the unfinished Retma box, an observer watched as 'some gunner started banging away like mad... It was the whole of Rommel's command in full cry straight for us.'[62] The position quickly fell.

Sergeant Ray Ellis (South Notts Hussars) waited with apprehension for the struggle to begin.

> I was tired, physically tired; and tired of battles, fighting, deserts and killing – sick of the whole thing. My gun crew were new and this was their first experience of warfare. I felt sorry for them... I was only 22, but as far as warfare went, I was an old man.[63]

Karl Susenberger stormed a British stronghold that afternoon.

> [It] fell and we counted 1,800 prisoners... [later] We saw now the havoc wrought by our heavy weapons; dead lay everywhere, burnt out tanks, lorries, guns etc.[64]

Scattered British formations independently engaged the oncoming enemy. Corbett later described how 'Ritchie's armour fought without its vital motor infantry component.'[65] Minus armoured support, the infantry could do little in unconnected, poorly coordinated counterattacks.

Targeting enemy armour, gunner Ray Ellis was immersed in his role:

> You take scant notice of the tank you've just fired at because you're looking at the next. You're very excited, not afraid, it's before and after that you're afraid. In the actual battle you're not so much afraid as excited and trying to get things done quickly. If a high explosive 25-pounder shell hits the track of a tank it is going to blow the track off and the tank will slew and stop. That means you can put another one into it, bang on into the back and he'll explode and brew up.[66]

A shell splinter injured Major Hans von Luck (3rd Panzer Reconnaissance Battalion) in the groin. Continuing to issue orders with the assistance of morphine injections, the wound soon became infected. Later taken to a Derna casualty clearing station, he recalled: 'two sisters held me tight, the [Italian] doctor, who seemed to me like a butcher, began to cut away at my wound. I cried out like an animal and thought I would faint with pain.'[67] Invalided home on a hospital ship, von Luck returned to Africa in mid-September 1942 to re-join his battalion.

Venezia began to slow. Bir Hacheim's defenders repulsed the Ariete Division with thirty-two M13 tanks lost, eighteen to mines. A captured Italian officer recalled Rommel 'absolutely livid with rage at the failure'.[68] Casualties among the 1ère Brigade Française Libre, under Général de Brigade Marie-Pierre Kœnig, were slight.[69] Their spirited stand, Susan Travers remembers, brought a message 'that we were no longer to be known as the Free French, but *La France Combattante*, the Fighting French…a name that never really struck, but the honour was appreciated.'[70]

Generalleutnant Ludwig Crüwell was taken prisoner the next day (29 May) when his *Storch* reconnaissance aircraft was forced down by ground fire. 'As though by a miracle', Crüwell recounted,

> the machine did not crash but flattened out and made a perfect crash landing, smashing the undercarriage to pieces. The fuselage cracked and splintered around me but to my good fortune the door did not jam. I was in the foremost line of the box held by the 150th Brigade.[71]

Alan Moorehead later observed 'his dead pilot's [Unteroffizier Rudolf Jordan] blood…still splashed on his boots when I saw him at Gambut.'[72] 'What a pity Rommel wasn't with him', a British *Movietone* narrator noted.[73]

The combat debut of the Eighth Army's Grant tank, one of the best-armed tanks of the day, came as a shock to the Germans. Up until this time, as Rommel stated, 'our tanks had in general been superior in quality to the corresponding British types. This was now no longer true, at least not to the same extent.'[74]

Leading a Grant into combat, Brigadier George Philip 'Pip' Roberts' (3rd RTR) tank was hit.

> The shell that hit my tank went through the nose of the tank plumb in the centre, passed between the driver's legs,

through the gear box (bits of which went into the driver's legs but not seriously), under my legs and between the 37-mm gunner and loader, through the engine and out at the back.[75]

Trooper Jack Merewood, The Bays (2nd Dragoon Guards), also in a Grant, was less fortunate.

> Through my periscope I saw a spurt of sand from the ground in front of us. Within seconds the next shell hit us... It came straight through the front of the tank and exploded inside. I looked at Jim; he had taken the full blast of the shell in his face and was dead. I had blood on my face and arms but what was hurting most was my leg... On looking at it I saw a hole in my thigh an inch or more across.[76]

Major John Sylvanus (Royal Army Medical Corps) later evacuated his camp when enemy tanks appeared at dusk. Steering a careful course beside a minefield, Sylvanus was called over to a truck to treat a man 'with his leg practically blown off. I amputated it with a pair of stretcher-bearer's scissors. He had stepped on a mine.'[77]

'Seriously worried'

German losses were climbing. By the evening of the third day's fighting Rommel had lost 200 tanks; his formations now low on fuel and ammunition. Axis formations were also widely, and dangerously, dispersed on the British side of the Gazala Line. With his supply columns effectively cut off, the situation was becoming critical; even Rommel admitted that he was 'seriously worried'.[78] Withdrawing into an area infamously known as 'the Cauldron', north of Bir Hacheim, the Germans screened themselves with anti-tank guns, fending off successive attacks.

The Line began to crack. 'Rommel', General Tuker later wrote,

> sat back on the defensive in the Cauldron, opened up a safer supply artery, and while doing so invited the piecemeal armoured attacks which the British obligingly delivered,

whereby he reduced the enemy's armoured superiority to the point where he felt strong enough to resume the offensive.[79]

Concerted Axis ground and aerial attacks overwhelmed the gallant Northumbrians of 150th Brigade, defending an important box north of Bir Hacheim. Back in Cairo, Auchinleck was naturally alarmed. He advised Ritchie that he was pleased that 'the situation is still favourable to us and is improving', but cautioned:

> I view the destruction of 150th Brigade and the consolidation by the enemy of a broad and deep wedge in the middle of your position with some misgiving… Situated as he is, he is rapidly becoming able to regain the initiative.[80]

Astounded by Ritchie's underestimation of Rommel's capabilities, Dorman-Smith urged Auchinleck, in vain, to dismiss Ritchie and assume command of the Eighth Army as Churchill had suggested as early as 20 May.

Rommel's challenge was to secure his southern flank by neutralising Bir Hacheim, derided by propagandist Leutnant Alfred-Ingemar Berndt as 'Gaullists, swashbucklers, and criminals of twenty different nations', before continuing the offensive.[81] An American AFS driver was eyewitness to the ferocity of the Axis siege:

> It was absolutely impossible to step out of the dugouts, the shelling and machine-gunning were so continuous. During the greater part of the attack, the Germans were throwing in at least 12,000 to 15,000 shells a day, as well as the tremendous weight of bombs which were rained down in the daily raids…
> It wasn't long before we got into the habit of always keeping our mouths open against the concussion of near-by shells.[82]

'Poor Pierre', Travers wrote of her lover, the citadel's commander, 'His features were creased with dust and I could see the tiredness in his sunken eyes… He was bearing such a heavy burden.'[83] Branded a traitor by the Vichy government, his band of Free French rebels, wrote Alan Moorehead, 'had come together from the strangest places…from Indo-China…from France…some had come up through the Congo jungles in the south, or enlisted in Syria and Egypt, some had got away from the Balkans or crossed from America. There were regular soldiers and diplomats, Spahis and sapiers-pompiers, businessmen and Foreign Legionaries, sailors, and farmers, black and white.'[84] Thrust into the spotlight, the world closely monitored the plight of the besieged outpost.

Rommel's onslaught, according to Richard McMillian (United Press correspondent), was the 'greatest dive-bomber raid ever seen in the desert... Between the avalanches of bombs, the Axis artillery hammered Bir Hacheim, and German armoured forces smashed the French minefield and barbed wire defences within minutes of the great raid by Stukas.'[85]

Exhausted and short of ammunition, 11 June brought a 'another hellish day. Water, Water, Water!! That's the scream of the injured, the cry of the survivors', a captured diary later attested.[86] That night 2,400 Frenchmen – and Susan Travers – broke through the Axis encirclement. Bir Hacheim surrendered the next day. French losses were 141 dead, 229 wounded and 814 men taken prisoner; Axis losses were significant: 3,300 dead or wounded, 227 captured, 164 vehicles and 49 aircraft destroyed. The 'gallant Allies' had bought time for the Eighth Army.[87] 'In the whole course of the desert war,' von Mellenthin recollected, 'we never encountered a more heroic and well-sustained defence.'[88]

'I fear we have not very good generals'

5 June. Ritchie ordered Operation Aberdeen – a badly planned assault that saw armour and infantry operating independently of one another. Inflicting heavy casualties, Rommel broke out of the Cauldron.

Poring over reports of Rommel's march, Churchill confided to Eden, 'I fear we have not very good generals.'[89]

Breaches in the Gazala defences continued with the annihilation of the 10th Brigade, 5th Indian Division. Generalmajor Walter Nehring (Rommel's second in command after Crüwell's misfortune) reported the capture of 3,100 men. One of those taken prisoner, Brigadier Desmond Young, watched as a Kübelwagen pulled up.

> Out of it jumped a short, stocky but wiry figure, correctly dressed, unlike the rest of us, in jacket and breeches. I noticed that he had a bright blue eye, a firm jaw and an air of command... I looked at the general and saw, as I thought,

the ghost of a smile. At any rate his intervention seemed to be worth a salute. I cut him one before I stepped back into the ranks to be driven off into captivity.[90]

In the frontlines, Sergeant Quentin Smythe (1st SA Infantry Division) took charge of a platoon after his commanding officer was seriously wounded. Badly wounded by a shrapnel gash to his forehead, Smythe continued to stalk an enemy machine gun nest, which he destroyed using hand grenades, capturing the crew. Weakened by blood loss, he also managed to assail and single-handedly capture an anti-tank position, killing and bayoneting several enemy troops. In danger of encirclement, he successfully withdrew his men.[91] Smythe's bravery was recognised with South Africa's first VC of the war.

'Pip' Roberts was in another Grant that fell foul of an anti-tank gun. He gathered his surviving crewmembers outside the stricken vehicle.

> The 75-mm gunner was quite blown to bits and hardly recognisable; he was a heavy man and his body undoubtedly saved Peter Burr [his adjutant] who was burnt on his exposed areas – i.e. arms and knees. The 37-mm gunner came out with only his boots on and he seemed to have been scorched all over with flash [he died later]. The wireless operator was very badly wounded and yelling as he couldn't get himself out... I had my epaulettes with rank badge blown off and also my beret.[92]

Cyril Joly's crew, also in the heat of battle, knocked out a Panzer III, spraying the crew with machine-gun fire as they bailed out. To his left a Grant 'was in flames... We watched it blow up with such a roar and concussion as we had not known before.' Shortly afterwards, Joly's tank received several hits, one killing the driver.

> A minute or two later another shot chipped the edge of the aperture where the driver's hatch had been and broke into fragments, one of which entered the side of Rogers' head, killing him instantly. With a cool courage which I had not suspected of him, Harden pushed aside the dead bodies... and then continued to load and fire the [75-mm] gun

himself... [Later] I helped them put bodies in [graves] and watched while the earth was shovelled over them. I left as they were fixing crude crosses to some stone-filled petrol tins.[93]

Three American-manned tanks (with volunteer crews) made their debut at Acroma on 11 June – the 'first US armed forces that made actual contact with Germans on land.'[94]Their commander, Major Henry C. Lodge, described the fighting: '[The crews were] attacked by German tanks at a range of about 4,000 yards. All day the American crews kept up a withering fire...[and] knocked out at least eight German Panzers before the Germans brought up their 88-mm guns and the British gave the order to retreat.'[95]

With his own tank hit, Lieutenant Colonel Henry Foote (7th RTR) continued to lead his battalion, riding on the outside of another tank where he received a neck wound.

Stanley Aylett was one of the surgeons attending to British wounded in a forward dressing station.

> We've worked flat out just snatching an hour's rest now and then. Once again, we have all the awfulness of shattered bodies lying on the floor head to head with not an inch between them, waiting their turn to come to the surgeon. Limbs bent and unnatural in their brokenness, faces that look like smashed pulp, heads where the brain oozes out, the little room set aside for the dying, the stink, the filth, the flies, the absolute shambles, following a night's work, of blood and dressings and plaster and cut-off clothes.[96]

Dr Alfons Selmayr also depicted the carnage, callousness and misery of men locked in battle:

> We encountered the first English tanks at Bir Hamat. The collision was blood. Oberstleutnant von Hülsen was killed by a round to the head... We captured an English brigade order that stated that no German prisoners were to be given water until they talked... Rommel then ordered that issuance of water to English prisoners was to stop until the order was

rescinded. These gentlemen, who appear to have borrowed their humanity from elsewhere, soon came to their senses… We ran into an English troop transporter that had been blown apart by a high explosive round. A horrible picture. Badly wounded, ripped-off limbs and dead and, between them, cans of [fruit] preserves. My people were no slouches; they immediately began to collect the cans. That disgusted me so much that I forbade them… I went back with one of our youngest soldiers, who had been badly burnt. It was very moving how he told me about his grandmother and his home area, neither of which he would ever see again.[97]

Helmut Wolf dispaired.

Whoever gets out of this hell can thank the Lord. I've been ordered for duty in the casualty clearing station. This morning I fainted, whether from hunger or at the sight of the wounded I don't know. My child, I feel so lonely. Does anyone think of the Germans in Africa – no air support, no food, no ammunition, no mail: nothing.[98]

When asked 'why the great tank battle on 12 June was lost', Robin Dunn (2nd Armoured Brigade), again raised the matter of inferior equipment and technology inexorably tied to receding morale.

Our tank crews were fighting an enemy better equipped than themselves, in tanks better armoured and more important with longer range guns… The first time they met the Germans they would go in with tremendous dash and courage, and very few of them would come out. One by one the morale of these proud regiments was broken... It was more than flesh and blood and nerves could stand always to be asked to fight at such fearful odds.[99]

Henry Foote returned to the fighting on 13 June with orders to slow enemy tanks and allow the Guards Brigade to be withdrawn. After the first wave of British tanks had been knocked out, Foote regrouped the remaining vehicles, 'going on foot from one tank to another to encourage the crews under intense artillery and anti-tank fire.' He positioned his own tank, though badly damaged with all guns smashed, standing tall in the turret as an example to his men. By keeping a corridor open, the brigade fell back. Foote's action won him a VC.[100]

In desperate fighting, neither side had yet to land a knock-out blow. Rommel turned to eliminate the Knightsbridge box, manned by the defiant Gurkha Brigade. Pinned down by the Italian Trieste Motorised Division, the 22nd Armoured Brigade was savaged by the 21st Panzer Division, which then joined with 15th Panzer Division in crushing the 7th Armoured Division.

Clare Boothe, of *Life*, covered the fighting for a US readership:

> Suddenly the picture changed as the German tanks faded away and bewildered Ritchie met a great battery, a mass formation, of Rommel's 88-mm guns firing point-blank, head on... Brilliant new Rommelian tactics or old-fashioned ambush – nevertheless in this encounter Rommel, 'the Trapped' trapped, captured and destroyed hundreds of Ritchie's tanks... Circling, swirling, thrusting ahead, Rommel lost neither his head nor his forward momentum.[101]

Perhaps driven by sheer desperation, an 'enterprising [British] gunner' installed four 3.7-inch anti-aircraft guns in an 'unfamiliar' anti-tank role. Withdrawing from this position, two of the guns were stuck in heavy sand and abandoned. Severely reprimanded by Cairo HQ 'for his temerity', this 'one tactical innovation', as Tuker put it, 'would have brought victory...instead of defeat and shame.'[102]

Flying Officer Geoff Chinchen (who had earlier damaged Hans-Joachim Marseille's aircraft in a dogfight on 13 May) was leading a flight of No. 3 Squadron RAAF P-40 Kittyhawks when suddenly, as he described it, 'all hell broke loose'. With his aircraft alight and wounds to his legs and arm, Chinchen bailed out. Taken prisoner on landing, he was placed in the custody of a German meteorological officer. Rommel quizzed the captured airmen; in Chinchen's words, 'He asked me a lot of questions but, of course, I couldn't tell him anything. He then said: "For you the war is over," to which I replied: "I don't know about that," and he laughed.'[103]

Tobruk, which had become a 'symbol of British resistance', now lay firmly in his sights.[104]

'A general feeling of optimism'

Rommel could now write: 'Now our forces were free. Despite all the courage' shown by the British and French troops, Ritchie 'had been badly mistaken if he had thought to wear down my forces by these pitched battles.'[105]

Anxious not to squander his remaining armour, Ritchie gave the order on 14 June to retire to a new defensive line incorporating Tobruk. We can only imagine what the retreating infantry would have thought when readers of London's *Times* were informed on 16 June that the Eighth Army was 'still full of fight', while an 'impotent' Rommel threatened 'no serious harm'.[106] A Cairo dispatch read:

> Fierce fighting is proceeding, but whatever the outcome, there is not a shadow of a doubt that Rommel's plans for his initial offensive have gone completely awry and have cost him dearly in men and material.[107]

Listening to similarly reassuring BBC broadcasts, US war correspondent Frank Gervasi concluded: 'We were really winning, not losing the war.'[108] Perhaps such confidence sprung from reading Crüwell's seized diary, which signalled Rommel's plan to take Tobruk on the fourth day of the attack – 1 June.

Regardless, Gott began planning for Tobruk to again be invested. Satisfied by what saw, he notified Ritchie that the defences were a 'nice tidy show' in comparison to 1941.[109] He also expressed his desire to be given command of the fortress – his observation was accepted, his proposal rejected. Instead, Ritchie selected the commander of the 2nd South African Infantry (SAI) Division – General Hendrik Balzazer Klopper. He was a 'first class soldier', Ritchie declared, 'I cannot want a better man for the defence of Tobruk.'[110]

Writing from within the fortress, Klopper exuded confidence.

> Things are going very well indeed with us here, as spirits are very high, and I do not think morale could be better under present circumstances. There is a general feeling of optimism, and I think there is every reason for it, although

we expect to put up a strong fight. We are looking forward to a good stand, and we are supported by the very best of British troops.[111]

Klopper was a young commander, supported by a largely inexperienced staff, of a division largely untried in battle. Meeting with his brigade commanders on 15 June, he announced that Tobruk was to be held for at least three months, though without mention of a tactical plan. Watching on, Colonel Max H. Gooler (US military observer) was eyewitness to a 'decided lack of co-operation' within a dysfunctional HQ

> [where] staff openly complained that General Klopper did not have the correct picture of the enemy situation or [realise] its serious potentialities. And what was more serious, apparently did not trust his chiefs of sections. In my opinion he was not in touch with the situation.[112]

Curiously, there seemed no sense of impending danger. The British Guards Brigade even travelled to the coastal 'retreat' to relax after the intense fighting at the Knightsbridge Box – hardly a regrouping before battle.

But while senior commanders reassured each other, *esprit de corps* within the lower ranks sagged. South African censors scrutinising soldiers' correspondence noted frequent references to adversity: 'tortured by dirt, dust, heat, thirst, cold, vermin and insects and bereft of all the freedom, individuality, amenities, associates and privileges of their normal lives', one soldier carped.[113]

Alan Moorehead found the mood within Tobruk 'altogether different' from 1941 – new occupants in a strange house – 'bundled pell-mell into the fortress at the last moment...tired and hungry and embittered from their setbacks of the past five days.'[114] Sergeant Fred Geldenhuis's regiment entered Tobruk, only to find the town deserted. There were 'no anti-aircraft guns pointing into the air, just empty gun pits.'[115] Heightening any sense of foreboding was the transfer of troops *out* of Tobruk. Moorehead observed that 'it can scarcely have contributed to the morale of the defenders to see hundreds of lorries [filled with the troops of the 1st SAI Division] passing straight through the garrison and on to the east.'[116] Eighteen 3.7-inch heavy anti-aircraft guns, earmarked for an anti-tank role, and six Grant tanks were also removed – clearly a sign of the higher authorities' thinking.

'As ever in the fog of battle', Reverend Chutter recalled, 'rumours were rife and repeated and distorted, according to the imaginative powers of the narrator.'[117] The 2,000 African Bantu people (2nd SAI Division), all fervent believers in witchcraft, or *tagati*, were dispirited after a Zulu witch doctor's forewarning that *Mkizi* (the Bantu term for the Germans) 'will come and take us all away.'[118] The native prophecy was apparently taken as a joke by the rest of the Springboks, until a 'disastrous and insane' BBC broadcast – also received by Axis listeners – blithely announced that Tobruk was 'no longer of any strategic importance.'[119] A soldier turned to his immediate circle, grumbling, 'That's our preliminary death notice'; another laconically remarked 'they are softening up the British public for the shock that the fall of Tobruk may be to them.'[120] One of Klopper's last cables, allegedly, was to complain: 'I cannot carry on if the BBC is allowed to make these statements.'[121]

Although Auchinleck reassured London as late as 20 June that the 'defences were in good order',[122] the 'fortress' was now a shadow of its former self. Tens of thousands of mines had already been lifted in readiness for General Scobie's breakout in November 1941 and later stripped for the Gazala defences. South African Brigadier Eric P. Hartshorn recalled after the war how SAI troops, among others, appropriated 'anything they needed from the Tobruk defences for the purpose of strengthening the Gazala Line. Mines, wire, steel pickets – anything that could be of use – were being removed in a spirit of "Help yourselves, boys, they won't be wanted here again."'[123]

Sections of the June 1942 minefields were practically non-existent, and of the remaining mines, many had already begun to deteriorate after an extended period in the ground.[124] An estimated 20,000 mines were needed to restore the defences to a reasonable state, though only 4,000 were available. Damning evidence from Lieutenant Colonel George E. Bastin (Assistant Quartermaster-General) – ordered out of Tobruk on a ship carrying 24,000 gallons of petrol – in the later Court of Enquiry exposed Klopper's ignorance of 'gaps in the [mine]fields which tanks could go through.'[125] The Court furthermore concluded that minefields insufficiently guarded and not covered by fire may offer

Right: *March 1937. Italian dictator Benito Mussolini and Air Marshal Italo Balbo (left) at the opening of the new coastal highway extending across the north of Libya. The 1,100 mile road was named the* Litoranea Balbo *or* Via Balbia.

Below: *Italian prisoners of war cross a bridge over the wadi Maaten El Bardi following the Battle of Bardia, January 1941.*

An Australian motorcyclist passes abandoned Italian light tanks at Bardia.

A German Panzer I, still in its dark grey European camouflage, is unloaded at Tripoli. The obsolete 5.4 ton light tank, with a two man crew, was prone to overheating.

Newly arrived— Generalleutnant Erwin Rommel (centre) and Oberst Rudolf Schmundt, Hitler's adjutant (left).

A German Sd.Kfz.231 heavy reconnaissance armoured car is paraded through Tripoli past Rommel and senior Italian officers.

Group portrait. A widely-held myth in Allied circles at the time held that German troops were acclimatised to desert conditions by marching through giant continental hothouses.

Photo opportunity with a 'ship of the desert'.

German propaganda images. A Luftwaffe motorcyclist poses with his BMW R12.

Tobruk! Useless in battle, Tropenhelm (tropical helmets) were quickly discarded by frontline troops.

H Nr. 12

2.JUNI-AFLEVERING 1941

Signaal

Tegen elk
klimaat bestand.
In Afrika :

Het gezicht
van den Duitschen soldaat
achter het zandmasker

Resistant to any climate in Africa', exclaimed the front cover of Signal (Dutch edition) magazine, June 1941.

Above and below: *A sandstorm approaches. Reducing visibility to only yards, these springs storms could generate electrical disturbances, rendereding compasses useless.*

Above, below left and below right: *Winter storms with flash flooding were another hazard for the unwary.*

Field maintenance. Germans vehicles designed for European conditions suffered in desert conditions from overheating and decreased engine life.

Above left and above right: *Contrary to propaganda and Hollywood imagery, German soldiers discovered the Western Desert to be desolate, flat and treeless.*

Above: *Digging a slit trench for shelter. Note the widely spaced vehicles in case of aerial attack.*

Right: *Refuse was to be buried to prevent the spread of infection. Though as a British veteran recalled, German 'units were close to and sometimes intermingled with the Italians, whose peasant style of sanitation provided the fly with too frequent a paradise.'*

Above left: *The lure of the Orient quickly faded, with the monotony of existence often leading to attacks of homesickness.*

Above right: *Tinned sardines formed part of the German soldiers' regular diet with fruit and vegetables virtually unknown.*

The white cross on this Wehrmacht-Einheitskanister (or 'Jerrycan' to the Allies) denotes its use as a water carrier. The gun is a captured 2-pounder portée (carried on the back of a truck).

A catastrophic internal explosion has destroyed this Panzer III. Note the unexploded ammunition in the foreground.

Knocked-out British Matilda II Infantry tank with multiple turret penetrations.

The horror of war. The bodies of severely burned Italian soldiers prior to burial.

The decapitated body of a German soldier. Private snapshots rarely featured the dead.

Fallen German gunners beside their 5.0 cm Pak 38 anti-tank gun.

Hunter and hunted—a knocked-out British Crusader III. Armed with a 6-pounder gun, some 100 of these tanks first saw action in the Second Battle of El Alamein (23 October- 11 November 1942)

Above: *German troops examine an American-built M3 Grant tank. The hull-mounted 75 mm gun brought much-needed firepower to British tankers.*

Right: *Under new ownership- a captured 25-pounder gun.*

The scourge of British armour; a knocked out 8.8 cm gun in ground combat role.

Above: *Australian 9th Division troops pictured at the El Alamein railway station.*

Left: *British Prime Minister Winston Churchill visited frontline troops in August 1942. In the so-called 'Cairo Purge', he appointed General Sir Harold Alexander to take over from General Sir Claude Auchinleck. Following the death of General William 'Strafer' Gott, General Bernard Law Montgomery, was appointed to lead the 8th Army.*

Right: *Lieutenant Colonel Geoffrey Keyes was buried by the Germans with fully military honours.*

Below: *General Bernard Law Montgomery, a man the 8th Army would know as 'Monty', shares a cup of tea with British tankers.*

Above: *A dummy M3 Grant tank…*

Left: *…and a warning not to stray any into an enemy minefield.*

a false sense of security, even aiding the enemy more than defenders.[126] But mines were not the only problem. The perimeter anti-tank ditch had succumbed to the elements and months of neglect. Indeed, what lay ahead of the Indian 2nd Mahratta Light Infantry, positioned along the southeast sector of the perimeter, was now a token obstacle that 'would hardly have interfered with the progress of a garden roller.'[127]

Beyond the state of the defences was the uncertainty, Brigadier Frederick H. Kisch, Eighth Army chief engineer, recalled, as to 'whether Tobruk was going to be defended or not.'[128] Numerous contradictory signals had passed between Auchinleck, his GHQ and London. Earlier on 19 January 1942, Auchinleck had issued Operational Instruction No.110, which advised in the event of another general retreat that he would not try to permanently hold Tobruk, or any position west of the frontier.[129] In the aftermath of the Gazala battle, however, Ritchie notified Auchinleck on 14 June that the risk of a temporary investment now existed – only to be informed that the 'defences of TOBRUK and other strong places will be used as pivots of manoeuvre but on no account will any part of Eighth Army be allowed to be surrounded in TOBRUK and your Army is to remain a mobile field army.'[130] The Auk's signal closed with a challenge to Ritchie: 'If you feel you can not accept the responsibility of holding this position you must say so.'[131] Ritchie's policy was to fight alongside Tobruk. In the event it was *temporarily* invested, he reasoned the garrison could hold out for two months.[132]

Similar to 1941, Churchill also weighed in, pressuring his C-in-C to stand firm: 'As long as Tobruk is held, no serious enemy advance into Egypt is possible. We went through all this in April 1941.'[133] Its loss would be disastrous. Major General John Kennedy noted in his diary: 'The limelight had been on the place so much that its political and prestige value had now become very great.'[134]

Rather than a solitary bastion, Tobruk's primary value now lay in its harbour installations, refrigerating plants and workshops as the Eighth Army's principal supply base. Auchinleck, who after the war declared that Tobruk now 'had no strategic value at all', responded to the premier's bluster by stating he did not intend Eighth Army to be besieged inside Tobruk; moreover, he had 'no intention whatever of giving it up.'[135]

Privately though, the Auk believed Tobruk would fall and ordered sufficient transport to evacuate the entire garrison should a breakout eventuate. He revised his original orders – sanctioning the possibility of Tobruk becoming *isolated*, though he remained firm in his policy of no siege.[136] A memo to Ritchie read: 'Although I have made it clear to you TOBRUK must not be invested I realise that its garrison may be *isolated* for short periods until our counter-offensive can be launched.' Ritchie, after consultation with Gott, expressed his confidence in accepting 'investment for short periods with every opportunity of success.'[137]

At the same time, Auchinleck held that Rommel's troops were verging on exhaustion with insufficient formations to both 'invest Tobruk and mask our troops in the frontier positions'; a view also shared by Eighth Army intelligence.[138]

In reality, Rommel had issued orders for his troops advancing east to 'push on as fast as they could to the western edge of Tobruk.' A shuttle service with many newly-captured vehicles was organised to bring these men forward with 'quick regrouping for the investment of Tobruk…now the most urgent necessity.'[139]

18 June. Grave news was received at Eighth Army HQ that Sidi Rezegh, El Adem and Belhamed had been overrun. Crucially, Klopper never received the codeword, *Lamphrey*, advising him that the last British troops covering his flank had been withdrawn. It was only after the Umvoti Mounted Rifles discovered Axis columns nearing Tobruk that the magnitude of the situation became apparent. During the morning, the 21st Panzer Division severed the *Via Balbia*. What Auchinleck had tried to forestall since the beginning of the year, now transpired. Tobruk was again invested. Turning to his diary, Sir Alexander Cadogan, Undersecretary of the British Foreign Office, and Churchill's chief advisor, noted dourly that 'Libya is evidently a complete disaster – we are out-generalled everywhere.'[140] *The Times*'s military correspondent also hinted at a possible blow: 'If Tobruk should now be assaulted it will be put to a test far more severe than on the last occasion.'[141]

'A scene of apocalyptic confusion and doom'

18 June. Rommel reached Tobruk. He wasted no time giving instructions and marshalling his troops before a final reconnaissance. Exhausted, he

dashed off a letter to his wife: 'Only two hours sleep last night. This is the really decisive day. Hope my luck holds.'[142]

Rommel's Axis assailing force was his strongest to date. It included the 15th and 21st Panzer Divisions, the 90th Light Infantry Division plus three Italian Army Corps: The Italian XXI Corps – 7th Bersaglieri Regiment, 60th Infantry Division Sabratha and 102nd Motorised Division Trento; the Italian X Corps – 27th Infantry Division Brescia and 17th Infantry Division Pavia (in reserve); and the Italian XX Motorised Corps – 101st Motorised Division Trieste; 132nd Armoured Division Ariete and the newly arrived 133rd Armoured Division Littorio.

German artillerymen took up their former positions on the El Adem escarpment. To their amazement, they discovered abandoned ammunition dumps with thousands of rounds undisturbed from the previous November. It was a different story inside Tobruk where Brigadier H.F. Johnson convinced Klopper to use artillery, in place of infantry, to prevent Axis troops from forming up. The subsequent barrage failed to disperse the enemy and possibly led to subsequent ammunition rationing during the forthcoming battle.

Inside fortress HQ, a poised Klopper notified Ritchie that his 'position was very satisfactory and that his harassing of the enemy was being effective.'[143] His heterogeneous garrison of 33,000 men comprised the 2nd SAI Division (4th and the 6th SA Infantry Brigades and a battalion from 1st SA Division including 2,000 native non-combatants) and the 11th Indian Brigade. The garrison's mobile force consisted of the 32nd Army Tank Brigade and 201st Guards Brigade. On paper, Klopper's garrison possessed numerical superiority in practically every area relative to May 1941. While numerically similar in firepower, Major Philip Tower (25th Field Regiment) painted a telling distinction between the operational capabilities of the 1941 and 1942 garrisons – the latter was in 'no sense built into a tightly woven flexible fighting machine like its predecessor. The chain of command was vague, fire plans were complicated and obscure, and, above all, communications were indifferent.'[144] Moreover, the highly trained RHA Regiment was ordered out of Tobruk on 16 June. 'Much would have been given for their presence', Brigadier Johnson later disclosed.[145]

	1 May 1941	18 June 1942
Infantry		
Infantry battalions	11	14
Motorised battalions	1	2
Machine Gun battalions	1	1
Total	13	17
Armoured Fighting Vehicles		
Infantry	16	77
Cruiser	28	
Light	33	
Armoured cars	31	Unknown
Total	108	77
Artillery		
Field	72	72
Medium		29
2-pounder anti-tank	16	41
6-pounder anti-tank	0	23
47-mm (captured Cannone da 47/32 mod. 1935)	25	0
Total	41	64
Anti-Aircraft Artillery		
Heavy	16	16
Light	53	60
Total	69	76

Figure 1. Comparative strength of the Tobruk garrison in May 1941 and June 1942.

Rommel planned to 'storm the fortress' using a plan from the previous year. A feint attack would be launched in the southwest while he belted the [vulnerable] south-eastern front with a 'heavy dive bomber and artillery bombardment' before overrunning the surprised enemy; 'we were now going to finish it off for good.'[146]

Siegfried Westphal remembered the night of June 19/20 – 'loud with rattlings and thunderings, suppressed shouts, whispered commands; there was no light but the occasional red or green signal of a pocket

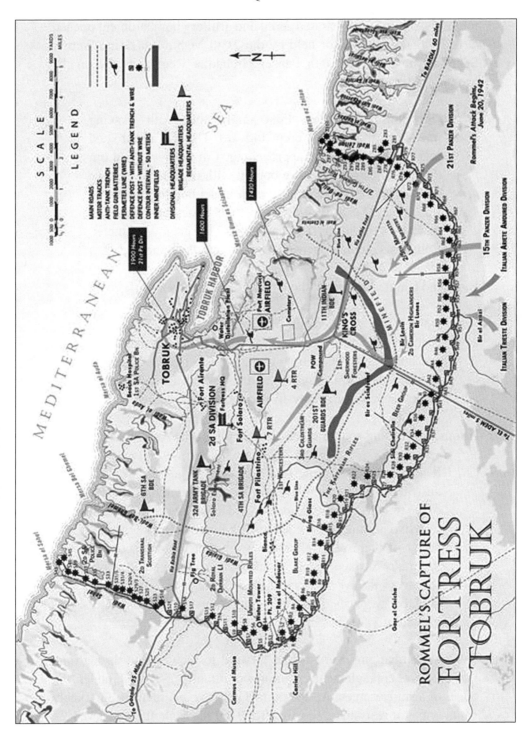

ROMMEL'S CAPTURE OF
FORTRESS
TOBRUK

torch.'[147] A tightly orchestrated aerial and artillery bombardment opened at 0520 against the sector held by the 2/5th Mahrattas. Heinz-Werner Schmidt (now in the 115th Panzer Grenadier Regiment) lay on the ground waiting.

> Our guns opened up. First singly, then with growing intensity…the barrage crept forward. Then a full throated roar: our Stukas were approaching. Carefully we laid out the identification strips we bought with us. Before now we had been given a taste of our own Stuka bombs. The battle was on… The Stukas dropped their noses and swooped down over our heads. They plunged at the enemy perimeter. Bombs screamed down and crashed into the minefield.[148]

Reverend Chutter described the terror of being targeted:

> Down they whistled, always, it seemed to the anxious watching and prostrate observer, directly at him: then there was apparent a little curtsy in the bomb's flight – a strange illusion of tensed nerves – and it passed up and over to explode twelve or twenty-five feet away.[149]

Another defending soldier endured the 'hell' of the Axis artillery.

> It seems fantastic now that so many of us got through unscathed. Shells were bursting all round, making the sides of the trench crumble in upon us… They made a whistle and roar like a train, and the shrapnel a horrible tearing sound. Many of them also fell short, exploding on contact with the rocky surface round about. But our main danger and fear were the AP [armour-piercing] shells bursting in the air. How we wished our tin helmets were 12 ft in diameter instead of 12 inches.[150]

German combat engineers moved forward to blow a path through the barbed wire entanglements. Motorised infantry followed under the cover of a smokescreen. Although the Germans recorded a 'remarkably small scale' of resistance, shortly after 0700 the Mahratta's reserve rifle company, supported by the 2/7th Gurkha carrier platoon, launched a 'most gallant counter-attack' that briefly checked the advance.[151] But, as Schmidt adds, 'they were swept down, swept aside, swept back' by heavy machine gun, anti-tank and mortar fire.[152]

Spearheading the assault, the 21st Panzer Division ripped a gaping breach in the perimeter with most of the bunkers between Posts 58 and 69 falling in quick succession. In the vanguard of the attack, Leutnant Dr. Kurt Wolff (5th Panzer Regiment) recalled how the 'spirit of the attack had gripped everyone so thoroughly, and the thought of Tobruk let them forget everything else – even their lives.'[153]

The assault proceeded faster than expected and with relatively light casualties. The first prisoners taken were sent to the rear. Schmidt was surprised by the garrison's artillery, which 'only began to lay down concentrated fire after 0730....too late.'[154] In place of the 1941 garrison's captured anti-tank guns was a new and unfamiliar weapon – the 29-mm Spigot Mortar (also known as a Blacker Bombard). With only two rounds allowed for familiarisation, the heavy, low-velocity stopgap weapon was generally disliked, its effectiveness dubious at best. A Gurkha officer recalled:

> To fire a spigot mortar, one jams the canister onto an instrument which resembles a blunt marline spike. The bomb hits some unpredictable distance away, precipitates itself along the ground like a prehistoric monster, belching fire as it goes, until it finishes its career in an ear-shattering explosion... They scared off any tank that looked as though it wished to try conclusions with us.[155]

Safely ensconced in his underground HQ, Klopper's reaction and that of his senior officers belied the gravity of the situation. Through a catastrophic communications breakdown, Klopper had yet to receive a single report from the frontline Indian Brigade. Uninformed of the enemy dive bombing, he wrongly assumed that the perimeter posts were holding out, when the German armour had in fact overrun the 11th Indian Brigade and 25th Field Regiment HQ.[156] Lieutenant Colonel P.L. Kriek, for one, had downplayed the distant thunder of bombardment as routine Luftwaffe attention. Precious hours had been lost. Not until 0840 was the sleeping squadron commander of the 4th RTR awakened with news of the assault. And not until 0930 did the British Coldstream Guards receive orders to counterattack (although their supporting armour had independently moved forward). Another hour would pass before they engaged enemy tanks.

Because the Italian XX (motorised) Corps had failed to push forward to Ras el Medauuar, the Ariete Division's tanks were swung behind the 15th Panzer Division, which began pushing northwest. The SA Infantry, meanwhile, languished in positions never attacked. The Springboks, much to their frustration, would barely feature in the fighting.

In the absence of frontline reports, Klopper maintained a 'sanguine appearance' before his fellow officers.[157] A self-assured outlook also prevailed in the harbour area where four Indian Mahratta soldiers who swam across from the southern shore to report approaching enemy tanks were labelled as deserters.

As late as at 1100 hours, Klopper complained of being 'completely in the dark.'[158] Were the perimeter posts still holding out? Not until mid-afternoon did news of looming catastrophe filter into fortress HQ – now a 'scene of apocalyptic confusion and doom.'[159] A later report by Brigadier A.C. Willison (a veteran of the 1941 siege) received sometime mid-afternoon signalled the destruction of the entire British armoured reserve force. Symptomatic of the unfolding disaster, the 6th SA Infantry Brigade had still received no word from Divisional HQ. As Brigadier F.W. Cooper relates, it was only 'towards evening' when Klopper suddenly appeared bearing news that his headquarters had been overrun.[160]

Leutnant Wolff's tanks reached a commanding position overlooking the harbour: 'Tobruk! Tobruk!... Remnants of the garrison had fled onto boats in the harbour and attempted to escape.'[161] Rommel called for anti-aircraft and artillery fire to target vessels attempting to escape, sinking six. Overcoming a strongpoint that fought with 'extraordinary stubbornness', the 21st Panzer Division began occupying the town and harbour.[162] By nightfall, two-thirds of the fortress had fallen.

'What a night!', Wolff exclaimed. 'And what a day! Tobruk, which the Afrikakorps had struggled so hard to take, was in our hands! Fire all around…burning ships…but the circled wagons of a tank battalion in the middle, a tank battalion that had earned the highest laurels… We had decided a battle.'[163]

In his appreciation of the day's fighting to the War Office, Auchinleck concluded:

> [I] Realise that this sudden and unexpected enemy success at Tobruk looks like being a major defeat, consequences of which will be most grave. Naturally I accept full responsibility for this lamentable occurrence.[164]

'It is foolish to carry on'

A tense conference that night at Cooper's headquarters revealed the hopelessness of the situation. The garrison's artillery, Colonel H. McA. Richards explained, 'only had ammunition for fifteen minutes' of fighting; an offer by Cooper to distribute ammunition from the dump was rejected.[165] Plans were tabled for the garrison to break out, as Klopper later elaborated, however his transport in the harbour area was destroyed during the seven hours it took for permission to be received. Instead it was agreed to form a new defensive line – a redoubt in the west that would hold out until a relieving force reached Tobruk. But as Cooper points out, these eleventh-hour attempts 'to throw up fortifications were not very successful as the ground was frightfully hard... The men kept at it all night, working like Trojans.'[166]

Klopper signalled Eighth Army at 0200 that it was

> not possible to hold until tomorrow. Mobile troops nearly naught. Enemy captured vehicles. Will resist to the last man.[167]

Ritchie's magnanimous response arrived an hour later.

> Whole of Eighth Army has watched with admiration your gallant fight. You are an example to us all and I know South Africa will be proud of you.[168]

Brigadier George Erskine, who was Gott's deputy, later interviewed a number of men captured at Tobruk. All concurred that by early afternoon on 21 June Klopper was a 'beaten man with his head in his hands, bewailing that his "shell" had been broken... His useless staff stood around, ineffective and inactive.'[169]

Faced with a desperate fight or flight decision, Klopper accepted that further resistance along the improvised defensive line was futile and accepted defeat: 'I am sorry boys, but we have to pack up. It is foolish to carry on. Gentlemen, I propose to surrender to save useless bloodshed.'[170] A representative under a white flag offered the garrison's surrender the next morning at 0630. The longest day of the year had also been Klopper's as he advised Eighth Army HQ that he was 'doing the worst'.[171]

'The smashing of Tobruk,' Morehead underscored, 'had taken just one day.'[172] Lieutenant A.N. Goldman recounted his astonishment when told 'they have surrendered', believing it to be the enemy; 'I had not for a moment thought that we would surrender. It seemed fantastic. We had not fired a shot.'[173]

The Queen's Own Cameron Highlanders and 7th Ghurkhas, who had stubbornly resisted, were bypassed islands in a hostile ocean, gallantly resisting for a further thirty-six hours until the situation became hopeless and they too surrendered. It was a bittersweet moment for the victors, Siegfried Westphal recalled:

> This was the first time that German soldiers had trodden the soil of Tobruk, so long the object of bloody and bitter fighting. For more than a year besieger and besieged had suffered in this barren waterless region of rock and dust, tormented by flies, parched by the sun, without cover, without room for manoeuvre... Long rows of crosses stand today to testify to the bitterness of the struggle. Now at last this hell was over, for both sides.[174]

'A blessing in disguise'

Britain's reaction to the surrender is perhaps best summed up by an Eighth Army officer then en route to the Middle East: 'There is a cold hand on my heart. I feel sick and utterly miserable.'[175]

Shockwaves from the surrender were global, recriminations immediate. The Australians were fiercely critical of the defeat, given their successful defence of Tobruk in 1941. South Africa's largest military reversal was a 'dark day' for the country's prime minster and C-in-C, General Jan Smuts, who called for his countrymen to unite and 'seek retribution'.[176] Smuts also telegraphed Churchill on 30 June with a request that 'the RAF instead of bombing German towns should concentrate maximum of its bombing force against Rommel and pound his army and African ports to pieces.'[177]

British headquarters at Cairo was in a state of panic, later dubbed 'the Flap'. Scenes ranged from dread in the European quarters to jubilation within the general populace for the 'great general' to liberate Egypt. Clerks incinerated scores of sensitive documents in a panicky disposal later dubbed 'Ash Wednesday'. Half-charred papers stamped TOP SCERET became convenient cones for peanut vendors, while Europeans crowded into whatever transport was headed for the safety of Palestine. Rumours abounded. Propaganda broadcasts beamed in Arabic asked: 'Who of us Arabs has not been proud of Rommel? Who of us is not sympathising with him?'[178] Via Radio Berlin the Grand Mufti declared: 'The Arabs believe that the Axis Powers are fighting against a common enemy, namely the British and the Jews.'[179]

Within Cairo, Anwar Sadat and Gamal Nasser (both future presidents of Egypt) drew up plans for an anti-British rebellion and prepared a draft treaty with Germany to recognise an independent, pro-Axis Egypt, promising that 'no British soldier would leave Cairo alive.' But it was not to be, the aircraft carrying their overture was mistaken for an RAF aircraft and shot down.[180]

Tobruk's loss was deeply humiliating for Churchill. When Churchill discussed the Middle East, the Soviet ambassador Ivan Maĭskiĭ observed: 'He immediately came to life. It was obvious that the Middle East is his "darling", that it dominates his mind.'[181] When asked why the fortress fell, Churchill conceded that 'the 'Germans wage war better than we do. Especially tank wars. Also, we lack the "Russian spirit": die but don't surrender!' Blame also was levelled at Klopper for his failed handling of the battle. 'I'd have a general like that shot on the spot!', Maĭskiĭ blurted out. 'I'd have done the same', the prime minister retorted, 'But just you try!'[182]

Brigadier Cooper recalled how the blow was especially hard for SAI troops along the coast and the western perimeter sector, largely bypassed in the fighting, though 'it was quite obvious to those in the know that the position was really hopeless.'[183] Astonished Springboks levelled blame at Klopper, as Chutter observed first-hand: 'The first to curse and denounce him were his own troops: his own Division. He has been accused of every military failing, from lack of courage to base treachery. He was hissed by his own Afrikaners.'[184] In a later PoW camp 'tribunal' known as the 'Bari Postmortem', Klopper and his divisional staff were deemed responsible. It was recalled how any suggestion of contingency planning was panned as being 'windy', (implying nervousness) and a mocking suggestion, should they wish to evacuate, that a hospital ship was leaving from the harbour.[185] But while damning evidence mounted, a later Court of Enquiry exonerated Klopper from blame, ascribing Tobruk's fall to:

> the eleventh-hour reversal of policy leading to the decision to hold the Fortress, regardless of the fact that Eighth Army was then in full retreat in the face of an enemy who had been uniformly successful and whose morale must in consequence have been high. It was impossible in the time available to make adequate preparations for the completely new role imposed upon the Garrison, which up to then had only been concerned with prevention of raids by land, air or sea.[186]

A boon to the Axis, Japan's ambassador in Berlin cabled: the 'campaign has been a great victory surpassing expectations.' Count Ciano foretold of 'new developments' that would now unfold while Mussolini flew to Libya with his prized white charger to ceremoniously ride into Cairo.[187] Joseph Goebbels naturally seized upon the victory, taking aim at Churchill who did not have a 'single general who has shown himself a real commander, on any current field of battle…everyone a failure.'[188]

A tragic day for the Allies, the *New York Times* reported. Tobruk's capitulation had enveloped Washington in a 'sober and realistic mood'. The caustic headline asserted: 'Rommel lectures the British on tactics.'[189] The American public, according to a Gallup poll in early July 1942, believed the 'loss of Tobruk and other British reverses in Africa' were primarily due to a shortage of men and equipment (twenty-six per cent); incompetent leadership; superior German strategy (twenty-five per cent); and the British being slow and unprepared (ten per cent).[190] Some commentators in Washington, however, viewed Tobruk as a blessing in disguise that would finally arouse America to the 'grim realities of the [British] military situation.'[191] Churchill, who had invited himself to the nation's capital again in mid-1942, was given news of Tobruk's capitulation personally by Roosevelt in the White House Oval Office. Brooke penned in his diary that it was a 'staggering blow'; Henry L. Stimson, head of the War Department, noted that Churchill was 'evidently staggered...and showed it in his speech and manner, although he bore up bravely. He did not attempt to excuse it because of overwhelming numbers or anything of that sort but he said it was just plain bad leadership; that Rommel had out-generalled them and out-fought them and had supplied his troops with better weapons.'[192]

'What can we do to help?', the President asked. To help check the growing danger to Egypt, General George C. Marshall, US Chief of Staff, raised the possibility of an armoured division before offering instead 300 new M4 Sherman tanks and 100 M7 105-mm self-propelled guns (known by the British as the 'Priest'), together with 150 maintenance personnel. They would be sent to Suez aboard six of the fastest available ships. The Desert Air Force would also be strengthened with US fighter aircraft and heavy and medium bombers originally bound for India, Australia, the Soviet Union and the Far East.

Across the Atlantic, London's *Daily Mail* directed an accusative finger at 'British strategy, faulty leadership and a lack of plans.'[193] British political commentators foresaw a 'first class political crisis' and Churchill's 'impending fall' from power.[194] The premier returned home to a censure motion tabled by Sir John Wardlaw-Milne. It closed with the rejection of a no-confidence motion – 476 votes to 25 (with some 40 conscious abstentions). 'Good for you', Roosevelt cabled.[195] In his explanatory speech to the House of Commons, Churchill refrained from lauding Rommel's leadership, instead acknowledging that with a 'disproportionate destruction of our armour Rommel became decisively the stronger. The battlefield [then] passed into the hands of the enemy.'[196] The insinuation was clear: the reason for defeat rested with his commanders.

*****

131

As early as 30 June, US heavy bombers began pounding Rommel's tenuous supply lines stretching far across the desert. But as British war correspondent Richard McMillan bemoaned in a biting front-page critique: 'We allowed the enemy in Libya to make every move... Rommel has become the bogey in the desert and is the biggest bogey of all to many of the high-ups themselves.'[197] In McMillan's view, a 'lack of aggressive spirit in the general direction of the fighting was the main cause of failure... The Imperial forces' trend was, "I wonder where Rommel is going to strike next?" instead of "I wonder where we will hit Rommel next?"'[198] Flushed with success, Rommel eyed Cairo.

Chapter Five

'Now it is imperative to completely destroy the enemy'

There's a Devil in the dawn
Horrific spawn of last night's hideous moon,
That hung above the gun's inferno
And smiled on men who died too soon
                    –Bombardier F.E. Hughes[1]

The Gazala Line had shattered, Tobruk had fallen and Britain was in a state of shock. As one English editorial warned: 'We shall do ourselves no good here by pretending that the position in Egypt is anything but serious, disturbing, even alarming.'[2]

For Hitler, 'the goddess of fortune' had smiled, and should a commander fail to seize the opportunity, he cautioned, she 'frequently never smiles again.'[3] In appreciation, he promoted Rommel to Generalfeldmarschall – Nazi Germany's youngest. The spirit of his beleaguered *Volk*, after nearly three years of war, 'rose at once to a peak not experienced since the conclusion of the battle of France in 1940.'[4] Tobruk was the gold mine Rommel needed: 'gigantic spoils of war in ammunition, fuel, rations and material of all types' – 2,000 vehicles and 3,800 tons of foodstuff – that 'strengthened my resolve to exploit the weakness of the British… by thrusting forward as far as I could into Egypt.'[5] And for Halder, one of Rommel's most vocal critics, this was a 'victory that is of equal value from the military and political aspect.'[6]

'Destiny…has given us an opening that will never again become available'

21 June. Morale within the Axis camp now soared with the gates to the Nile now seemingly within reach. Rommel urged his army forward in

one last push: 'Now it is imperative to completely destroy the enemy. We do not want to rest until we have defeated the last elements of the Eighth Army.'[7]

In a letter to the Duce on 23 June, Hitler proclaimed: 'Destiny…has given us an opening that will never again become available in the same theatre of operations… The British Eighth army is virtually destroyed.' From his 'deeply concerned heart', Mussolini endorsed the appeal and encouraged Comando Supremo to push Operation *Herkules*, the invasion of Malta, back until September. The Germans, the Duce opined, 'will be full of Teutonic pride when they reach the Pyramids, like Napoleon.'[8] But at the same time he was anxious for the efforts of both the Italian and German soldier to be 'equally represented in the advance to the canal.'[9]

Rommel received word from Generalleutnant Enno von Rintelen on the morning of 24 June that the 'Duce is in agreement with the Panzerarmee's plan of following the enemy into Egypt.'[10] Orders for rest days were cancelled as Rommel harried his men to move off again. The Eighth Army, still recovering from recent blows, recoiled east after failing to halt the Axis at Sollum and Sidi Barrani. The Panzerarmee's daily report for 24 June recorded a rapid advance, although 'it had not been possible to bring the enemy's main body to battle.'[11]

Alan Moorehead set out for the front, only to find the road jammed with withdrawing British troops. 'It was nerve-wracking to see them drive by. There seemed to be no end to the hundreds and thousands who kept pouring back in such haste that they were making no attempt to obey the order that at least a hundred yards should be kept between each vehicle on the road.'[12]

The British newspaper audience learned through a Vichy shortwave broadcast – 'Axis Rumours of Eighth Army Changes' – that Auchinleck had stepped in to personally take over command from the luckless Ritchie.[13] 'The danger of complete catastrophe', the Auk mulled over afterwards, was 'too great for me to leave the responsibility with a subordinate already subjected for several weeks to extraordinary strain.'[14]

Auchinleck arrived at Eighth Army HQ at Maaten Baggush on 27 June to be confronted by possibly the most desperate situation of any British commander in the war. He decided not to hold Mersa Matruh, which fell on 29 June, along with another 8,000 British troops. Instead he would stand and fight further east at a dusty railhead known by the Bedouin as 'El Alamein' – ironically meaning the 'the place of two flags'.

South of Mersa Matruh, Private Adam Wakenshaw (Durham Light Infantry) was waging a desperate rearguard action. After knocking out one enemy tracked vehicle, he became the target of another self-propelled gun, which attacked, killing or seriously wounded the rest of his 2-pounder anti-tank gun crew. Under intense artillery and mortar fire, Wakenshaw crawled back to the gun. Although his left arm was a bloodied stump, severed below the elbow, he succeeded in loading and firing the gun six times – setting the enemy vehicle on fire. Another near miss tossed Wakenshaw from his weapon, further wounding him. Dragging himself back to the gun, he had placed another round in the breech when a direct hit exploded ammunition, killing him and wrecking the gun.[15] Wakenshaw was posthumously awarded the VC for 'conspicuous gallantry'.

Surrounded by Axis forces and facing defeat, the encircled New Zealand 4th and 5th Brigades, plus Divisional Headquarters, managed, in ferocious close-quarter fighting, to break through the enemy cordon at Minqar Qaim on the night of 27/8 June. Lieutenant Colonel J.T. Burrows later reported:

> A most amazing and thrilling thing happened. To a man the whole [Fourth] brigade charged forward. No orders were given; no urging forward by officers or NCOs. With shouting, cheering and war cries, every man broke into a run as if he knew exactly what was expected of him.[16]

Dan Davin described the 'savage grunt behind the bayonets shoved home, the inhuman high-pitched scream of the enemy. The flash from the muzzles of weapons fired at close range, the roar and singe of a burning vehicle.'[17] Captain Charles H. Upham VC (20th Battalion, NZEF) 'was covered in blood... From the grenades he had been distributing on the enemy he had at the same time peppered himself with grenade fragments'; his taciturn commentary: 'This show will make bloody history.'[18]

In an ugly incident that evening, the 28th (Māori) Battalion overran a German dressing station, bayoneting medical staff and wounded. Lord Haw Haw was quick to deride the New Zealanders as 'Freyberg's butchers'. Captured Kiwi soldiers were afterwards segregated from other British prisoners, stripped of their personal belongings and made to stand in the sun for six hours. German anger lingered. A Kiwi officer later captured on 15 July 1942 was abused at 21st Panzer Division HQ and told that his countrymen 'no longer fight like "Gentlemen" but fill themselves up with cognac and fight like Bolsheviks.'[19] Rommel later raised the allegations of 'gangster' methods with New Zealander Brigadier George Clifton, captured by Italian troops (much to his disgust) on 3 September, who 'said it was probably due to the large number of Maoris.'[20]

For the Eighth Army, 'this period of retreat was a most depressing time. It was difficult to get news of the bigger picture', to quote an officer from the 3rd County of London Yeomanry (CLY).[21] In an unfortunate incident of 'friendly-fire' on 27 June, RAF Wellingtons bombed units of the 3rd The King's Own Hussars, 4th CLY and 7th Armoured Division during a two-hour raid near Mersa Matruh. More than 359 troops were killed and 560 others were wounded. Rommel noted: 'The RAF bombed their own troops, and, with tracer flying in all directions, German units fired on each other.' The next morning 'we found a number of lorries full of the mangled corpses…killed by British bombs.'[22]

Mussolini expectantly flew to Libya on 29 June, with a train of party leaders and journalists, primed to enter Cairo. Hopeful of vanquishing the British at Alamein, he remained in Egypt until 20 July. Tellingly, Rommel opted not to visit him during his entire stay. In an act of show, the Duce left his luggage behind for when he would return for his parade. But as Ciano noted, his return home 'convinces the public that many rosy dreams about Egypt have faded, at least for the time being.'[23]

As Italian preparations continued for the future governing of Egypt, Auchinleck endeavoured to inspire his embattled troops. He circulated a message on 30 June that Rommel 'thinks we are a broken army' and 'hopes to get to Egypt by bluff… Show him where to get off.'

In Cairo, Croswell Bowen noted a sombre and threatening mood hanging over the Egyptian capital.

> The despair is weary and deep-rooted. It is apprehension at the possible collapse of a world we believed in. The danger is not only across the Nile out in the desert but, as the soldiers say, the "wogs" are ready to turn on us at the

slightest opportunity. They say it's in the look in their eyes and their muttered insults as they pass in the streets. We have lost face with them and for a very simple reason: we are not the victors in battle.[24]

British censorship summaries revealed flagging morale, noting that 'the withdrawal into Egypt has provoked expressions of very bitter disappointment from all ranks of the Eighth Army, accompanied by admissions of weariness and fatigue.'[25] Even at the end of July, after Rommel had been brought to a halt, it was reported that 'many of the troops are beginning to lose interest in the war, to some in fact the reason for the war itself has become dimmed.'[26] In unison with the army's lack of drive was an increased rate of sickness and a jump in psychological casualties. For some men, the stress of active service proved too much. AFS driver Captain Andrew Geer observed one distraught individual

completely bomb happy [army slang for shock, and in no way derogatory]. He was crying hysterically; his limbs jerked and twitched; he was soaked in perspiration. His history showed a previous cracking up, and he was evacuated.[27]

Brigadier T.C. Hunt (consultant physician) later discussed anxiety states in a wartime lecture. Amazed by just how much the human spirit could endure, he also questioned whether it was explicable for men, on occasion, to succumb to the merciless strain of combat:

To me, however, it was almost more remarkable to see not how many men broke down in battle, but how much the human mind and body were able to stand without collapse. A soldier lay under a truck with his friend while being bombed; his friend crawled half out to look around, and when, a little later, the man pulled him back, his head had completely disappeared. Is it surprising that the survivor developed an intense hysterical blindness?[28]

A widespread perception at the time, shared by many medical staff, was that 'nervous' cases – the condition termed 'shell shock' during the First World War – were likely to be cowards or malingerers. At the beginning of the campaign these men received the 'disgraced' diagnosis 'Lack of Moral Fibre' (LMF). Captain James Graham (RAMC working with 7th Armoured Division), however, felt that LMF was an insensitive label, later disclosing:

> I felt that no man who had fought with a tank or gun or worked in close support deserved the designation LMF. It was a contradiction in terms. I had to "smuggle" one major, one sergeant and five other ranks out of harm's way. This way they retained their self-respect and came back for more after a rest. To have applied the label would have upset the tank crews and aroused a feeling of distrust and resentment that would have had the worst possible effect on morale.[29]

The diagnosis of LMF, however, was short-lived and replaced by the label 'Not Yet Diagnosed (Nervous)'. By the middle of 1942 the most commonly used diagnostic term was 'exhaustion'.[30]

To increase his soldiers' 'fight' and diminish the number listed as 'missing', Auchinleck even called for the reintroduction of the death penalty, abolished in 1930, for 'desertion in the field' and 'misbehaving in the face of the enemy in such a manner as to show cowardice.' It would, he believed, act as a 'salutary deterrent'.[31]

The Eighth Army set to work consolidating its defensive positions at El Alamein, an obvious 'last-ditch' position to protect the Nile. Lieutenant General James R. Marshall-Cornwall had earlier reconnoitred the area in 1940 and some unfinished earthworks still remained. Captain Tom Witherby (23rd Armoured Brigade) described the works in progress.

> There were three [defensive 'box'] posts. The most important of these surrounded Alamein Railway Station and had been likened to a small Tobruk… These three posts were too far apart to be mutually supporting and it was intended that strong armoured forces would manoeuvre round them.[32]

Auchinleck summoned General David Belchem on the night of 27 June to deliver a personal message to General Morshead, then in Alexandria.

The 9th Australian Division, fresh from re-forming in Palestine, was to move to the northern sector of the El Alamein line as part of XXX Corps. Of Alamein, Sergeant Joseph Stokes, 2/7th Australian Field Regiment, noted sarcastically: 'We must have passed through it without noticing it. No wonder... there was nothing there.'[33]

On 1 July Rommel's vanguard also reached El Alamein – the apex of his African adventure. His tenuous line of communication, however, was now desperate. Supplies to his German troops fell to just 5,000 tons in June, against 34,000 tons in May. By August 1942, Tobruk had become the Axis' primary port in North Africa, receiving 248 vehicles, 10,931 tons of fuel and 4,379 tons of matériel.[34] Still, Rommel expected more and held that a five-fold increase was possible. (The British quartermaster received 254 tanks, 446 guns, 3,289 vehicles and 72,192 tons of stores on the busy Suez docks in August.) Allied aircraft routinely hammered Tobruk. It was bombed thirty-three times in July, mostly at night, by the RAF Wellingtons and by the newly established US Army Middle East Air Force. Another 1,600 sorties followed in August. Air power would be key in defeating the Axis, Major General Charles L. Scott, a US military observer, explained: 'What we need out here is two to three hundred more bombers, for with them we can bag the Hun lock stock and barrel and settle the Libyan campaign.'[35]

Frank Gervasi flew as an observer on an American B-24 during a bombing strike on Tobruk. He afterwards reflected on the mission: 'It never occurred to me at the time that we were killing and maiming men. No, we were surgeons removing a cancerous growth, the enemy.'[36]

Gervasi's 'enemy' assembled on the night of 30 June in readiness for a new headlong assault. In place of a wide flanking movement, Rommel favoured a boldfaced frontal charge reminiscent of his assault on Tobruk. If successful, it was possible that another British flight would be triggered. An intercepted dispatch from Colonel Fellers revealing considerable panic in Cairo was surely encouraging. At the same time, and reminiscent of April 1941, German intelligence was ignorant of the British defences – on this ocassion, Auchinleck's defensive network. Weakened and exhausted, the Panzerarmee could manoeuvre, but it had little punch in reserve for heavy fighting. Moreover, Ultra was privy to its intentions.

'Both officers and men reached the limit of human endurance'

1 July 1942. Exhausted German troops battled to deploy through a violent sandstorm across rugged terrain. Their morale had begun to ebb. Pressing on, behind schedule, the 21st Panzer Division was hit by a 'colossal [RAF] bombing attack'.[37] The Germans were also struggling with a reliance upon plundered fuel, food, ammunition, even uniforms. Up to eighty-five per cent of their vehicles *wurden als Beute erfasst* (were captured booty), likewise requiring captured fuel stocks. Rommel later acknowledged the extraordinary demands in this period placed on 'both officers and men [who had] reached the limit of human endurance.'[38] A swathe of illness thinned their ranks, incapacitating nearly half of the forward Axis troops. To quote a 1944 British hygiene report:

> The enemy appears to have no conception of the most elementary measures and has a dysentery/diarrhoea rate so very much higher than ours that it is believed that the poor physical condition of his troops played a great part [in the outcome at El Alamein].[39]

An inventory of the 90th Light Afrika Division attests to an attendant matériel deficit. With a combat strength of seventy-six officers and 1,603 other ranks, it could muster only 19 field guns (four captured 25-pounders and seven ex-Russian 76.2-mm guns) and 32 anti-tank guns (twelve ex-Russian pieces and two British six-pounders). The DAK, similarly, could field only 55 tanks – including a solitary Panzer IV – plus a similar assortment of German, Russian and British artillery. Another nightmare for the quartermaster.

Surprise was absent on the morning of 1 July. British radio and aerial intelligence detected the forthcoming Axis attack and related diversion – a day Dorman-Smith later marked in his diary as 'The battle of El Alamein.'[40]

Rommel's penultimate attack began on an inauspicious note. British artillery halted the 90th Light Afrika Division in its attempt to push northeast on the coastal road, leading to panic among the veteran combatants. Nehring's 21st Panzer Division, however, successfully assaulted the Deir el Shein box, occupied by the 18th Indian Brigade (two of its three battalions untried in battle). 'Visibility was very bad', a wartime narrative told:

> and the defenders were often unable to see for more than a few yards. The enemy naturally took advantage of this cover, and during the afternoon, the minefield was penetrated… At 1700 the tanks swept around onto the Sikhs where a troop of 2-pounders destroyed two Panzers before they closed. Four 25-pounders were still in action and they too took their toll. The tanks were too close, however, and the guns were immediately knocked out. The German tank crews found the mess tent and stopped to drink up the beer.[41]

An SOS from the Indian Brigade was received too late at XXX Corps HQ and a counterattack never eventuated. The capture of Deir el Shein gave Rommel cause for optimism. In reality, the day had ended in a brutal setback. The loss of eighteen tanks had effectively blunted the DAK's offensive capability and, having failed to outmanoeuvre the British, Rommel would now face a crushing battle of attrition. The lack of fuel and ammunition was critical; as the DAK's diary noted: 'Replenishment is urgently needed.'[42] An afternoon message for the Littorio Division to continue the pursuit generated the curt response: it 'has fuel for only 20 km, to Alexandria 150 km!'[43]

Axis plans for the second day of fighting called for the isolation of the Alamein box and opening up the coast road. Both failed.

Leutnant Wolff was injured in the fighting. After knocking out a British Bren Gun carrier,

> a high explosive round from an American [Grant] impacted next to me. I was able to pull my head in time, reflexively, and then I felt a small, biting pain on right arm… A small piece of shrapnel… What happened next was like a mirage… [An] entire New Zealand battle group surrendered… Our commander was laughing. Finally a catch… Four burning tanks, perhaps ten shot-up prime movers, eight guns, a number of carriers, machine guns, antitank guns…[44]

Determined resistance, repeated enemy air attacks by bombers with strong fighter support, and supply and ammunition shortages, resulted in only modest Axis headway. Hauptmann Kleiböhmer, diary keeper for the 90th Light Africa Division, feared that his fellow soldiers were no longer capable of taking 'this last British stronghold forward of the Nile Delta by themselves'. The Italian formations, so far largely removed from the fighting, offered a 'last hope', though he expected little of them.[45]

Wolff described the scene that evening: 'Tired, unwashed, greasy, faces moistened by the nightly dew of the desert. We pull guard for Germany in the middle of a star-filled African night.' There was little sleep.

> Dear God, when I think about the 2nd of July, my eyes start to burn!... During the night, New Zealanders entered the sector... Two men were put on guard on each tank – one at the weapons, one outside with a submachine gun, straining his ears and staring into the night.[46]

Rommel's attempted drive around the Alamein box on 3 July brought another reverse. Although some headway was made at Ruweistat Ridge, the New Zealanders assailed Ariete from their Qaret el Abd box, taking 350 prisoners and its artillery complement of 44 guns. Frontline German units reported Italian troops streaming back, 'mostly unarmed'.[47] In the eyes of the Panzerarmee diarist, the Italians bore full responsibility:

> Although the attack of the German Divisions had gained some ground, even on this day no decisive breakthrough had been achieved. The reason lay in the complete failure of Panzer Div. Ariete which had offered no serious resistance to the enemy.[48]

Rommel's position on the morning of 4 July was 'perilous'. With only thirty-six operational tanks, it was questionable whether the Axis could have endured a determined confrontation at this time. 'We survived', von Mellenthin later wrote, 'with no real damage except to our nerves.'[49] 'Things are not going as I should like them', Rommel wrote home.[50]

Mussolini's earlier enthusiasm had tapered off. On 6 July he pressed for the fighting to continue, though with the lesser objective of

Alexandria – 'an important centre, and its capture will [still] make an impression on the world.'[51]

For a moment there was a lull in the fighting. Lieutenant Colonel Hugh Murray Reid watched as tank crews brewed tea beside their vehicles: 'Evidence of the recent engagement was all about, and the crew of one tank had just buried their commander. Twenty minutes before he was standing in his turret…when a shell hit the top of the turret and passed right through him.'[52]

A renewed Axis attack in the south on 10 July coincided with a strong attack by the Australians in the north against the unprepared Sabratha Division, the Italians retreating 'in haste' with most taken prisoner.[53] A remarkable win came with the capture of Hauptman Alfred Seeböhm's 621st Radio Intercept Company (Rommel's radio intelligence unit) by the Australian 2/24th Battalion. Radio Cairo afterwards reported: 'We are much obliged for the extensive amount of excellent materiel we captured.'[54] Seized files revealed lax radio security and manifold leaks from British military traffic as well as a spy ring operating in Egypt. The cipher that Fellers (now stateside) used to communicate with Washington was changed – another massive blow to Rommel's intelligence feed. The loss of Seeböhm's unit was a 'catastrophe' with consequences even more serious than the 'Good Source drying up'.[55] Rommel was 'absolutely furious' upon receiving the news.[56] Unaware of the British regrouping and introduction of new weapons, 'the great general now had to rely upon himself and his reconnaissance at the front.'[57]

Still incensed by Italian battlefield performance, Rommel reported on 12 July 'alarming symptoms of deteriorating morale'. The day before he called upon Italian commanders 'not to shrink from [enacting] the death penalty.'[58] Meanwhile, German troops of the newly arrived 104th Infantry Regiment fought a furious battle to break through at Tel el Eisa. Australian machine gunner Corporal Victor Knight helped to see off the attack:

> We had to urinate on the barrels to keep them cool enough to keep firing. We had oil available and we simply poured it from a four-gallon drum into the working parts, keeping the guns firing all the time.[59]

Rolf Krengel, whom we last saw wounded at Mechili the previous year, was in a forward position on the afternoon of 12 July when Rommel suddenly arrived. With his armoured car drawing enemy fire, the Feldmarschall jumped 'like a young boy',

> from one hole into the next, then crouches behind a Pak shield, looks with his binoculars, shouts orders, and even directs a Pak to fire on an enemy tank in the distance. He even helps the crew pull the gun around… Just before dark, the General mounts an NSU [motorcycle] and drives to the south, his armoured car shot to bits by British tank gunners.[60]

Rommel directed the 21st Panzer Division against the Alamein Box on 13 July, supported by Ju 87 dive-bombing and artillery, aiming to seize this key position and isolate the Australians at Tel el Eisa. Resolutely defended by the 1st Royal Durban Light Infantry, the Germans fell back. A change in direction the next day, with an attempt to breakthrough to the coast, was also resisted. As von Mellenthin explained: 'The attacking infantry moved too late so that the paralysing effects of the bombing were lost… Fighting continued until long after dark and the Australian infantry showed that they were the same redoubtable opponents we had met in the first siege of Tobruk.'[61] It was with an air of resignation that Rommel wrote his combat report:

> Two months of continuous hard campaigning had reduced the strength of the German formations to such a degree that they could not resume the offensive immediately. This fact, and the failure of the Italians, forced Panzerarmee to the decision to go over to the defensive in its present positions until the formations were completely refreshed.[62]

The transfer of the 21st Panzer Division towards the coast prompted Auchinleck to undertake a major assault in the central sector of the Alamein Line. Although the best part of the Italian X Corps (Brescia and Pavia Divisions) were captured or destroyed, the 4th New Zealand Infantry Brigade suffered 1,405 casualties and over 1,200 men taken prisoner – the heaviest loss sustained by the New Zealanders during the entire campaign. Tank-infantry coordination was later panned by

Major General Howard Kippenberger (5th New Zealand Brigade), who described a 'most intense distrust, almost hatred, of our armour. Everywhere one heard tales of the other arms being let down; it was regarded as axiomatic that the tanks would not be where they were wanted in time.'[63]

Rommel had cause for concern with the performance of his allies, who several times had 'deserted their positions under the effect of artillery fire' and failed to heed their officers' call to 'stand up to the enemy'.[64] Rommel's criticism, in a letter to Hitler to 'straighten things out', riled Mussolini, who would 'never forgive' him. Italian troops, after all, were exhausted, having 'marched hundreds of kilometres... always on foot.'[65]

The weary Eighth Army settled into a period of static warfare, expanding trenches and laying mines. Kippenberger elaborated:

> We set to work to lay minefields, to clear or mark the Italian minefields that we were sitting among, and to dig ourselves in. One truck carrying a load of mines struck a mine and blew up, leaving no trace of the laying party. The ground was very hard, and except in patches it was impossible to get deeper than eighteen inches without a compressor, so that most of the work had to be done at night and progress was slow... For the troops in the line, who all day long had to remain in their narrow slits, it was purgatory. After sunset the air became deliciously cool and pleasant and everyone came to life.[66]

Lieutenant R.W. Johnston (AFS) waited behind the frontlines in his Dodge ambulance, sympathetic to the plight of the 'the poor infantry' and the struggle to transport the wounded over rocky terrain under fire:

> They are dug in and don't dare show themselves during the day and only get food when its dark. With the heat, the flies, and the lack of everything, I really do not see how they stand it and retain their sanity.[67]

Captain Charles Upham VC was again in the midst of the fighting, leading a company of troops into combat on the night 14-15 July. Wounded twice, once while assailing and destroying a truck carrying German soldiers with hand grenades, Upham was firm in guiding his men in a final assault on El Ruweisat Ridge. When communications broke down with the advancing troops, he rushed ahead, armed with a captured German MG-34 machine gun, past enemy machine-gun nests, to learn of their progress. Nearing his goal, Upham was stopped by an enemy strongpoint before dawn. Aggressively taking the lead – his voice 'heard above the din of battle' – Upham inspired his men, hurling grenades and single-handedly knocking out a tank, several guns and vehicles. Shot through the elbow and carrying a broken arm, he continued to lead his men through a fierce counterattack to win his objective. Weakened by blood loss, his wounds dressed, Upham returned to his men where he was once more severely injured while under heavy mortar and artillery fire. Unable to move, he was taken prisoner. Labelled an 'incorrigible German hater' by his captors, the habitual escapee was finally incarcerated in Colditz castle.[68] Upham received the Bar to his VC in September 1945.

Sergeant Keith Elliott (22nd Battalion) was another New Zealander to distinguish himself on 15 July at Ruweisat. Under heavy tank, machine-gun and artillery fire, Elliott was wounded in the chest. Regardless of his injury, he 'led seven men in a bayonet charge across 500 yards of open ground in the face of heavy fire and captured four enemy machine-gun posts and an anti-tank gun, killing a number of the enemy and taking fifty prisoners.' Severely wounded, Elliott 'refused to leave his men until he had reformed them, handed over his prisoners, which now numbered 130, and had arranged for his men to re-join their Battalion.'[69]

Auchinleck, only too aware of Churchill's prying and concern for Britain losing Iraq (and its oil reserves) should the 'Russian Front break', notified the premier on 15 July that he was 'doing his utmost to defeat the enemy in the West or drive him back sufficiently to lessen the threat to Egypt.'[70]

A follow-up attack by the 9th Australian Division, 1st South African Division, 161st Indian Brigade and 6th New Zealand Brigade during the night of 21 July made substantial headway.

Private Arthur Stanley 'Stan' Gurney (2/48th Battalion) crossed the start line at Tel-el-Eisa in the early hours on 22 July 1942 lugging a cumbersome Boys anti-tank rifle. Running into oppressive machine-gun fire, his platoon commander, Lieutenant Jim Wearing-Smith, directed: 'For Christ sake drop that bloody Boys, you'll do better with a rifle!'[71] Seconds later Wearing-Smith was badly wounded, his platoon sergeant killed. At once, Gurney took the initiative and charged across open ground under a hail of fire, to the nearest enemy post where he bayoneted three men, silencing the position. He assailed a second post, bayoneting two more machine-gunners and taking a third prisoner. Despite being knocked off his feet by the blast of a stick grenade, Gurney picked himself up and charged a third post. He was last seen by his fellow 'diggers', 'using the bayonet with great vigour' before disappearing from view. His body was later found in an enemy post. Gurney was posthumously awarded the VC.[72]

British fortunes changed soon after daybreak with the 15th Panzer Division fighting back. The newly arrived Valentine tanks of the British 23rd Armoured Brigade, in what was described as 'a real balaclava' charge, raced into a tremendous hail of anti-tank fire before blundering onto a minefield.[73] The brigade pressed on, only to face determined opposition. Well over 100 British tanks were lost and 1,400 men taken prisoner.

An officer of the British 9th Lancers found some of his men at the point of mental collapse.

> The constant battles and lack of sleep is having its effect; most of us are at the extreme limit and it is getting hard to even think clearly. Yesterday three men – all normal stout-hearted men – went temporarily out of their minds and others were showing the same signs of mental and physical strain.[74]

Operation Manhood was a final attempt by Auchinleck to seize Miteiriya Ridge, known colloquially as Ruin Ridge, by the 9th Australian Division and the 69th Brigade, 50th (Northumbrian) Division. Launched on 27 July, it too ended in disaster with the loss of more than 1,000 men. One of the many critics, Major Donald Jackson (Australian 24th Brigade), later criticised the ambitious plan for smacking 'a little of someone with a small map and large chinagraph pencil.'[75]

'The man was completely undone'

In the absence of a decisive victory, the slog of attrition continued. Reporting from Africa, A.J. Berndt (Reich Propaganda Ministry) could only inform readers that Rommel's advance was halted 'for the time being'.[76] After an inspection tour at the front, Generalleutnant Walter Warlimont (Deputy Chief of the Operations Staff) presented to Hitler's HQ the challenge of the German-Italo army, facing 'an enemy who, from the point of view of both equipment and ammunition supply, had become considerably superior on land, on sea and in the air.'[77] But while Auchinleck fielded the stronger of the two sides, he notified Whitehall that it 'badly needs either a reinforcement of well-trained formations or a quiet period in which to train.'[78] Churchill thought otherwise. Shouldering the political pressure of Gazala and Tobruk, the prime minister, once again, sought a change at the top. He would see to it personally.

Churchill, accompanied by Brooke, touched down at Burg el Arab (outside Alexandria) on 5 August. Dorman-Smith at once sensed the 'chill', for 'this was not going to be a nice visit.'[79] Churchill's hostility was immediate. He paid no attention to a briefing given by Auchinleck and Dorman-Smith, instead

> [he] quickly began to demand that the Eighth Army should attack afresh. He thrust his stubby fingers against the talc; 'Here,' he said, 'or here.' We were alone with him and it was a little like being caged with a gorilla. Eventually Auchinleck said quietly and finally, 'No, Sir we cannot attack again yet.' Churchill, rose, gruntled, stumped down from the caravan and stood alone in the sand, back turned to us.[80]

Suntanned troops gathered to see a lilywhite 'Mr Bullfinch' tour the front-lines in his white suit and white sun umbrella looking 'pugnacious, confident, cheerful, firm and powerful.'[81] Henry T. Gorrell, United Press war correspondent, watched as troops recognised their unexpected guest: 'Blimey, its Winnie'; 'The undreamed-of sight of the prime minister, complete with cigar, thumping the ground with his stick as he sidestepped shell and bomb craters.'[82] He stopped to meet with the men of the Australian 2/23rd Battalion, giving the 'V for Victory' sign. Private Stan Collins stepped forward, saluted, and asked, 'How about a cigar, sir?'[83] Smiling, the premier obligingly took one from his pocket. Out of his earshot, an Antipodean anti-aircraft gunner called out, much to the amusement of those around, 'When are you going to send us home, you fat old bastard?'[84]

To another observer: 'We all thought he had rather the air of a pleasant headmaster who had come along to see how his pupils were getting on; only one wasn't too sure that he hadn't a birch concealed somewhere. Perhaps it was the fly-whisk he carried which fostered this idea.'[85] Churchill, however, would wield the stick within his upper echelon. Retracing his steps back to Cairo at the end of a long day, he 'remained sunk in his own thoughts. He did not speak once.'[86] In his room, he wrote of the cheerful and confident Australian and South Africans troops that he'd met, men 'bewildered at having been baulked of victory on repeated occasions' – a telling commentary. That night he drafted a memo calling for 'drastic and immediate change'.[87]

In yet another leadership shake-up, the so-called 'Cairo Purge', Churchill appointed General Sir Harold Alexander to take Auchinleck's place, with General William 'Strafer' Gott as commander of the Eighth Army.[88] Colonel Ian Jacob (who accompanied Churchill on this visit) recorded the rationale for the Auk's removal:

> General Auchinleck [has] universal respect… Nevertheless, he has not created a coherent Army, and most of the criticisms and explanations which people give are directed to the matters which are his immediate concern… The great expansion of the Army meant that formations arriving in the Middle East were very inexperienced, and there was no method by which they could be introduced gradually into battle… The discipline of the Army is no longer what it used to be… There is a need for new blood, and a more rapid interchange between the Middle East and home.[89]

Moran's diary held a similar perspective, shared by Brooke, that for a 'man of many talents' and 'great strength of character', he had so dispersed our forces in the desert that Rommel, with his more effective tanks and guns, had little difficulty in defeating the scattered fragments piecemeal. [But] there is another reason: 'The Auk does not understand Winston.'[90]

Jacob delivered the letter to the C-in-C informing him of his removal. 'He opened it and read it through two or three times in silence. He did not move a muscle, and remained outwardly calm.'[91] Meeting later with Brooke, Moran watched the two in conversation across the lush British

149

Embassy lawn. Auchinleck, he observed, 'sat with his forearms on his thighs, his hands hanging down between his knees, his head drooping forward like a flower on a broken stalk. His long, lean limbs were relaxed; the whole attitude expressed grief: the man was completely undone.'[92]

In another tragic twist, Gott was killed when his aircraft was shot down flying to Cairo (on the same route Churchill had taken two days before). Receiving the news, Churchill 'stood staring at the carpet, then very slowly he pulled himself up the stairs.'[93] Brooke later persuaded the premier to instead appoint his protégé for the role – Lieutenant General Bernard Law Montgomery, a man the Eighth Army would simply know as 'Monty'.

'I am convinced that [Gott's] appointment was not sound', Montgomery later reckoned, adding that it 'might have led to disaster.' Captain Tom Witherby (23rd Armoured Brigade) concurred, believing: 'We would have been defeated at Alam Halfa… Gott was a brave man, but he was tired and simply did not have the intellectual stature for the command.' General Sir Harold Pyman (7th Armoured Division) drew attention to another shortcoming: 'I was never certain that he understood the correct use of artillery fire, or that he had that decisive grasp of timing that is essential to any commander.'[94]

'Renewed optimism and confidence'

Montgomery's orders from Alexander were 'quite simple; they were to destroy Rommel and his Army.'[95] He assumed command of the shaken Eighth Army on 13 August. Monty knew his first task was to raise morale. Privately he noted, 'The troops had their tails right down and there was no confidence in the higher command. It was clear that ROMMEL was preparing further attacks and the troops were looking over their shoulders for rear lines to which to withdraw.'[96]

Writing on British morale at this time, Lieutenant Colonel H.S. Gear witnessed

> pitiless men soaked in war fully trained and experienced, but dispirited. To do this rhythmical rushing forwards and backwards seemed to contain no promise of finality. It was no longer a European but a Desert Army, with its own

cultivated and characteristic attitudes and habits. It was an Imperial and not a British Army, and partly for this reason was the finest and most finished instrument of war thus fashioned by the Allies. Because of its peculiar constitution and unusual experience it needed an exceptional commander if its qualities were to be most advantageously exercised. For this position General Montgomery was chosen.[97]

'He took a grip immediately', Major General Francis 'Freddie' de Guingand recalled. 'You suddenly felt here was leadership... He told us the bad days were over and he was now determined that it was going to be a success.'[98] Within weeks, British censors noticed an immediate and positive change of tone in soldiers' mail leaving Egypt – 'renewed optimism and confidence were everywhere... The old aggressive spirit... is in the process of being recovered.'[99]

Moorehead observed the new commander inspecting the front lines; he was a 'queer little bloke who stood up in his car and waved at every passing group of soldiers as though he had known them for a long time. No saluting, none of that beefy, red-blooded look usually associated with red tabs.'[100] During a field visit on 14 August, Monty requested a slouch hat, 'because it was an exceedingly good hat for the desert – complete with the iconic "rising sun" badge.'[101] Various unit badges soon adorned it, though reactions were 'mixed' over his adoption of an 'Australian bush hat'. In its place, Sergeant James Fraser (6th RTR) offered Monty a black beret.[102] Bearing an officers' cloth badge and metal RTR tank badge, it quickly became his signature headdress.[103]

Suitably impressed by the new commander, Morshead pulled Brigadier Victor Windeyer (20th Brigade) aside: 'This man really is a breath of fresh air. Things are going to be different soon.'[104] Belchem believed this period was Montgomery's 'finest hour':

> None of us has been able to adequately describe all that he accomplished in such a short time... The first task which he undertook was to tour the whole of the El Alamein region, and to visit every formation in the Army, studying the ground and defences at the same time. Wherever conditions permitted, he gathered officers and men about him and personally explained to them his new defensive policy.[105]

Churchill again visited Egypt on 19 August (on the return leg of a meeting with Stalin) where Monty was hounded to open a Second Front. Moran overheard Churchill in high spirits singing in his bath (on the day of the bloody fiasco at the German-occupied port of Dieppe) when Alexander arrived to drive him to the front. A tour of the high ground, where the next battle would be fought, followed. To Churchill's amazement, the troops were 'naked, except for a loin-cloth… burnt brown by months under the Africa sun.' Turning to his physician, he exclaimed, 'Forty-four years ago it was a military offence to appear without a path helmet… Why don't these fellows here get sunstroke and heatstroke?'[106] 'How fashions change', his memoirs later told.[107]

Preparations for the prime minister's visit to Montgomery's HQ at Burg-el-Arab revealed a dilemma: no brandy was on hand. As de Guingand describes, 'An ADC was sent to Alexandria to buy some. A local product was found, and to drink this one had to have a cast-iron stomach, and a very good head.'[108] An element of subterfuge was employed with the local liquor decanted into the bottle of a well-known French brand.

Brooke was impressed by Montgomery's energy and grasp of the situation. But Monty was not to be rushed. He explained to his party the need for six weeks' thorough preparation, reforming divisions into three army corps, 'breaking-in' the new American Sherman tanks and using artillery 'as had never been possible before in the desert.' His chosen date for an offensive was at the end of September. This 'disappointed' Churchill, who later wrote: 'Although I was always impatient for offensive action on our part at the earliest moment, I welcomed the prospect of Rommel breaking his teeth upon us before our main attack was launched.'[109]

To gain an edge over the enemy, Montgomery showed special interest in the drug Benzedrine sulphate – likely because of its reputation as a 'confidence drug' or 'pep drug' and its potential as a 'pharmacological morale boost'.[110] Psychologists were already aware of the drug's effects on the nervous system, as well as its shortcomings, 'a variety of psychologic reactions which are unpredictable and at times paradoxic.'[111] Nevertheless Brigadier Quentin Wallace (X Corps) believed that 'pep pills, properly administered, would be a powerful weapon against the enemy.'[112] Field tests using methamphetamine and amphetamine over 48 hours were conducted on 7 September to determine any improvement in marching speed and arithmetic scores. Another bevy of tests at the end of September put two infantry squads through a series of tasks such as shooting, trench digging, signalling and machine gun reassembly with no sleep and only short rest periods. This was followed by a seven-mile march in which the 'Benzedrine squad' beat its placebo counterpart by 11 minutes, marching with 'snap and zest'.[113] The results supported a pharmacologically-enhanced fight with 100,000 5 mg tablets ordered for distribution to combat units in the forthcoming battle.

Interestingly, the corresponding use of methamphetamine in the Wehrmacht at this time was declining, with drugs such as *Pervitin* restricted to 'emergency' use and listed as 'dangerously addictive'.

In contrast to his sprightly opponent, Rommel was now exhausted. Barely able to review and sign the reports placed before him, the 'Desert Fox' would fall into bed early. Siegfried Westphal wrote of the burden he carried:

> He was not only the soul but also the motive power of the North African war. Frugal and abstemious as he was, he would never have incurred the cardiac weakness which afflicted him in 1942 if it had not been for the continual over-activity to which he forces himself. His responsibility for the war theatre and for his troops lay heavy on him.[114]

Rommel's personal physician Professor Hans Horsters (Würzberg University) diagnosed the 'symptoms of low blood pressure, with a tendency to fainting fits. His present condition is due to stomach and intestinal complaints he has had for a long time, aggravated by the unfavourable climate.'[115] Writing home, Rommel explained his need to convalesce in Germany. He closed with the comment that having used up five generals per division for eighteen months, his time for an 'overhaul' had come.[116]

*****

As both sides recovered their strength, BBC correspondent Godfrey Talbot toured the surrounding terrain.

> The tank fighting left its marks upon the southern stony plain beyond those vast, wired-off minefields of ours... The tanks lay twisted and black as they had died, heaps

of torn and fire-charred metal strewn about the flat desert and the humps of rising ground. Broken guns, trucks, shell cases, and soldiers' clothing lay about; but it was the tanks you remembered... Turrets and tracks had been torn off and flung fifty feet away to lie beside helmets, boots, torn uniform jackets, burned socks and cartridge belts. Whole machines had been ripped open wide by explosions.[117]

Talbot also spent several days with Tomahawk pilots of the 5th South African Fighter Squadron. He found them scheming. How might they best 'spread terror in the enemy lines'?

Their agile brains produced such novel methods as dropping beer bottles from their diving aircraft, because as they hurtled to the ground they emitted a spooky, spine-crawling shriek... Another trick, finally banned by an order stating that 'No more pamphlets are to be dropped over the enemy lines', was the hurling of rolls of toilet paper from aircraft, on which were scrawled such slogans as *'Fur der Fuhrer unt der Reich* – South African compliments'.[118]

Chapter Six

'Big things at stake'

What did I see in the desert to-day,
In the cold, pale light of dawn?
I saw the Honeys creaking out,
Their brave, bright pennants torn;
And heads were high against the sky,
And faces were grim and drawn.

–Bombardier L. Challoner

Rommel made one last attempt to reach the Nile Delta in 1942. 'There are big things at stake', he wrote to 'Dearest Lu… It might go some way towards deciding the whole course of the war. If it fails, at least I hope to give the enemy a pretty thorough beating.'[1] Badly needed reinforcements had arrived in August including the 164th Light Africa Division from Crete (without transport) plus the parachutists of the Fallschirmjäger-Brigade Ramcke and Italian Folgore Division.

Dr Selmayr optimistically jotted in his diary: 'Already dreaming of Alexandria and Cairo.' Preparations were underway to burst through the British minefields,

> and roll them up from the rear. The tanks were dug in deeply and covered with camouflage nets. Under the death penalty it was forbidden to walk around in the open during the day. Final conference with the commander: go easy on the fuel and ammunition. How could that mean anything good for an attack?[2]

Across the (dummy and real) minefields de Guingand hatched a deceptive plan to lure Rommel into a trap using a doctored map. With nearly perfect (Ultra) intelligence regarding his intents, de Guingand secretly falsified a

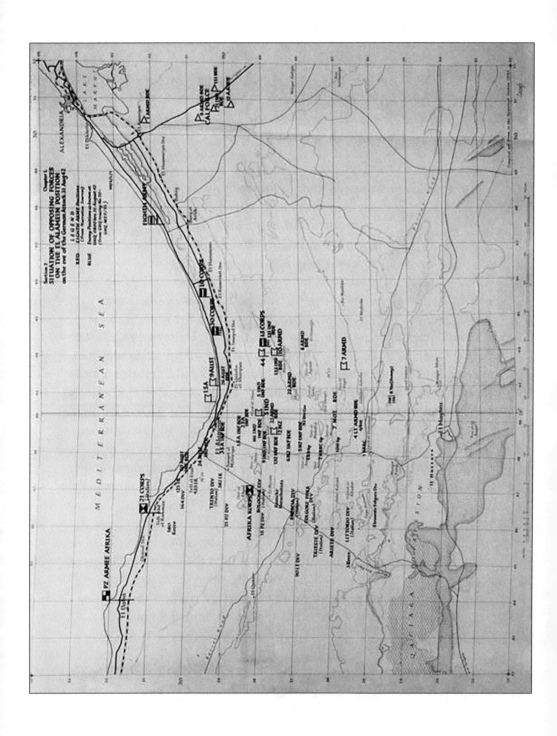

map illustrating the terrain south of Alam Halfa, an area of very soft sand, as 'good going'. This would (hopefully) divert the assault northwards to 'where preparations had been made to receive them'.[3] In place of a 'good gallop', Rommel would 'find himself wallowing in deep sand.'[4] Suitably aged, creased and tea-stained, the fake 'going map' was planted in a soldier's haversack and left in an abandoned scout car 'knocked-out' by a mine. It was duly recovered and examined by Rommel's staff.

The battle of Alam Halfa began on the night of 30/31 August. Ciano believed the British would be caught unprepared, settling down for the evening to a 'whisky'.[5] Rommel manoeuvred by moonlight to the south of the El Alamein bottleneck until his assault force, as he later described, was 'held up far too long by the strong and hitherto unsuspected mine barriers'; 'surprise...had been lost.'[6] Losses escalated on both sides. As de Guingand anticipated, Rommel now wheeled north, only to encounter the fabricated area of 'good going' – a sand belt that tripled his Panzers' fuel consumption. (Whether or not this was a consequence of the ruse or an autonomous decision by Rommel, however, remains open to conjecture.)[7] 'Painfully grinding their way through the soft sand,' the DAK's fuel stocks 'were soon badly depleted and at 1600 hours we called off the attack on Hill 132.'[8]

Practically undisturbed, Allied aircraft pounded the fuel-starved enemy formations. Rolf Krengel endured a sleepless night in a wadi: 'About 2,000 bombs fall in our vicinity. We have three men KIA, several wounded and we lose three guns from a battery of four.'[9] British and US bombers on 1 September undertook 111 sorties, dropping nearly 80 tonnes of bombs in neat formation. Aside from the heavy toll on vehicles and equipment, seven DAK staff officers including Generalmajor Georg von Bismarck were killed. Generalmajor Walter Nehring was also severely wounded. Throwing himself into a slit trench, during one of six bombing raids, Rommel survived unscathed from the 'red hot metal fragment [that] fell beside me in the trench.'[10]

'We had never experienced anything quite like that before', Dr Selmayr wrote. The RAF 'flew past us in air-show formation and dropped their loads wherever there were even just a few vehicles close together.'[11] Superior numbers of enemy aircraft, however, never troubled Hans-Joachim Marseille, who shot down seventeen Allied aircraft on 1 September. Something of a maverick, his commanding officer, Oberst Eduard Neumann, later said that he was 'too fast and too mercurial to be a good leader and teacher, but his pilots adored him. He thanked them by protecting them and bringing them home safely.'[12]

An attack by the New Zealanders and British 132nd Infantry Brigade on 3 September was beaten off with nearly 1,000 casualties.

The severity of the supply situation finally persuaded Rommel that he could not sustain his offensive. He even debated whether to abandon it altogether. Montgomery cautiously chose not to use his massed armour, forfeiting what von Mellenthin assessed as 'an excellent opportunity of cutting off and destroying' the DAK.[13] Instead, the British commander would conserve and train his troops for a forthcoming counter-offensive, as he later explained:

> I soon realised that although the Eighth Army was composed of magnificent material, it was untrained; it had done much fighting but little training. We had just won a decisive victory, but it had been a static battle; I was not prepared to launch the troops into an all-out offensive without prior training.[14]

The battle was over by 6 September. The 'Six-day Race', as German troops referred to it (after a famous bicycle race), was, von Mellenthin decided, the 'turning point of the desert war, and the first of the long series of defeats on every front.'[15] In his *Papers*, Rommel conceded that 'our last chance of gaining the Suez Canal had gone.'[16] Schmidt similarly entertained, 'serious doubts as to whether I should ever, as a soldier, set eyes on the Pyramids.'[17]

The Axis assault force withdrew, successfully, to its starting position. Rommel estimated his losses at 3,000 men, 50 tanks and 400 other vehicles. He also lost fifty anti-tank and field guns. General Alexander's losses were 110 officers, 1,640 men and sixty-eight tanks.[18]

Montgomery was satisfied: 'Thus the Battle of Alam Halfa ended in the way we wanted.'[19] Holding all the intelligence aces close to his chest, Churchill wrote:

> We know that Rommel was in dire straits, and of his insistent demands for help. We know too that he was a wearied ailing man at that time. The consequences of Alam Halfa were effective two months later.[20]

A 'most grateful' prime minister notified Roosevelt that 193 Sherman tanks had been unloaded at Suez in 'record time'; 'I have good hopes about all the Egyptian fighting and believe Rommel is hard pressed.'[21]

A new phase in the desert war commenced with Axis troops now digging in on the defensive. Throughout September and October almost 500,000 Teller anti-tank and smaller anti-personnel mines (some captured at Tobruk) were planted in fields up to five miles deep – a deadly barrier Rommel called his *Minegarten*.[22] The pause in the fighting also presented many German soldiers with their first period of rest in months. Concerts and a comedy troupe provided entertainment while milestones, such as the 155th Artillery Regiment's 80,000th shell fired, or the four millionth loaf of bread distributed by the 15th Panzer Division's bakers, were celebrated.

Rolf Krengel was up early on the morning of 21 September in readiness for an inspection tour by Rommel:

> Two Fieseler *Storch*s land and three Stukas afterwards. Several other generals are with Rommel; we give them a precise salute… It's time for them to take off. To show his appreciation, he [Rommel] orders the three Stukas to dive on our position with blaring sirens as a farewell greeting.[23]

The next day Rommel left for treatment at Wiener Neustadt (site of the War Academy he commanded before the war) for medical treatment. Schmidt noticed his ailing appearance, 'he looked more finely drawn each time I saw him…he had now undergone twenty months of continuous mental and physical drain in the Desert…Rommel was a spent force.'[24]

Tinged with the pain of knowing an Allied offensive was imminent, and certain that only a successful German thrust in the Caucasus could avert it, Rommel passed his command to General der Panzertruppe Georg Stumme. A veteran tank commander unfamiliar with North Africa, in poor health and recently court martialled and relieved of his command in Russia, Stumme nevertheless set to work with zeal, advancing Rommel's defensive works and forging relations with Italian authorities.

Lieutenant General Brian Horrocks (XIII Corps) led the next engagement, Operation Braganza, a brigade-sized assault on the night of 29 September, aiming to retake Deir el Munassib, for extra artillery deployment, and to focus Axis attention southwards. The 131st (Queens)

Infantry Brigade, supported by tanks of the 4th Armoured Brigade, nine field regiments and one medium artillery battery, had difficulty in locating enemy positions and was driven off by the Folgore Division who bore the brunt of the attack. Ernest Norris (NCO in the 1/5th Queens) recounted the shock of being fired at once the preliminary barrage had finished:

> You feel so naked and you can't describe it. In a matter of seconds they were firing tracer bullets at us. It was still dark and I was aware of the tracer coming towards us – they seemed too slow to be bullets. But there were men getting killed and wounded all around... It was almost daylight. We got down behind what cover we could find. I looked around. Captain Clark was dead. Mr Cole-Biroth was pretty badly wounded and Mr Whittaker had most of his face shot away. We had no officers left. [25]

Little gain was for made for 328 casualties; the Italians even received a rare compliment from the DAK.

Hans-Joachim Marseille – Germany's top scoring desert ace with 158 confirmed aerial victories – was killed on 30 September while bailing out of his Bf-109G fighter and striking the aircraft's tail. Unable to open his parachute, he died on impact.[26]

That night Hitler presented Rommel with his Feldmarschall's baton. The *Wüstenfuchs* (Desert Fox) was honoured at a rally at the Berliner *Sportpalast*, an event broadcast to millions. Goebbels gushed in his diary the following day that Rommel was 'ideologically sound... He is a National Socialist; he is a troop leader with a gift for improvisation, personally courageous and extraordinarily inventive. These are the kinds of soldiers we need. Rommel is the coming Supreme Commander of the Army.'[27] He was also a welcome distraction from the bloody war mired on the Eastern Front – 'The deciding front'.

Back in Egypt, Monty launched Bertram, an elaborate and cunning operation to convince his foe that the bulk of the Eighth Army was positioned in the south, while concealing the scale of his preparations in the north. Imitation tanks and artillery appeared in strength while a bogus pipeline complete with pump-houses was 'laid'. Colonel Geoffrey Barkas (No. 85 Camouflage Company) observed a 'formidable total of more than 400 dummy Grant tanks, 100 dummy guns, and nearly

2,000 dummy vehicles.'[28] To the north, thousands of tons of stores were covered from view while hessian sheeting disguised some four hundred 25-pounder guns as ordinary trucks. Also lying in wait, hidden under detachable covers, were tanks secretly camouflaged as trucks.

Republican and informal envoy for President Franklin D. Roosevelt, Wendell L. Willkie accepted an invitation from Montgomery to view preparations at the front. 'It was my first lesson in the strategy and tactics of desert warfare', Willkie recorded. Without mincing his words, Monty summed up the situation:

> With the superiority in tanks and planes that I have established as a result of this battle and with Rommel's inability to get reinforcements of matériel across the eastern Mediterranean – for our air forces are destroying four out of five of his matériel transports – it is now mathematically certain that I will eventually destroy Rommel.[29]

Writing from Europe, Rommel shared the Axis dictators' grandiloquent designs with Stumme: 'first to hold the positions gained in North Africa and then, but only after thorough stockpiling, replenishment...and the provision of more forces, to go over to the attack.'[30] As the Suez docks groaned under the weight of more and more Allied matériel, the under-resourced Stumme could only advise his senior commanders that the Allies were 'by no means certain of victory'. Crippled by a dearth of supplies – with insufficient fuel for even his own supply units – he called for 'complete moral superiority over the enemy', a noble rekindling in spirit 'awakened and fostered in every soldier'.[31]

'Let no man surrender so long as he is unwounded and can fight'

Montgomery elected to open his forthcoming offensive at night. This would, Moorehead summarised,

> allow the infantry to find cover in the darkness but it would not be so dark under the moon that they lost contact with one another. For the last few hours before dawn they would

be able to pick up mines, dig into the sand and remain there under cover to repel daylight counter-attacks until the following night. Then they would advance again.[32]

The date was set for 23 October once meteorologists confirmed a waxing moon and favourable conditions. Set on 'pinning down and annihilating' the (renamed) Deutsche-Italienische Panzerarmee, Monty enjoyed a nearly 2:1 manpower advantage. His 195,000-strong multinational Allied force included: XXX Corps (Lieutenant General Oliver Leese) – 51st (Highland) Division; 9th Australian Division, 2nd New Zealand Division, 1st South African Division and 4th Indian Division; Horrocks' XIII Corps – 7th Armoured Division, 50th (Northumbrian) Division, 44th (Home Counties) Division, 1st Greek Brigade and 1st Independent Free French Brigade; and General Herbert Lumsden's X Corps – 1st Armoured Division, 10th Armoured Division, 8th Armoured Division (HQ Staff).

Approximately 152,000 Axis troops were present in Egypt – of these 48,854 German and 50,000 Italians troops fell under Panzerarmee command, a total of four German and eight Italian Divisions, the remainder being Luftwaffe and Kriegsmarine personnel. Rommel's frontline formations comprised (from the north): XXI Corps – 164th Light Africa Division, 102nd Trento, 25th Bologna Divisions plus two Ramcke parachute battalions; and X Corps – 27th Brescia, 17th Pavia, 185th Folgore (parachute) and two Ramcke battalions. The 133rd Littorio Armoured and 15th Panzer Divisions were positioned behind XXI Corps; the 21st Panzer and 132nd Ariete Divisions behind X Corps. Held in reserve along the coast near Mersa Matruh were the 90th Light Africa and 101st Trieste Divisions plus the 288th Sonderverband (special operations unit) and 580th Reconnaissance Battalion.

Montgomery enjoyed a hefty superiority in armour with 1,029 operational tanks (252 M4 Sherman, 170 M3 Grant, 216 Crusader, 194 Valentine, 119 M3 Stuart and 78 Cruiser Mk III) and 435 armoured cars against 547 Axis tanks (31 Panzer II, 173 Panzer III, 38 Panzer IV, 7 command tanks, 278 M13 Italian tanks and 20 light tanks) and 192 armoured cars. Eighth Army artillery stood at 908 guns and 1,451 anti-tank guns versus 552 artillery pieces and 496 anti-tank guns. The Western Desert Air Force would have mastery of the skies.

'This thing can't go wrong', Sergeant J.A. Brown (1/3rd Transvaal Scottish Regiment) pencilled in his diary, 'We outnumber the enemy two-to-one in tanks and five-to-one in the air.'[33]

Montgomery's offensive was organised down to the smallest detail with nothing left to chance. Operation Lightfoot – a curious play on words given the task ahead of infiltrating the extensive Axis minefields – would open with a colossal artillery bombardment. Leese's XXX Corps would attack the more heavily defended northern sector, in tandem with Horrocks' XIII Corps' diversionary assault in the south. Lumsden's armour – in a plan that sat uneasily with all three Dominion commanders (Morshead, Freyberg and General Dan H. Pienaar) – would penetrate the minefields and form a defensive belt against Axis tanks. By exploiting his numerical superior, Monty hoped to 'crumble' the enemy line. His tanks would then go on the offensive. The battle would be fought in three stages: the break-in, the 'dogfight' and the breakout. The battle, Montgomery predicted, would be over in ten days.

Exuding confidence, in private Montgomery was more circumspect. He noted in his diary of having

> an untrained army due to Auchinleck… and I had to be careful what I did with it. Commanders especially did not know how to fight a good enemy in a real dogfight; they had been used to dispersion and to battle groups and tip-and-run tactics…there had been no firm doctrine of war on which to base training. The troops must have confidence in their commanders and must have the light of battle in their eyes.[34]

On the cusp of battle, Moorehead took note of the 'momentous and awful quiet in the Army':

> In the unbearable strain of waiting it was apparent to everyone that this was to be a major battle, that many would be killed and wounded and that all the future was intensely doubtful.[35]

Tank gunner Jack Merewood (Queen's Bays, 1st Armoured Division) had recovered from his injuries in the Gazala Battle. He turned to his diary:

> Well, now dawns the great day. Troop Leader gave us all the 'dope'… After dinner got tank all fixed up for the beginning of the fight. Played cards in the afternoon. Supposed to sleep but none of us can.[36]

Hungry troops were advised not to eat. This would give them a better chance of survival in the event of a stomach wound. A rousing message from Monty was circulated in the afternoon – the Eighth Army was about to engage in 'one of the decisive battles of history... the turning point of the war... And let no man surrender so long as he is unwounded and can fight.'[37] Every man felt that he was necessary, Murray Reid recalled, and 'resolved to do his utmost to assist (using a cricketing analogy) in "Hitting the enemy for six, right out of Africa".'[38]

While British troops formed up in their assembly areas, Stumme forbade his artillery from targeting them, through the need to conserve ammunition. Richard Gorle (51st Highland Division), conversely, looked on as British gunners made their final preparations:

A drop of oil on a breech block, one or more box of ammunition opened and the shells stacked ready, a peep through the sights to confirm the crosswire was dead on the aiming lamp, and then there remained but to wait. Slowly the minutes ticked by...[39]

A wartime bulletin described the scene:

All is silent across the vast wastes of the moonlight desert. Over a front of six miles General Montgomery has ranged one 25-pounder gun every 23 yards.[40]

Reid repeatedly checked his watch. At 2135, 'I looked at it for the last time...until the guns opened fire. Bang! Bang! Bang!'[41] The combined firepower of nearly 900 guns suddenly lit up the sky. 'A great and heartening sight', de Guingand noted in awe.[42] Reporting from the front, Godfrey Talbot continues:

For a very long period there wasn't a single second when not one gun but many were blazing away – heavy stuff. We had the BBC recording truck up there with the guns; when very near, explosions from the batteries almost lifted our gear up in the air.[43]

In his forward HQ, General Freyberg turned to a staff officer: 'If there was ever justice in a cause this is it... Mind you this is going to be a stiff fight.'[44] Meanwhile, his infantry lay on the cold sand in the dark, feeling the thump of recoiling guns, the air thick with the acrid smell of burning cordite. Men on the tanks 'were muffled because of the cold; at the guns the men were stripped to the waist and perspiring from the heat.'[45]

Leutnant Ralph Ringler (104th Panzergrenadier Regiment) had celebrated his battalion commander's birthday. 'It was peaceful', when suddenly, 'the whole desert horizon seemed to burn and to shudder... No one knew what was up, we could only hope and wait in our miserable foxholes.'[46] The rolling bombardment 'was just horrible', Martin Ranft (220th Artillery Regiment, DAK) recounted. 'We thought then that the world was coming to an end.'[47] 'A mighty roar like a thunder clap tore the moonlit desert night... It was as if a giant had banged his fist down on the table', a German report chronicled.[48]

The desert sky was dramatically lit. Searchlights beamed vertically provided a point of reference for the Allied troops while friendly tracer delineated boundaries for brigades and battalions painstaking probing a path through the minefields.

'We had been in action before at Alam Halfa', Lieutenant Douglas Sladden reminisced, 'but a set-piece attack was "something else".'[49] Shadowing the creeping barrage, the first wave of infantry advanced – a scene reminiscent of the Great War, though with more deadly weaponry. From afar, Churchill was naturally pleased that the offensive had opened. 'Greedily he devoured the reports from the desert', his physician wrote. 'It appeared that everyone in the Eighth Army was cock-a-hoop when the battle began on October 23.'[50] The premier notified Roosevelt with news:

> The Battle in Egypt began tonight... The whole force of the Army will be engaged... A victory there will be most fruitful to our main enterprise. All the Shermans and one zero five [self-propelled] guns which you gave me on that dark Tobruk morning will play their part.[51]

Against the backdrop of thunderous shellfire, Stumme grew impatient. With telephone lines severed by the opening bombardment and specially equipped RAF Wellington bombers jamming radio telephony, he was blind to what was happening at the front. To assess the situation first-hand, Stumme drove to the forward positions with his chief intelligence officer, Oberst Andreas Büchting, minus the usual escort and radio vehicle that Rommel used. Ambushed in the open by British infantry and anti-tank guns, Büchting died from a head wound while Stumme is believed to have suffered a fatal heart attack.

Ritter von Thoma stepped in to fill the Panzerarmee command vacuum while Rommel, who was still not well, received word from Hitler early the next morning to return to Africa.

Captain David Smiley (Royal Armoured Car Regiment) had cleared the Axis minefields and was approaching the forward enemy positions: 'There were dead Italians everywhere', he wrote: 'I can remember seeing a man in his trench with his mess tin in front of him. He was dead. The barrage had opened so suddenly, it caught them well and truly unprepared.'[52]

Lieutenant Colonel Guy Jackson from the Warwickshire Yeomanry (9th Armoured Brigade) was leading a regiment of tanks into combat for the first time. There was some delay while the sappers cleared a gap through the minefield with six tanks damaged in the process. 'Then the fire came', Jackson later narrated, 'from the front and the flanks. Anti-tank guns spluttered evilly, the heavier 88-mm guns fired at close range, and behind the guns were enemy tanks milling about and bringing down fire… It was a terrific fight.'[53]

Sister Dulcie Thompson was working at the 2/3rd Australian Casualty Clearing Station when the first casualties were brought in:

> Arms blown off, legs blown off, lots of shocking leg wounds… stomach wounds and head wounds, every kind of casualty that you can imagine, sometimes two or three on one person. I have a very vivid picture of one Greek officer who had neither face nor hands as far as I could see'.[54]

Assaulting Miteiriya Ridge, 39-year-old British-born Sergeant William 'Bill' Kibby (Australian 2/48th Battalion) assumed control of his platoon after his commanding officer was killed. Encountering strong resistance, he dashed ahead, firing his Thompson sub-machine gun, killing three and capturing twelve others. His company continued its advance.

Elsewhere on the battle ground, as one soldier reported, there was an almighty explosion:

> Something flew past my head; it was a leg with a boot on it. A round of H.E. [high explosive] had taken Chalky

White's leg off. He was looking at me with astonishment and pointing to the raw, bleeding stump with the white bone sticking through. I went towards him with the idea of helping him, I think. Just then the machine gun opened up and poor Chalky got it full in the face.[55]

Disturbing reports reached Eighth Army HQ during the night of 24 October that the 10th Armoured Division was making little progress through the congested lanes being cleared through the minefields. Confronted with the dangerous prospect of tanks exposed or trapped at daybreak, de Guingand woke a soundly sleeping Monty for an immediate conference. Amid the strained atmosphere, and a sense that the armour should be withdrawn, Montgomery stood firm. He telephoned the divisional commander, making it clear that 'there would be no alteration to his orders. The armour could and must get through.'[56]

The 'chaotic' battlefield, Colonel Charles Richardson wrote, was 'absolutely unbelievable', with tanks jammed in a close-combat zone, having failed to make inroads through Axis positions.[57]

Monty's amphetamine tablets were not the panacea he expected. Judgement was impaired and rational decision making was diminished. Numbness and hallucinations were reported with tank crews experiencing delusions such as tanks driving sideways. With fighting efficiency compromised, one captain later stated that the drug had been 'abused by certain units with deleterious results'.[58] Nevertheless, reports of increased confidence and energy prompted Middle East Command to authorise use of up to 20 mg of amphetamine (twice the amount recommended for RAF pilots) a day for five days.[59]

The slog continued. At one point in the fighting, a voice with a German accent came over the radio in Colonel Guy Jackson's tank (9th Armoured Brigade), goading: 'It is very good to see your nice new tanks burning.' But 'I think that German (sic) lived to regret his remark more than we did', the colonel later remarked.[60]

Monty now extracted the 10th Armoured Division from the southwest and transferred it north, aiming to draw Rommel's armour into battle and then to encircle his soft-skin vehicles.

For Jack Merewood this had been 'the worst day of my life'. After his regiment retired from the fighting, he examined his battle-scared

Sherman tank. 'We had been hit in at least six places, and we were in no doubt that we were the luckiest crew on earth because one hit had taken a huge chunk out of the side, right over the petrol tank... Why the tank didn't catch fire we'd never know.' His regiment had suffered heavily. His troop leader, Lieutenant Stephen Christie-Miller, was 'cut in two' by a shell.[61] Only twelve out of twenty-nine tanks had survived the day's combat.

Australian troops assaulted 'Trig 29' (also known as Hill 28) at Miteiriya Ridge on the night of 25/26 October. Private Percival 'Percy' Gratwick's company (2/48th Battalion) was held up by intense enemy fire. With his platoon reduced to seven men, Gratwick charged a mortar post with hand grenades, killing all. Rushing a machine-gun nest with rifle and bayonet, he inflicted further casualties before being cut down by machine-gun fire. Gratwick's bravery was recognised with a posthumous VC.[62]

Rommel's return to Africa, Hans von Luck recalled, 'put fresh heart into our people.'[63] Without delay he counter-attacked. But as Schmidt describes, 'it was smashed up by our old enemies, the medium bombers and the 25-pounders... He lost Panzers he could ill afford.'[64] Not until 26 October did Panzerarmee HQ recognise that the main thrust of the British offensive actually lay in the north, where Montgomery had staged a head-on breakthrough, in place of a southerly flanking movement. Rommel was forced to transfer troops to north, to where Australian infantry had formed a salient. Montgomery, meanwhile, was preparing his second act – Operation Supercharge.

Mindful of Rommel's escalating supply crisis (via Ultra), a restless Churchill monitored British divisions being withdrawn from the front in readiness for the next attack.[65] In the meantime, Monty's bloody 'dogfight' continued. Written under the strain of sustained bombing and artillery fire, a German dispatch rider's diary read:

> In the evening we get busy digging slit trenches for ourselves. All hell broke loose during the night. One bomb attack after another; artillery fire, too. About 0400 we were hauled out of the slit trenches. Tommy has broken through on our sector. We move to the new sector and dig in again and wait for the attack. More bombing attacks. There are crashes behind us now, and the front is two

kilometres away. Nothing to eat or drink. Our tanks are drawn up ready for a counter-attack. Will we succeed in cutting off Tommy?

An hour of barrage fire on our position. Six more bombing attacks, 18 planes at a time. We bury our casualties. Shells blew them to pieces in their slit trenches. We prepare to move to a new position. It is dark. The moon is rising, and with the moon the English artillery. It starts its evensong, and we lie in our slit trenches. Flares and bombs.[66]

The desert, wrote Brigadier C.E. Lucas Phillips, was 'quivering with heat.'

Gun detachments and the platoons squatted in their pits and trenches, the sweat running in rivers down their dust-caked faces. There was a terrible stench. The flies swarmed in black clouds upon the dead bodies and excreta and tormented the wounded. The place was strewn with burning tanks and carriers, wrecked guns and vehicles, and over all drifted the smoke and the dust from bursting high explosives and from the blasts of guns.[67]

Lieutenant Colonel Victor Turner successfully directed the 2nd Battalion of the Rifle Brigade (Prince Consort's Own) across 4,000 yards of enemy territory on the night of 26 October to his objective at 'Kidney Ridge' (actually a depression), code named 'Snipe'. With forty enemy troops captured, all-round defence was organised for the anticipated response, which came in spades. Continuously attacked the following day from 0530 to 1900, Turner excelled in motivating his men, manning thirteen 6-pounder anti-tank guns against ninety enemy tanks. Isolated and unable to be replenished, Sergeant Charles Calistan (later awarded the DCM) recounted the battle:

Our colonel kept going from gun to gun. How he inspired us! When the first attack came in, the colonel was acting as loader by my gun. He got wounded in the head, a nasty one, and we wanted [to] bind it up, but he wouldn't hear of it. 'Keep firing,' that's what he went on saying.[68]

An extract from the War Diary of the 133rd Regiment, Littorio Division reads:

> The [12th] battalion attacks. In spite of the violent enemy fire and the resultant initial losses of tanks and men the battalion advances firmly but keeping a certain distance from the anti-tank guns which are extremely well dug in and camouflaged. Suddenly there is most violent fire from another 8 or 10 anti-tank guns hidden... A number of victims in the battalion, which halts too suddenly. Enemy fire becomes more and more violent.[69]

By the end of the engagement, Turner's men had knocked out 57 tanks and self-propelled guns. The Rifle Brigade had suffered 72 casualties. Rommel afterwards detailed the 'murderous fire' from the 'immensely powerful anti-tank defence' that had resisted his largest counterattack against XXX Corps.[70] Turner's leadership and gallantry was recognised with a VC.[71]

'The present battle is a life-and-death struggle'

Rommel circulated a message to his commanders on October 28: 'The present battle is a life-and-death struggle. I therefore require that...every officer and man give his utmost and thereby contribute to its success.'[72] Neither side continued the attacks during daylight hours but at 2200 hours a brigade from the Australian 9th Division attacked north towards the coastal road. Richard Weston (a veteran of the 1941 siege of Tobruk and now in the 3rd Anti-Tank Regiment) was trailing tanks and infantry:

> We were facing heavy machine gun fire with tracer bullets everywhere plus mortar fire. One of my crew got a bullet through his chest but he seemed okay and I sent him out on a tank that was herding prisoners back to our lines. Just then the prisoners decided to break loose, so the tanks mashed a couple of hundred of them with machine gun and cannon fire.[73]

Weston was subsequently wounded during a German bombardment. After waiting several hours on his back, he was taken by ambulance to an underground surgical centre.

> All the surgeons were nearly dead on their feet, blood from head to toe, but he said he would do his best. And when I came to, I was pleased to see I still had two arms, even though the left one was useless.[74]

British surgeons dealt with a large number of abdominal injuries, a consequence of the static 'slogging match'. Complex eight-hour operations were not uncommon.[75] Erik de Mauny (New Zealand Medical Corps and future BBC correspondent) observed:

> Their eyes dark with fatigue, cutting away sections of blood-soaked uniform, trimming, probing and sewing up the gaping flesh with calm and studious concentration.[76]

A young German soldier with multiple intestinal wounds was brought to a casualty clearing station.

> Yards of intestine were hauled out on a metal side tray, each perforation was neatly sutured, then the whole lot unceremoniously shoved back into the open space of the abdomen. It was like watching a seemingly impossible repair of a badly punctured bicycle tyre.[77]

Allan Prince, another volunteer AFS driver, remembered, how it was 'pretty gory, bleeding...all over the place. You did your best.'[78]

'I am fighting a terrific battle with Rommel'

Montgomery adjourned to his caravan on 30 October to finalise Supercharge: 'I always wrote such orders myself and never let the staff do it', he conceitedly wrote in his memoirs. 'This was the master plan and only the master could write it.'[79] On the eve of the operation he penned a letter to Major Tom Reynolds (headmaster of Amesbury School and unofficial guardian to his son):

> I am fighting a terrific battle with Rommel. It began on 23 October and he is resisting desperately. I hold the initiative. But it has become a real solid and bloody killing match. I do not think he can go much longer. I am dealing him a terrific blow in the very early hours of tomorrow... and it may well be that that will knock him off his perch. I hope so.[80]

Sergeant Bill Kibby's 2/48th Battalion attacked Ring Contour 25 behind enemy lines that night. His No. 17 Platoon was mown down from point blank range by 'the most withering enemy machine-gun fire'. Kibby went forward singlehandedly to silence the gun, hurling grenades at the enemy, now only yards away. Killed by a burst of machine-gun fire, Kibby's 'outstanding courage' was recognised with a posthumous VC. [81]

Rommel was now in a precarious position. Although a small amount of fuel had reached the front via Tobruk, the ammunition shortage was critical with the strictest economy enforced. His available armour had dwindled to 90 German and 140 Italian tanks. After a week of 'very, very hard fighting', he awaited the next British onslaught.[82]

Supercharge was launched at 0105 on 2 November, north of 'Kidney Ridge' and south of the 21st Panzer Division, which could no longer freely manoeuvre through lack of fuel. With a path forced open, British armour poured through the enemy line. Rommel counterattacked with some success, causing a 'severe' dent in Monty's armour. Every available German gun was brought to bear, preventing, for the moment, further British infiltration.

Rommel, however, was uninformed of what was happening, with communication lines shot up and wireless communication jammed. Despite their hopeless situation, Axis troops fought hard. The 90th Light Africa Division recorded:

> Smoke and dust covered the battlefield, and visibility became so bad that the general picture was of one immense cloud of smoke and dust. Tanks engaged in single combat; in these few hours the battle of Alamein was decided.[83]

Rommel watched the fighting from a hill: 'British tanks were shooting up one after the other of the Littorio's and Trieste's tanks.'[84] Ariete's armour was also moved north. Its destruction was a familiar story, Soldato Antonio Tomba recalled: 'Our poor M13s with their 47-mm guns could never be effective against [the British tanks] – we could only hope to hit their tracks in order to immobilise them at least; our shells just bounced off their armour.'[85]

The Panzerarmee's supply emergency worsened. Against 450 tons of ammunition fired, only 190 tons was delivered. Allied air supremacy blocked all efforts to bring stores forward. The (aforementioned) German dispatch rider despondently recorded: 'Nothing but bombing raids every day and night. Last night we had bombing attacks for ten hours on end. Big bombs fell around our position. Naturally there was no sleep.'[86]

The DAK could now field only thirty-five serviceable tanks. From this hopeless position, Rommel planned to slip away. His enemy's 'often incomprehensible caution' might save at least a portion of his infantry.[87] He signalled Hitler of impending annihilation, a portentous message duly intercepted and placed in Montgomery's hands the following morning (3 November):

> In spite of today's defensive victory, the capabilities of the army are exhausted after ten days of exceedingly severe battle against a multiple superiority of British air and ground forces. The army therefore will no longer be able to repel a renewed breakthrough attempt by strong British armoured forces during the coming night or tomorrow. Owing to the lack of adequate motor transportation, an orderly withdrawal of the six Italian and two German non-motorised divisions and brigades is impossible. Large parts of these forces will probably be captured by the fully motorised hostile forces…
> In this situation the gradual destruction of the army must be expected in spite of the heroic resistance offered and in spite of the excellent troop morale.[88]

Hitler's HQ received a teletype message from Rome at around 0300 hours regarding the pitiful state of the Deutsche-Italienische Panzerarmee. The duty officer overlooked a crucial cipher outlining Rommel's intention to 'break off the battle because the situation was gradually becoming untenable, to give up the El Alamein position and begin withdrawal.' The Führer, Oberstleutnant Eckhard Christian witnessed, was furious at the 'careless handling of the vital message…[with] an immediate court-martial'. An order of the day was promptly radioed to Rommel, ordering him to hold his old position 'to the last man'. [89]

Caught in a tactical cul-de-sac, weeks later Rommel related his hopeless position to Hans von Luck:

> [He] wavered between doing his duty of absolute obedience to the oath he had taken, and the reality at the front, with the threatening destruction that implied of the whole Africa Army.[90]

Hitler's order to hold fast – 'You can show your troops no other road but that to victory or death' – was conveyed to his commanders; his men were not to know. Rommel was profoundly frustrated, but for the present he obeyed the Führer.'[91]

A letter to 'Dearest Lu' depicted a battle raging with 'unspent fury' and little chance of success.[92]

Ensnared in the hopeless maelstrom, Leutnant Ralph Ringer (104th Panzer Grenadier Regiment) contemplated his future:

> It is morning again. I'm hungry and cold. Corporal Franken was blown to bits... The cold has passed but hunger remains. And now in addition comes thirst. We are here, a few grenadiers in our foxholes. Every 20 yards and in places at about 50 lie a few men. Two anti-tank guns, that is all. No. 9 Company must be somewhere to the left. Eight miles away is the sea, and behind us, nothing! And to the south, nothing! And facing us an armada of tanks. Will it be the end for me today too?[93]

4 November. Another hour-long bombardment preceded a morning attack that the DAK and the 90th Light Afrika Division managed to fend off, though the twenty remaining Panzers still faced nearly 600 Eighth Army tanks. Generalfeldmarschall Albert Kesselring flew to Rommel's HQ, where 'angry words passed' and the possibility of skirting the

Führer's 'Victory or Death' order was broached.[94] The afternoon saw British tanks swing through the open right flank. Carnage ensued. Dr Alfons Selmay watched the valiant demise of Ariete's assault guns: 'Despite their poor armour, they advanced boldly. Of course, they were blown to bits in a miserable fashion.'[95] By the evening the 'gallant' Italian XX Corps ceased to exist. News was later received via a British radio broadcast that General der Panzertruppe Wilhelm Ritter von Thoma had been taken prisoner.[96]

Challenged by enemy forces moving west, with no reserves, and encirclement threatening, Rommel finally issued orders at 1530 hours for a general retreat. His forces were in full flight by the time formal permission to withdraw was received.

A new crisis for the Axis erupted on 8 November when 80,000 US and 25,000 British troops in two armoured and five infantry divisions landed in Morocco and Algeria. The substantive Anglo-American invasion – Operation Torch – would facilitate a pincer movement from the west against the retreating Axis forces.

'This is a complete and absolute victory'

The silence that had fallen upon the battlefield, the first 'sweet silence' since 23 October, struck Springbok soldier James Ambrose Brown. To 'satisfy a morbid curiosity' he walked across the ground so stubbornly contested.

> I was sated and disgusted, and not a little saddened. All those men and all those fine machines utterly destroyed. More than a score of heavy tanks stood dotted over the plain. Most of them had been rendered helpless, losing their tracks in the minefields and then being pitilessly pounded by anti-tank shells... The interiors of the tanks were for the most part masses of twisted steel, shattered and blackened by fire. But others, unburned, were filled with flies, scraps of bloody clothing, spilled oil and pieces of flesh.[97]

5 November. Montgomery assembled Middle East war correspondents for a briefing on the outcome of the offensive. He 'toyed with his cap.

He exchanged light-heartedly a few banalities and suddenly he said, "Gentlemen. This is a complete and absolute victory." His audience stared at him incredulously.' Prepared to hear of difficulties, perhaps even an admission of defeat given the nature of the fighting, his 'flat and arrogant assertion' of success came as a bombshell.[98]

Both sides had suffered heavily. The Eighth Army's casualties were 2,350 men killed, 8,950 wounded and 2,260 reported missing. The Panzerarmee's losses, based on Ultra intercepts, were 1,149 Germans killed, 3,886 wounded and 8,050 men captured; Italian casualties were 971 men killed, 933 wounded and 15,552 men captured.

*****

Hitler's War in Africa entered a new phase. As General Alexander wrote in his memoirs, the British 1st, 7th and 10th Armoured Divisions were now 'freely operating in the open desert, some miles beyond the original minefield area; the Afrikakorps itself was in full retreat… the long attrition of Alamein suddenly ceased to be a battle; the problem was now one of pursuit.'[99]

Bibliography

A. Unpublished Sources

Archives
Australia – The National Archives

AWM 54 423/5/69 [Intelligence - Captured Documents and Translations:] Translations of extracts from German Diary captured near Tobruk - Diary of Lieutenant Schorm, 5 Tank Regiment, April 1941.

AWM 54 523/7/19. A brief history of Tobruk: March–August 1941.

AWM, 3DRL2632/72 Morshead Papers 1940 to 1944, Lecture on Tobruch part 2.

AWM 54 523/7/36. [The Siege of Tobruk - Reports:] Patrol Reports - Tobruk, June-July 1941.

AWM 523/7/11 9th Australian Division, Special Information Summary No 1 - Information from March 1941-August 1941, Part 1: Brief History of Tobruk.

AWM 54 523/7/28 Brief History of the 9th Division (Aust) in the Middle East 1941-1942.

AWM 54, 523/7/43 Narrative of operations in Cyrenaica during the period April 7-14 by Lt-Gen Sir John Lavarack.

AWM 54 522/7/8 Main movements ordered and made Western Desert and Tobruk with chronology of AIF Units involved in operations- Libya and Tobruk (April-May 1941).

AWM 523/7/9 24th Aust. Inf. Bde. History of activities at Tobruk, 1 Feb. to 25 Sep. 1941.

AWM 54 523/7/29 Reports on 9th Division Operations in Cyrenaica by Lieutenant-Gen. Sir L.J. Morshead, March to October 1941, Part 1.

AWM 54 492/4/77 Stumme to Lower Formations, 20 October 1942, Translation of Appendices to Panzerarmee Afrika War Diary.

AWM B5505 Army Training Memorandum (War) (Australia) No. 28.

NAA: A2684, 556 Relief of 9th Division at Tobruk (1941) also publication of despatch of General Sir Claude Auchinleck (1945-46).

NAA A5954 528/6 Australian Forces - communiques of military operations in North Africa, Greece, Crete.

NAA: A5954, 2400/3 Press Release: Despatch of General Sir Claude Auchinleck on Operations in the Middle East (Tobruk) during Period Aug-Oct 1941 - published in *London Gazette* - with observations of Commonwealth Government requested to be published in full.

Britain - The National Archives

CAB 106/718 Western Desert: Studies on the Decision to Hold Tobruk and the Fall of El Adem 1942

CAB 106/834 Western Desert: summary of the battle of Tobruk 1941 Jan.

WO 201/345 Capture of Tobruk: Report by 13th Corps Commander.

WO 106/2238 A Fall of Tobruk; Court of Enquiry, Vol. I, Part III.

WO 169/1173 7th Armoured Division General Intelligence Summary No. 2

WO 204/7977 Notes on deception practised by 8 Army prior to the offensive of October 1942 at El Alamein (Plan Bertram)

CAB 65/30/22 1. Military Situation - Middle East

CAB 44/421 Fall of Tobruk, June 1942

CAB 79/86/2 Despatch of Cruiser Tanks to the Middle East

CAB 65/18/77 1. Overload Security - Censorship of Diplomatic of Communications from this Country.

FO 954/15A/171 Middle East: High Commissioner, South Africa telegram to Dominions Office No 1170. General Smuts to Prime Minister Proposes RAF should switch bombing activities from Germany to Rommel.

FO 954/15A/212 Middle East: Prime Minister to President, No 146. Arrival of tanks for Egypt.

FO 954/16A /Private Office Papers of Sir Anthony Eden, Earl of Avon, Secretary of State for Foreign Affairs.

FO 954/31B/300 War (General): General Auchinleck to the Prime Minister Review of military situation.

IWM AL 1517 Extracts from German diaries and reports, North Africa, 1941.

BIBLIOGRAPHY

IWM 87/12/1 J.H. Witte, 'The One that Didn't Get Away'.

Tobruk Court of Enquiry, "Operations in the Western Desert 27 May-2 July". Court of Enquiry, 1942.

King's College London. O'CONNOR 4/3/18 Copies of comments by Brig. J.F.B. Combe on the account of operations in Cyrenaica by Neame, and on various letters of Neame and O'Connor.

British Information Services, African Victory with the British Forces From El Alamein to Cape Bon. New York 1943.

Ministry of Information, Destruction of an Army, The First Campaign in Libya: Sept. 1940-Feb. 1941, HMSO, London 1941.

____ The Eighth Army: September 1941 to January 1943, London 1944.

____ RAF Middle East, HMSO, London 1945.

United States

Collection FDR-FDRMRP:

Map Room Papers (Roosevelt Administration), 1942-1945 Series:

Message Files, 1942 - 1945 File Unit:

Churchill to FDR - August-October 1942

Memo, Halifax [Earl, Ambassador the United States] to Franklin D. Roosevelt, April 17, 1941, Box 35, President's Secretary's File (PSF) Safe Files: State Dept., 1941, Franklin D. Roosevelt Library Digital Archives.

Records of the Central Intelligence Agency, File Unit: Fall 1959: 1-9-1: The Lost Keys to El Alamein: A German Cryptanalysis Presents His Own Version of the Reason Rommel was Beaten at the Gates of Egypt, by Wilhelm F. Flicke.

US Army Foreign Military Studies

Detwiler, D.S. ed. *World War II German Military Studies*, Vol. 14, Part VI, *The Mediterranean Theatre*, MS#B-495.

D-072. 'Report on My Activities as Commander of Rear Area of Army of North Africa' by Generalmajor Ernst Schnarrenberger; 15 pp; 1947. Part II, Nov. 1942-Apr. 1943.

D-084, Supplement to 'Reasons for Rommel's Success in Africa, 1941-42'.

D-172, 'El Alamein Crisis and Its After-Effects in the OKW' (23 Oct.-4 Nov. 1942) by Generalmajor Eckhard Christian.

D-216, 'The Operations under the Command of Marshal Graziani prior to the Arrival of the German Troops' (Aug.-Sep. 1940).

D-217, 'Italo-German Cooperation in Italian North Africa'.

D-400, 'Desert Warfare: A Comparison of the North African Desert Warfare with those of the South Russian Steppe'.

D-424, 'Command Techniques Employed by Feldmarschall Rommel in Africa'.

P-038 'German Radio Intelligence' by General der Nachrichtentruppe Albert Praun.

P-129 'Desert Warfare: German Experiences in World War II', by Generalmajor Alfred Toppe.

P-207 'German Exploitation of Arab Nationalist Movements in World War II.'

B. Published sources

Aandahl, F. et al. *Foreign Relations of the United States, The Conferences at Washington, 1941–1942, and Casablanca, 1943*. Washington 1958.

Agar-Hamilton, J.A.I. & L.C.F. Turner. *Crisis in The Desert*. Cape Town 1952.

_____ *The Sidi Rezegh Battles*, 1941. Cape Town 1957.

Alanbrooke, Lord. *War Diaries 1939-1945*. Berkeley 2003.

Aldrich, R.J. *Witness to War: Diaries of the Second World War in Europe and the Middle East*. London 2004.

Alexander, K. *Clive Caldwell, Air Ace*. Sydney 2006.

Allport, A. *Browned Off and Bloody-minded: The British Soldier Goes to War, 1939-1945*. New Haven 2015.

Andreas, P. *Killer High: A History of War in Six Drugs*. Oxford 2020.

Argent, J.N.L. *Target Tank: The History 2/3rd Australian Anti-Tank Regiment*. Parramatta [Sydney] 1957.

Arthur, M. *Forgotten Voices of The Second World War: A New History of the Second World War in the Words of the Men and Women Who Were There*. London 2005.

Asher, M. *Get Rommel: The Secret British Mission to Kill Hitler's Greatest general*. London, 2004.

Aylett, S. *Surgeon at War, 1939-1945*. London 2015.

Barber, J. *The War, the Whores and the Afrika Korps*. Sydney 1997.

Barclay, C.N. *Against Great Odds*. London 1955.

BIBLIOGRAPHY

Barkas, G. *The Camouflage Story: From Aintree to Alamein*. London 1952.

Barker, A.J. *Afrika Korps*, Lincoln 1978.

Barnett, C., *The Desert Generals*. New York 1961.

Barr, N. *Pendulum of War: Three Battles at El Alamein*. New York 2010

Barrett, J. *We Were There: Australian Soldiers of World War Two*. Melbourne 1987

Barter, M., *Far Above Battle: The Experience and Memory of Australian Soldiers in War 1939-1945*. Sydney 1994.

Bassett, J. *Guns and Brooches: Australian Army Nursing from the Boer War to the Gulf War*. Oxford 1992.

Bates, P. *Dance of War: The Story of the Battle of Egypt*. Barnsley 1992.

Beckett, I.F.W. *Rommel: A Reappraisal*. Barnsley 2013.

Behrendt, H-O., *Rommel's Intelligence in the Desert Campaign 1941-1943*. London 1985.

Belchem, D. *All in the Day's March*. London 1978.

Bennett, R. *Ultra and Mediterranean Strategy 1941-1945*. London 1989.

Best, B. *The Desert VCs: Extraordinary Valour in the North African Campaign in WWII*. Barnsley 2018.

Bharucha, P.C. *The North African campaign, 1940-43*. Calcutta 1956.

Bidwell, S. *Gunners at War: A Tactical Study of the Royal Artillery in the Twentieth Century*. London 1970.

Bierman, J. & C. Smith. *The Battle of Alamein: Turning Point of World War II*. London 2002.

Blum, G.P. *The Rise of Fascism in Europe*. Santa Barbara 1998.

Boog H. et al. ed. *Germany and the Second World War*, Vol. 6: *The Global War*. Oxford 2001.

Bowen, C. *Back from Tobruk*. Dulles [Virginia] 2013.

Bradford, G. *Rommel's Afrika Korps: El Agheila to El Alamein*. Mechanicsburg [Pennsylvania] 2009.

Bright, J. *The Ninth Queen's Royal Lancers, 1936-1945: The Story of an Armoured Regiment in Battle*. Aldershot 1951.

Brooks, S. ed. *Montgomery and the Eighth Army*. London 1991.

Brown, J.A. *One Man's War: A Soldier's War*. Aylesbury 1980.

Bryant, A. *The Turn of The Tide: A History of the War Years Based on the Diaries of Field Marshal Viscount Alanbrooke*. London 1957.

Bungay, S. *Alamein*. London 2002.

Burdick C. & H.A Jacobson, ed. *The Halder War Diary, 1939-1942*. Novato [Ca] 1988.

Burgwyn, J. *Mussolini Warlord: Failed Dreams of Empire, 1940-1943*. New York 2012.

Burn, L. *Down Ramps: Saga of the Eighth Armada*. London 1947.

Caccia-Dominioni, P. *Alamein 1933-1962*. London 1966.

Cadogan, A. *The Diaries of Sir Alexander Cadogan, O.M., 1938-1945*. New York 1972.

Cameron, C. *Breakout: Minqar Qaim, North Africa, 1942*. Christchurch 2006.

Carell, P. *Foxes of the Desert*. New York 1960.

Carter, M. *Anti-Tank: The Story of a Desert Gunner in the Second World War*. Barnsley 2012.

Carver, M. *El Alamein*. Hertfordshire 2000.

Casey, Lord. *Personal Experience 1939-1946*. New York 1962.

Christopherson, S. *An Englishman at War: The Wartime Diaries of Stanley Christopherson DSO MC TD 1939-1945*. London 2014.

Churchill, W., *The Second World War*, Vol. 2, *Their Finest Hour*. Boston 1949.

____ *The Second World War*, Vol. 3, *The Grand Alliance*. New York 1962.

____ *The Second World War*, Vol.4, *The Hinge of Fate*. Boston 1950.

____ *War Speeches*, London 1951.

____ *The Churchill War Papers: The Ever-Widening War 1941*. Vol. III. New York 1993.

Chutter, J.B., *Captivity Captive*. London 1954.

Clayton, T. & Craig, P., *The End of the Beginning*. London 2002.

Clifford, A.G. *Crusader: The Story of the Eighth Army's Offensive, Libya, 1941*. London 1942.

____ *The Conquest of North Africa 1940-1943*. Boston 1943.

____ *Three against Rommel*. London 1943.

Cody, J.F. *28 (Maori) Battalion*. Wellington 1956.

Coombes, D. *Morshead: Hero of Tobruk and El Alamein*. South Melbourne, 2001.

Connell, J. *Auchinleck: A Critical Biography*. London 1959.

____ *Wavell, Scholar and Soldier*. London 1964.

Converse, A. *Armies of Empire: The 9th Australian and 50th British Divisions in Battle 1939–1945*. Cambridge 2011.

Coox, A.D. & L. Van Loan Naisawald, *Survey of Allied Tank Casualties in World War II*. Baltimore, 1951.

Corvaja, S. *Hitler & Mussolini: The Secret Meetings*. New York 2008.

BIBLIOGRAPHY

Cox, G., *A Tale of Two Battles*. London 1987.

Crawford, R.J. *I was an Eighth Army Soldier*. London 1944.

Crisp, R., *Brazen Chariots: An Account of Tank Warfare in the Western Desert November-December 1941*. New York 1959.

Cull, B. *Hurricanes over Tobruk: The Pivotal Role of the Hurricane in the Defence of Tobruk, January-June 1941*. London 1999.

de Guingand, F. *Operation Victory*. London 1960.

_____ *Generals at War*. London 1964.

Delaforce, P. *Monty s Marauders: The 4th and 8th Armoured Brigades in the Second World War*. Barnsley 2008.

Delaney, J. *Fighting the Desert Fox*. London 1998.

Dimbleby, R. *The Frontiers Are Green*. London 1943.

Denniston, R. *Churchill's Secret War: Diplomatic Decrypts, The Foreign Office and Turkey 1942-1944*. Gloucestershire 1999.

Devine, J. *The Rats of Tobruk*. Sydney 1943.

Dimbleby, J. *Destiny in the Desert: The road to El Alamein - the Battle that Turned the Tide*. London 2012

Doherty, R. *British Armoured Divisions and their Commanders, 1939-1945*. Barnsley 2013.

Douglas, K.C. *Alamein to Zem Zem*. London 1966.

Douglas-Home, C. *Rommel*. London 1973.

Eden, A. *The Reckoning: The Memoirs of Anthony Eden*. Boston 1965.

Fearnside, G.H., ed., *Bayonets Abroad: A History of the 2/13th Battalion A.I.F. in the Second World War*. Perth 1993.

Fennell, J. *Combat and Morale in the North African Campaign: The Eighth Army and the Path to El Alamein*. Cambridge 2011.

Fielding, S. *They sought out Rommel: A Diary of the Libyan campaign, from November 16th to December 31st, 1941*. London 1942.

Forty, G. *Desert Rats at War: North Africa. Italy. Northwest Europe*. London 1975.

_____ *Afrika Korps at War*: Vol. 1. *The Road to Alexandria*. New York, 1978.

_____ *Afrika Korps at War*: Vol. 2. *The Long Road Back*. New York 1978.

_____ *Tank Warfare in World War II*. London 1998.

Foster, R.C.G. *History of the Queen's Royal Regiment*, Vol. 8. 1924-1948. Aldershot 1953.

Freudenberg, G. *Churchill and Australia*. Sydney 2008.

183

Fuller, J.F.C. *The Decisive Battles of the Western World, and Their Influence Upon History*. London 1954.

Fergusson, B. *The Trumpet in the Hall*. London 1971.

Fischer, B.J. *Albania at War, 1939-1945*. West Lafayette [Indiana] 1999.

Fischer, K.P. *Hitler and America*. Philadelphia 2011.

Fredborg, A. *Behind the Steel Wall*. Sydney 1944.

Gardiner, N. *Freyberg's Circus*. Auckland 1981.

Gallup, G. *The Gallup Poll: Public Opinion 1935-1948*, Vol. 1 *The Gallup Poll: Public Opinion 1935- 1971*. New York 1972.

Geer, A. *Mercy in Hell*. New York 1943.

Gibson, H., ed. *The Ciano Diaries 1939-1943*. New York 1946.

Gilbert, M., *Winston S. Churchill*, Vol. V, *1939-1941*, London 1983.

_____ *Winston S. Churchill*, Vol. VII, *1941-1945*, London 1986.

Glenn, J.G. *Tobruk to Tarakan: The Story of a Fighting Unit*. Adelaide 1960.

Goodhart, D. *The History of the 2/7th Australian Field Regiment*, Vol 2. Adelaide 1952.

Gordon, J. ed. *A Job to Do: New Zealand Soldiers of 'The Div' Write About Their World War Two*. Auckland 2014.

Gorrell, H.T. *Soldier of the Press: Covering the Front in Europe and North Africa, 1936-1943*, Vol. 1. Columbia [Missouri] 2009.

Gorle, R. *The Quiet Gunner at War: El Alamein to the Rhine with the Scottish Divisions*. Barnsley 2011.

Graham, A. *Sharpshooters at War: The 3rd, the 4th and the 3rd/4th County of London Yeomanry, 1939 to 1945*. London 1964.

Graham, J. & M. Mace. *Operations in North Africa and the Middle East 1939-1942: Tobruk, Crete, Syria and East Africa*. Barnsley 2015.

Greacen, Lavinia, *Chink: A Biography*. London 1989.

Gregory-Smith, F. *Red Tobruk: Memoirs of a World War II Destroyer Commander*. Barnsley 2008.

Greene, J. & A. Massignani. *Rommel's North African Campaign, September 1940-November 1942*. Pennsylvania 1994.

Gregory, D.A & W.R. Gehlen. *Two Soldiers, Two Lost Fronts: German War Diaries of the Stalingrad and North Africa Campaigns*. Drexel Hill [Philadelphia], 2009.

Hammond, B. *El Alamein: The Battle that Turned the Tide of the Second World War*. Oxford 2012.

Hancock, W.K. *Smuts: The Fields of Force 1919-1950*. London 1968.

Harper, G. *The Battle for North Africa: El Alamein and the Turning Point for World War II*. Bloomington [Indiana] 2017.

Hall, T. *Tobruk 1941*. Sydney 1984.

Halton, M., *Ten Years to Alamein*. Toronto 1944.

Hamilton, N. *Master of the battlefield: Monty's war years, 1942-1944*. London 1983.

_____ *Monty: the battles of Field Marshall Bernard Montgomery*. New York 1994.

_____ *The Mantle of Command: FDR at War, 1941–1942*. Boston 2014.

Handel, M.I. ed. *Strategic and Operational Deception in the Second World War*. Abingdon 2012

Harrison, M. *Medicine and Victory: British Military Medicine in the Second World War*. Oxford 2004.

Hart, P. *The South Notts Hussars The Western Desert, 1940-1942*. Barnsley 2010.

Hartmann, B. *Panzers in the Sand: The History of Panzer-Regiment 5*, Vol. 1 1935-1941. Barnsley 2010.

_____ *Panzers in the Sand: The History of Panzer-Regiment 5*, Vol. 2 1942-1945. Barnsley 2011.

Hartshorn, E.P. *Avenge Tobruk*. Cape Town 1960.

Heaton, C.D & A.M. Lewis. *The Star of Africa: The Story of Hans Marseille, the Rogue Luftwaffe Ace Who Dominated the WWII Skies*. London, 2012

Hinsley, H. *British Intelligence in the Second World War*: Vol. I, *Its influence on Strategy and Operations*. London 1979.

_____ et al. *British Intelligence in the Second World War*: Vol. II, *Its influence on Strategy and Operations*. Cambridge 1981.

Hinsley, H. & M.E. Howard. *British Intelligence in the Second World War*: Vol. 5, *Strategic Deception*. Cambridge 1990.

Hirszowicz, L. *The Third Reich and the Arab East*. Toronto 1966.

Hodson, J.L. *War in The Sun*. London 1942.

Holmes, R. *The World at War: The Landmark Oral History from the Classic TV Series*. London 2012.

Horrocks, B. *A Full life*. Madison [Wisconsin] 1974.

Hurley, F. *The Diaries of Frank Hurley*. New York 2011.

Irving, D. *The Trail of the Fox: The Life of Field-Marshal Erwin Rommel*. Hertfordshire 1977.

Jacobsen H.A. & J. Rohwer, ed. *Decisive Battles of World War II: The German View*. London 1965.

Jackson, W.G.F. *The Battle for North Africa 1940-1943*. New York 1975.

Jentz, T. *Panzer Truppen: The Complete Guide to the Creation & Combat of Germany's Tank Force, 1933-1942*. Atglen [PA] 1996.

____ *Tank Combat in North Africa: The Opening Rounds, Operations Sonnenblume, Brevity, Skorpion and Battleaxe February 1941- June 1941*. Atglen [PA] 1998.

Johnston, M. *At the Frontline: Experiences of Australian Soldiers in World War II*. Cambridge 1996.

____ *Anzacs in the Middle East: Australian Soldiers, Their Allies and the Local People in World War II*. Melbourne 2013.

____ *That Magnificent 9th: An illustrated history of the 9th Australian Division 1940-46*. Sydney 2005.

Johnston, M. & P. Stanley. *Alamein*. Melbourne 2002.

Joly, C. *Take These Men: Tank Warfare with the Desert Rats*. Barnsley 2019.

Jones, P.J. *Burning Tanks and an Empty Desert*. Bloomington 2015.

Jones, E. & S. Wessely. *Shell Shock to PTSD: Military Psychiatry from 1900 to the Gulf War*. London 2006.

Katz, D.B. *South Africans versus Rommel: The Untold Story of the Desert War in World War II*. Guilford [Connecticut] 2018.

Kaplan, P. *Fighter Aces of the Luftwaffe in World War II*. Barnsley 2007.

Kamieński, L. *Shooting Up: A Short History of Drugs and War*. Oxford 2016.

Kershaw, R. *Tank Men: The Human Side of Tanks at War*. London 2009.

Kesselring, A. *The Memoirs of Field-Marshal Kesselring*. London 1974.

Kippenberger, H. *Infantry Brigadier*. London 1949.

Knox, M. *Mussolini Unleashed: 1939-1941: Politics and Strategy in Fascist Italy's Last War*. New York 1982.

Korson, G. *At His Side: The Story of the American Red Cross Overseas in World War II*. New York 1945.

Latimer, J. *Alamein*. Cambridge 2002.

Lawrence, R.D. *The Green Trees Beyond*. New York, 1994.

Lee, D. *Up Close and Personal: The Reality of Close Quarter Fighting in World War II*. London 2006.

Lewin, R. *Rommel as Military Commander*. New York 1968.

____ *The war on land: the British Army in World War II: An Anthology of Personal Experience*. New York 1970.

____ *The Life and Death of the Afrika Korps*. London 1977.

____ *The Chief*. London 1980.

Liddell Hart, B.H. *History of the Second World War*. New York 1971.

____ *The German Generals Talk*. New York 1979.

____ *The Other Side of the Hill*. London 1983

____ ed. *The Rommel Papers*. London 1953.

____ et al. *A Battle Report: Alam Halfa*. Washington D.C. 1956.

Long, G. *To Benghazi*. Canberra 1986.

Lucas Phillips, C.E. *Alamein*. London 1962.

Lyman, R. *The Longest Siege: Tobruk, The Battle That Saved North Africa*. London 2009.

McLeave, H. *A Time to Heal: The life of Ian Aird, the Surgeon*. London 1964.

McLeod, J. *Myth & Reality: The New Zealand Soldier in World War II*. Auckland 1986.

McKenzie, C.G. *Gimme the Guns!: Recollections of El Alamein*. Ravenswood [Tasmania] 2003.

Mackenzie, C. *Eastern Epic*. London 1951.

Mackenzie-Smith, J.H.G. *Tobruk's Easter Battle 1941: The Forgotten Fifteenth's Date with Rommel's Champion*. Moorooka [QLD], 2011.

Mahlke, H. *Memoirs of a Stuka Pilot*. London 2013.

Maĭskiĭ, I.M. *The Complete Maisky Diaries*, Vol. 3. New Haven 2017.

Mallman, K-M.& M. Cüppers. *Nazi Palestine: The Plans for the Extermination of the Jews in Palestine*. New York 2010.

Marshal C.F. *Discovering the Rommel Murder: The Life and Death of the Desert Fox*. Mechanicsburg [Pennsylvania] 2002.

Martin, A.C. *The Durban Light Infantry*, Vol. II, *1935 to 1960*. Durban 1969.

Menzies, R. *Dark and Hurrying Days: Menzies' 1941 Diary*. Canberra 1993.

Merewood, J. *To War with The Bays: A Tank Gunner Remembers, 1939-1945*. Cardiff 1996.

Mitcham, S.W. Jr. *Hitler's Legions: The German Army Order of Battle, World War II*. Dorset 1985.

____ *Rommel's Greatest Victory: The Desert Fox and the Fall of Tobruk. Spring 1942*. Novato [California] 1998.

____ *Triumphant Fox: Erwin Rommel and the Rise of the Afrika Korps*. New York 1990.

Mitchelhill-Green, D. *Tobruk 1942*. Stroud [Gloucestershire], 2016.

____ *With Rommel in the Desert: Tripoli to El Alamein*. Barnsley 2017.

Montgomery, B.L. *The Memoirs of Field Marshal the Viscount Montgomery of Alamein, K.G.*, London 1958.

Moorehead, A. *Don't Blame the Generals*. New York 1943.

____ *Montgomery: A Biography*. London 1947.

____ *African Trilogy: The North African Campaign 1940-43*. London 1965.

Moran, Lord. *Winston Churchill: The Struggle for Survival 1940-1965*. London 1968.

Moseley, R. *Reporting War: How Foreign Correspondents Risked Capture, Torture and Death to Cover World War II*. New Haven, 2017.

Murphy, W.E. *The Relief of Tobruk, Official History of New Zealand in the Second World War 1939-45*. Wellington 1961.

Murray Reid, H. *The Turning Point: With the N.Z. Engineers at El Alamein*. Auckland 1944.

Naravane, A.S. *A Soldier's Life in War and Peace*. New Delhi 2004.

Nash, N.S. *Strafer Desert General: The Life and Killing of Lieutenant General W.H.E Gott*. Barnsley 2013.

Neame, P. *Playing with Strife*. London 1947.

North, J., ed. *The Memoirs of Field Marshal Earl Alexander of Tunis 1940-1945*. London 1962.

Orpen, N. *War in the Desert, South African Forces World War II*, Vol. III. Cape Town 1971.

Orpen, N. & H. J. Martin. *Salute the Sappers, South African Forces World War II*, Vol. VIII, Part 1. Johannesburg 1981.

Owen, D.L. *The Desert My Dwelling Place*. London 1957.

Peniakoff, P. *Private Army*. Oxford 1950.

Perversi, F.G. *From Tobruk to Borneo*. Kenthurst [NSW] 2002.

Pimlott, J., ed. *Rommel in His Own Words*. London 1994.

Pitt, B. *The Crucible of War: Western Desert 1941*. London 1980.

____ *The Crucible of War: Auchinleck's War*. London 2001.

Playfair, I.S.O. *The Mediterranean and Middle East: The Early Successes Against Italy (to May 1941)*. London 1954.

____ et al., *History of the Second World War: The Mediterranean and Middle East*, Vol. II: *The Germans Come to the Help of their Ally*. London 1956.

BIBLIOGRAPHY

_____ *History of the Second World War: The Mediterranean and Middle East*, Vol. III: *British Fortunes Reach Their Lowest Ebb*. London 1960.

_____ et al. *History of the Second World War: The Mediterranean and Middle East*, Vol. IV: *The Destruction of the Axis forces in Africa*. London 1960.

Rankin, N. *Churchill's Wizards: The British Genius for Deception 1914-1945*. London 2008.

Rasmussen, N. *On Speed: From Benzedrine to Adderall*. New York 2009.

Raugh, H.E. *Wavell in the Middle East: A Study in Generalship*. London 1993.

Rees, P. *Desert Boys*. Sydney 2011.

Reisch, M. *Out of the Rat Trap: Desert Adventures with Rommel*. Stroud [Gloucestershire], 2013.

Reuth, R.G. *Rommel: The End of a Legend*. London 2005.

Reynolds, Q. *Only the Stars Are Neutral*. New York 1942.

Richardson, C. *From Churchill's Secret Circle to the BBC: The Biography of Lieutenant General Sir Ian Jacob, GBE CB DL*, Lincoln 1991.

Roach, P. *The 8.15 to War: Memoirs of a Desert Rat*. London 1982.

Roberts, A. *The Storm of War: A New History of the Second World War*, London 2009.

Roberts, G. *From the Desert to the Baltic*. London, 1987.

Rock, G. *The History of the American Field Service, 1920-1955*. New York 1956.

Rodger, G., *Desert Journey*. London 1944.

Rosenthal, E. *Fortress on Sand*. London 1942.

Ross, A. *23 Battalion*. Wellington 1959.

Rota, J.L. *Luftwaffe in Africa, 1941-1943*. Philadelphia 2019.

Roy, K, ed. *The Indian Army in the Two World Wars*. Leiden, 2012.

Royle, T. *Montgomery: Lessons in Leadership from the Soldier's General*. New York 2010.

Sadat, A. *Revolt on the Nile*. New York 1957.

Sadler, J. *El Alamein: The Story of the Battle in the Words of the Soldiers*. Stroud [Gloucestershire] 2010.

Salter, J.C., *A Padre with the Rats of Tobruk*. Hobart, 1946

Schreiber G. et al. *Germany and the Second World War,* Vol. III, *The Mediterranean, South-East Europe, and North Africa 1939-1941*. Oxford 1995.

Scoullar, J.L. *Battle for Egypt: The Summer of 1942*. Wellington 1955.

Sears, S.W. *World War II: Desert War*. New York 1967.

Serle, R.P. ed. *The Second Twenty-Fourth Australian Infantry Battalion of the 9th Australian Division*. Brisbane 1963.

Seton-Watson, C. *Dunkirk, Alamein, Bologna: Letters and Diaries of an Artilleryman, 1939-1945*. London 1993.

Stevens, G.R. & W.G. Hingston. *The Tiger Kills: The Story of British and Indian Troops with the 8th Army in North Africa*. Bombay 1944.

Stevenson, W. *A Man Called Intrepid: The Secret War 1939-1945*. London 1984.

Stockings, C. *Bardia: Myth, Reality and the Heirs of Anzac*. Sydney 2009.

Strawson, J. *The Battle for North Africa*. New York 1969.

Stroud, R. *The Phantom Army of Alamein: The Men Who Hoodwinked Rommel*. London 2012.

Talbot, G. *Speaking from the Desert: A Record of the Eighth Army in Africa*. London 1944.

Taylor, F. ed. *The Goebbels Diaries 1939-1941*. London 1982.

Thompson, J. *Forgotten Voices: Desert Victory*. London 2012.

Thompson, R.W. *The Montgomery Legend*, Vol. 1. Sydney 1967.

Travers, Susan, *Tomorrow to be Brave*. London 2000.

Trevor-Roper, H.R. ed. *Hitler's War Directives 1939-1945*. London 1964.

Trye, R. *Mussolini's Afrika Korps: The Italian Army in North Africa 1940-1943*. New York 1999.

Tuker, F. *Approach to Battle*. London 1963.

Various. *Poems from the Desert: Verses by Members of the Eighth Army*. Sydney 1944.

Verney, G.L. *The Desert Rats*. London 1954.

von Luck, H. *Panzer Commander*. New York 1989.

von Mellenthin, F.W. *Panzer Battles*. New York 1956.

Wade, F.A. *A Midshipman's War: A Young Man in the Mediterranean Naval War 1941-1943*. Vancouver 1994.

Walker, A.S. *Middle East and Far East, Australia in the War of 1939-1945*, Series 5, Medical Vol. II, Middle East and Far East. Canberra 1953.

Warlimont, W. *Inside Hitler's Headquarters 1939-1945*. London 1964.

Warner, G. *Iraq and Syria 1941*. New Jersey 1979.

Warner, P. *Auchinleck: The Lonely Soldier*. London 1981.

Westphal, S. *The German Army in the West*. London 1951.

Whaley, B. *Practise to Deceive: Learning Curves of Military Deception Planners*. Annapolis 2015

Whitworth, A. *VCs of the North: Cumbria, Durham & Northumberland*. Barnsley 2015.

Willkie, W.L. *One World*. New York 1943.

Wilmot, C. *Tobruk*. Sydney 1945.

Winter, B. *Stalag Australia*. Sydney 1986.

Yeide, H. *Weapons of the Tankers: American Armor in World War II*. St. Paul 2006.

Yindrich, J. *Fortress Tobruk*. London 1951.

Young, D. *Rommel: The Desert Fox*. New York 1950.

Zaloga, S. *M3 Lee/Grant Medium Tank 1941–45*. Oxford 2005.

Journals and Papers

'German Psychological Warfare', *British Medical Journal*, 4 April 1942.

Aird, I. 'Military Surgery in Geographical Perspective: A Libyan Exercise in Surgical Strategy and Tactics', *Edinburgh Medical Journal*, April 1944.

Barclay, C.N. 'Early Desert Victory'. *Army*. Vol. 14, August 1963.

Bernhard, P. 'Behind the Battle Lines: Italian Atrocities and the Persecution of Arabs, Berbers, and Jews in North Africa during World War II.' *Holocaust and Genocide Studies* 26, No. 3 (Winter 2012).

Boothe, C. 'The Battle for Egypt', *Life*, 13 July 1942.

Citino, R. 'Drive to Nowhere: The Myth of the *Afrika Korps*, 1941-43'. *MHQ Magazine*, Summer 2012

Debenham, R.K. 'War Surgery in the Middle East', *British Medical Journal*, 21 August 1943.

Donald, C. 'With the Eighth Army in the Field', *British Medical Journal*, 27 May 1944.

Dovey, H.O. 'The False Going Map at Alam Halfa'. *Intelligence and National Security*, Vol. 4, No. 1 (January 1989).

Fennell, J. 'Steel my soldiers' hearts: El Alamein Reappraised'. *Journal of Military and Strategic Studies*, Vol. 14, No. 1, 2011.

_____ 'Courage and Cowardice in the North African Campaign: The Eighth Army and Defeat in the Summer of 1942.' *War in History*, Vol. 20, No. 1.

Gear, H.S. 'Hygiene Aspects of the El Alamein Victory, 1942', *British Medical Journal*, 18 March 1944.

Gear, H.S. 'Hygiene, Morale and Desert Victory', *British Medical Journal*, 18 March 1944.

Giblin, T. 'Abdominal Surgery in the Alamein Campaign', *The Australian and New Zealand Journal of Surgery*, July 1943, Vol. XIII, No.1

Gladman, B.W. 'Air Power and Intelligence in the Western Desert Campaign, 1940-43,' *Intelligence and National Security*, 1998, 13:4, 144-62.

Glass, C.H. 'Sidi Rezegh: Reminiscences of the late Gunner Cyril Herbert Glass, 143458, 3rd Field Regiment (Transvaal Horse Artillery).' *Military History Journal*, Vol. 14 No 5 - June 2009.

Horn, K. 'Narratives from North Africa: South African prisoner-of-war experience following the fall of Tobruk, June 1942'. *Historia*, 56, 2, November 2011.

Horn, K. & D. Katz. 'The Surrender of Tobruk in 1942: Press Reports and Soldiers' Memories'. *Scientia Militaria*, Vol. 44, No 1, 2016.

Hunt, T.C. Medical Experiences in North Africa 1943-4'. *British Medical Journal*, 14 October 1944.

Katz, D. 'The Greatest Military Reversal of South African Arms: The Fall of Tobruk 1942, an Avoidable Blunder or an Evitable Disaster?' *Journal for Contemporary History*, December 2012.

Kittel, Katrina, 'Capture in the Desert: 3 Anti-Tank Regiment at Mechili 1941 and Alamein 1942'. *Sabretache*, Vol. 54, No.1, March 2013.

Kozlovsky-Golan, Y. 'Childhood Memories from the Giado Detention Camp in Libya: Fragments from the Oeuvre of Nava T. Barazani'. *Shofar*, Spring 2020.

Low, R. 'I Saw the Blitzkrieg Stopped at Tobruk.' *Liberty*, June 21, 1941.

Matthews, D. 'With the 5th South African Infantry Brigade at Sidi Rezegh.' *Military History Journal*, Vol. 10 No 6 - December 1997.

Rasmussen, N. 'Medical Science and the Military: The Allies' Use of Amphetamine during World War II', *Journal of Interdisciplinary History*, September 2011.

_____ 'Amphetamine-type Stimulants: The Early History of Their Medical and Non-Medical Uses', *International Review of Neurobiology*, Vol. 120, 2015.

Rachel, S. 'It Could Have Happened There: The Jews of Libya during the Second World War', *Africana Journal*, Vol. 16, 1994.

Raugh, H.E. 'General Wavell and the Italian East African Campaign', *Military Review*, Vol. LXIII, July 1983.

Reifenstein E.C. & Davidoff. E., 'The Psychological Effects of Benzedrine Sulfate', *The American Journal of Psychology*, Vol. 52, No. 1. January 1939.

Riches, L. The Patrolling War in Tobruk', Australian War Memorial, Summer Scholars paper, 2012.

Scianna, B.M. 'Rommel Almighty? Italian Assessments of the "Desert Fox" during and after the Second World War', *The Journal of Military History*, 82 (January 2018): 125-46.

Stewart, A. 'The "Atomic" Dispatch: Field Marshal Auchinleck, the Fall of the Tobruk Garrison and Post-War Anglo-South African Relations', *Scientia Militaria*, Vol. 36, No. 1, 2008.

Townsend, N. 'Road to Ruin: 9th Australian Division and the First Battle of El Alamein, July 1942'. Australian War Memorial, SVSS paper, 2016

Westphal, S., 'Notes on the Campaign in North Africa', *Journal of the Royal United Service Institution*, Vol. 105, February 1960.

Academic Theses

Christie, H.R. Fallen Eagles: The Italian 10th Army In The Opening Campaign In The Western Desert, June 1940-December 1940, Master of Military Art and Science, Bloomsberg University, Pennsylvania, 1999.

Hickey, A.S., 'Departing for the Ends of the Earth to do My Humble Part: The Life of William A. Rich, Volunteer Ambulance Driver for the American Field Service, 1942-1945- A Study of War Letters' (2008). University of Pennsylvania, 2008.

McLeod, J.R. 'The New Zealand soldier in World War II: Myth and Reality'. Master of Arts in History at Massey University, New Zealand, 1980.

Newspapers and Periodicals

Army News
Birmingham Daily Post
Birmingham Mail
Brisbane Telegraph
Daily Advertiser
Daily Mirror

Dundee Courier
Dundee Evening Telegraph
Herald
History of the Second World War, Part 34, 'Tobruk Falls', London 1972.
Life
Liverpool Evening Express
Mount Barker and Denmark Record
Nambour Chronicle and North Coast Advertiser
Nottingham Journal
The Age
The Argus
The Times
The Sun
The Courier-Mail (Brisbane)
The Daily Telegraph (Sydney)
The Illustrated London News
The London Gazette (Supplement)
The Newcastle Sun
The New York Times
The Scotsman
The Sunday Telegraph
The Sydney Morning Herald
The Telegraph (Brisbane)
The Uralla Times
The West Australian
Warwick and Warwickshire Advertiser
Western Morning News

Film and Television
The World at War, Episode 8 - 'The Desert: North Africa (1940–1943)',
Thames Television 1973.
'Libya - Successes and Shocks', Movietone News.

Internet
Diary of Edmund Crawford Lecky. Australian War Memorial. Lecky's
letters: Saturday 26 April 1941. Accessed 1 January 1914.
3squadron.org.au/subpages/Chinchen.htm. Accessed 21 May 2020.
comandosupremo.com/siege-of-tobruk/. Accessed 21 May 2020.

BIBLIOGRAPHY

Brune, P. 'Gurney, Arthur Stanley (1908–1942)', Australian Dictionary of Biography, National Centre of Biography, Australian National University, adb.anu.edu.au/biography/gurney-arthur-stanley-10381/text18391, accessed 10 June 2020.

Unpublished Memoirs
Flak, J., *Pages from a Life*, NSW, 2/4th Field Company, Royal Australian Engineers.
Fletcher, A., *NX 20365*
Paget, F.M., *Tobruk to Tarakan*. 2/28th Infantry Battalion
Perversi, F.G., *Mirror of Time*, 2/32nd Infantry Battalion
Weston, R. *Nine Lives*. 24th Anti-Tank Company

Notes

Foreword

1. Quoted in *The Uralla Times*, 27 November 1941, p. 4.

Chapter One: Rommel's African Sideshow

1. D-217, 'Italo-German Cooperation in Italian North Africa', p. 12.
2. Stockings, *Bardia*, p. 79.
3. Blum, *The Rise of Fascism in Europe*, p. 55.
4. Mallman & Cüppers. *Nazi Palestine*, p. 56.
5. Burgwyn, *Mussolini Warlord*. p. 216.
6. Mallman & Cüppers. *Op. Cit.,* p. 57.
7. Thompson, *Forgotten Voices Desert Victory*, p. 7
8. Hammond, *El Alamein*, p. 11.
9. 'On the return from a reconnaissance flight over Egypt in an airplane piloted by himself, the Marshal approached Tobruk directly from the east, in violation of his own orders to circle out over the sea and approach the fortress from the west only. As he prepared to land, he was shot down by an Italian improvised anti-aircraft gun – a 75mm field piece mounted on a concrete block. The aircraft burst into flames and its passengers burned to death. The gun never scored another hit.' D-217, 'Italo-German Cooperation in Italian North Africa', written by Oberst Heinz Heggenreiner, p. 9.
10. Heggenreiner noted that 'a far-reaching difference of opinions on the offensive against the Suez Canal existed between the Marshal and the Duce.' D-216, 'The Operations under the Command of Marshal Graziani prior to the Arrival of the German Troops' (Aug.-Sep. 1940).

11. Knox, *Mussolini Unleashed*, p. 160.
12. Pitt, *The Crucible of War: Western Desert 1941*, p. 49.
13. Playfair, *The Mediterranean and Middle East*, p. 209.
14. Thompson, *Forgotten Voices Desert Victory*, p. 13
15. Raugh, *Wavell in the Middle East,* p. 85.
16. Thompson, *Forgotten Voices Desert Victory*, p. 14.
17. Burdick & Jacobson, *The Halder War Diary 1939–1942*, p. 240.
18. Ciano, *The Ciano Diaries*, p. 300.
19. Ibid.
20. Liddell Hart, *History of the Second World War*, p. 112.
21. The division was called 'The Desert Rats' because of its red jerboa (a nocturnal rodent from North Africa) emblem. Not to be confused with the 'Rats of Tobruk'. O'Connor explained that the '"Infantry" tanks from their name were there to assist the infantry's advance and help them in every possible way and they were obviously used for that.' Hammond, *El Alamein*, p. 13.
22. Connell, *Wavell, Scholar and Soldier*, p. 278.
23. Sears, *World War II: Desert War*, p. 16.
24. Kershaw, *Tank Men*, p. 142.
25. Hart, *The South Notts Hussars*, p. 88.
26. Liddell Hart, *History of the Second World War*, p. 117.
27. Knox, *Mussolini Unleashed,* p. 76.
28. Hart, *The South Notts Hussars*, p. 94.
29. Ibid, pp. 94-5.
30. Corvaja, *Hitler & Mussolini,* p. 149.
31. Ciano, *op. cit.*, p. 321.
32. Corvaja, *op. cit.*, p. 149.
33. Barter. *The 2/2 Australian Infantry Battalion*, p. 109.
34. Ciano, *op. cit.*, p. 332.
35. WO 201/345 Capture of Tobruk: Report by 13th Corps Commander.
36. *The Times*, 24 January 1941.
37. Barnett, *The Desert Generals*, p. 53. Quoted from General Michael Creagh, commander of the Seventh Armoured Division.
38. Raugh *op. cit.*, p. 118.
39. Kershaw, *Tank Men*, p. 147.
40. Ibid, p. 148.
41. Forty, *Desert Rats at War*, p. 60.
42. Barclay, *Against Great Odds*, p. 14.

43. Jackson, *The Battle for North Africa 1940-1943*, p. 69.
44. *Life*, 24 February 1941, p. 23.
45. Churchill, *The Grand Alliance*, p. 58.
46. *The World at War*, Episode 8, 'The Desert: North Africa (1940–1943)'.
47. Ultra was the name given by British military intelligence in June 1941 to signals intelligence attained by breaking high-level encrypted enemy radio and teleprinter communications. The breaking of the German Enigma keys at the Government Code and Cypher School (GC&CS) at Bletchley Park provided direct evidence of German planning and subsequently has been acknowledged as the 'single most important British advantage of the war'. Denniston, *Churchill's Secret War*, p. 45.

   Britain sent the British 1st Armoured Division, 6th and 7th Australian Infantry Division, 2nd New Zealand Infantry Division and Polish Independent (Carpathian) Infantry Brigade to Greece.
48. Fuller, *The Decisive Battles of the Western World, and Their Influence upon History*, p. 480. Fuller was an early British theorist of armoured warfare.
49. Trevor-Roper, *Hitler's War Directives 1939-1945*, pp. 98-9. Heinz Heggenreiner, who met with Marshal Balbo in May 1940, wrote in addition that the 'loss of Libya thus meant resignation to playing a defensive role in Mediterranean naval affairs, forgoing the offensive against the Suez Canal, forgetting about the resumption of direct contact with Abyssinia, and finally the collapse of its hard-won influence in the discontent Arab world. For Germany, the significance of Libya lay – aside from separating the French and British – for the time being only in the fact that it constituted an offensive basis of the Italian ally against the life-line of the British Empire: the Suez Canal.' D-217, 'Italo-German Cooperation in Italian North Africa', pp. 5-6.
50. Libya is divided into two territories: Cyrenaica in the east and Tripolitania in the west, although the Germans and Italians referred to the western part of the country as Cyrenaica and the area east of Gazala as Marmarica.
51. *The World at War*, Episode 8, 'The Desert: North Africa (1940–1943)'.
52. Reuth, *Rommel: The End of a Legend*, p. 47.

53. Burgwyn, *Mussolini Warlord*, p. 89.

54. Heckman, *Rommel's War in Africa*, p. 24.

55. Liddell Hart, *The Rommel Papers*, p. 100.

56. Ibid, p. 134.

57. Reuth, *op. cit.*, p. 113.

58. Schmidt, *With Rommel in the Desert*, pp. 16-17.

59. Schraepler, *At Rommel's Side,* p. 53.

60. Ibid.

61. Liddell Hart, *The Rommel Papers*, p. 101.

62. Rommel had flagged his intentions to General Enno von Rintelen, Hitler's military attaché in Rome, who advised against it, cautioning that it would lead to a loss of honour and reputation.

63. Liddell Hart, *The Rommel Papers*, p. 103.

64. Ibid, p. 200.

65. Schmidt, *op. cit.*, p. 16.

66. IWM AL 1517 Extracts from German diaries and reports, North Africa, 1941. 'The Via Balbia,' wrote Oberst Heinz Heggenreiner after the war, was 'a wide asphalt highway of superior construction, almost 2000 kilometres in length, that extended from Tunisia to the Egyptian frontier. That achievement of Balbo will outlive his name.' D-217, 'Italo-German Cooperation in Italian North Africa'.

67. Westphal, 'Notes on the Campaign in North Africa', p. 72.

68. Kershaw, *Tank Men*, p. 147-8

69. Fritz, *Frontsoldaten*, p. 127.

70. Mitchelhill-Green, *With Rommel in the Desert: Tripoli to El Alamein*, p. 28.

71. Forty, *Afrika Korps at War*, Vol.1, p. 117.

72. von Luck, *Panzer Commander*, p. 72.

73. Ibid.

74. IWM AL 1517 Extracts from German diaries and reports, North Africa, 1941. There were four main types of German tanks at this time – Pzkw I, II, III and IV (the German word for a tank is *Panzerkampfwagen*, abbreviated to Pzkw). Pzkw I and II were light tanks. In the medium class, Pzkw III mounted a 50-mm gun as its main armament, but with a shorter barrel than the anti-tank gun of the same calibre. It is obviously impossible to say how many successes this gun scored in the fighting between tanks.

The short 75-mm gun equipping the medium Pzkw IV was not designed as a tank-killer, although its 15-lb high-explosive shell could 'crack' British tanks at an unpleasantly long range; it was a support weapon, useful also against the British anti-tank guns.

75. Forty, *Tank Warfare in World War II*, pp. 188-9.
76. Reisch, *Out of the Rat Trap*, p. 34.
77. Schraepler, *op. cit.,* p. 79.
78. *The Telegraph*, 25 July 1942, p. 3.
79. Schraepler, *op. cit.*, p. 55.
80. Schmidt, *op. cit.*, p. 60.
81. Paget, *Tobruk to Tarakan*. Unpublished memoir.
82. Schmidt, *op. cit.*, pp. 98-9.
83. Schraepler, *op. cit.*, p. 106. Diary entry for 24 May 1941.
84. Hartmann, *Panzers in the Sand*, Vol. 1, p. 232.
85. Caccia-Dominioni, *Alamein 1933-1962*, p. 192.
86. Gear, 'Hygiene Aspects of the El Alamein Victory, 1942', pp. 386-7.
87. Debenham, 'War Surgery in the Middle East', p. 4311.
88. *The Scotsman*, 30 May 1942, p. 6.
89. *The Sun* 1 November 1942, p. 1.
90. Paget, *Tobruk to Tarakan*. Unpublished memoir.
91. Hammond, *El Alamein*, p. 25
92. Seton-Watson, *Dunkirk, Alamein, Bologna*, p. 93. A New Zealand officer recalled: 'Where they came from in the summer and went to in the winter none of us knew. So far I have not seen any description of those most persistent visitors which really does justice to the way they tormented us from daylight till dark. For days on end they made life a real misery.' Murray Reid, *The Turning Point*, p. 98.
93. AWM 52 8/3/13.
94. Bierman & Smith, *The Battle of Alamein*, p. 32.
95. Hammond, *El Alamein*, p. 24.
96. Hartmann, *Panzers in the Sand,* Vol. 2, p. 41.
97. Hammond, pp. 24-5.
98. Crawford, *I was an Eighth Army Soldier,* p. 51.
99. Fritz, *Frontsoldaten*, pp. 126-7.
100. Moorehead, *African Trilogy*, p. 381.
101. Fennell, *Combat and Morale in the North African Campaign*, pp. 129-30.
102. Schraepler, *op. cit.,* p. 71.

103. Liddell Hart, *The Rommel Papers*, p. 105.
104. Mitchelhill-Green, *With Rommel in the Desert*, p. 49.
105. Mahlke, *Memoirs of a Stuka Pilot*, p. 184.
106. AWM 52 8/3/13.
107. AWM 52 8/2/26.
108. Reid, *The Turning Point*, p. 144.
109. Hammond, *El Alamein*, p. 24.
110. Trye, *Mussolini's Afrika Korps*, p. 147.
111. Donald, 'With the Eighth Army in the Field', p. 710.
112. NA CAB 106/834 Western Desert: summary of the battle of Tobruk 1941 Jan; Keogh, *Middle East 1939-43*, p. 50.
113. Liddell Hart, *The Rommel Papers*, p. 133.
114. *The Age*, 16 September 1941, p. 7.
115. Hammond, *El Alamein*, p. 21.
116. Jones, *Burning Tanks and an Empty Desert*, p. 134.
117. Connell, *Auchinleck*, p. 421.
118. Thompson, *The Montgomery Legend*, Vol. 1, p. 254.
119. Travers, *Tomorrow to be Brave*, p. 136.
120. Schraepler, *op. cit.,* p, 54
121. *The Sydney Morning Herald*, 16 January 1943, p. 7.
122. IWM AL 1517 Extracts from German diaries and reports, North Africa, 1941.
123. Westphal, 'Notes on the Campaign in North Africa', *Journal of the Royal United Service Institution*, p. 73.
124. Fennell, *op. cit.*, p. 146.
125. Ibid. p. 147.
126. Reisch, *op. cit.*, p. 62.
127. Schraepler, *op. cit.,* p. 124.
128. Yindrich, *Fortress Tobruk*, p. 213. Epilogue by Generalleutnant Hans von Ravenstein.
129. P-129 'Desert Warfare: German Experiences in World War II'.
130. Maughan, *Tobruk and El Alamein,* p. 17.
131. Remarkably, Neame still remains the only recipient of both the Victoria Cross and an Olympic Gold medal.
132. AWM 54 523/7/19 Brief history of Tobruk, March to August 1941, Part 1.
133. Barker, *Afrika Korps*, p. 16.
134. Schraepler, *op. cit.,* p. 60. Diary entry for 6 March 1941.

135. *The London Gazette* (Supplement), 3 July 1946, p. 3441.

136. Connell, *Wavell, Scholar and Soldier*, p. 385.

137. Ibid, pp. 385-6.

138. Maughan, *op. cit.*, p. 44. Neame softened his stance after the war, writing of the 9th Division as a 'splendidly-led' formation that 'fought magnificently'.

139. Connell, *Wavell, Scholar and Soldier*, p. 386.

140. Lewin, *The Chief*, p. 103; Lewin, *The Life and Death of the Afrika Korps,* p. 41.

141. AWM 54 523/7/29 Reports on 9th Division Operations in Cyrenaica by Lieutenant-Gen. Sir L J Morshead, March to October 1941, 9 Aust Div Operation Instruction, No.1.

142. AWM 54 522/7/5 Summary of events, Defence in the Desert – The retreat. Wavell wrote to O'Connor in June 1945 that he did not believe the Germans were capable of building up their supply system between Tripoli and the frontier of Cyrenaica so quickly.

143. Liddell Hart, *The Rommel Papers*, p. 105.

144. Schraepler, *op. cit.*, p. 71.

145. IWM 87/12/1 J.H. Witte, 'The One that Didn't Get Away'.

146. Jackson, *The Battle for North Africa, 1940-43*, p. 97.

147. Gambier-Parry later told Combe that 'Rimington had lost his nerve at the end of the first war and that he had no faith in him and should have displaced him around Mersa Brega, but was sorry for him.' Quoted from John Combe, letter from Combe to Liddell Hart. O'CONNOR: 4/3/18 1940s Copies of comments by Brig J F B Combe on the account of operations in Cyrenaica by Neame, and on various letters of Neame and O'Connor.

148. Liddell Hart, *The Rommel Papers*, p. 111.

149. Ibid.

150. Schreiber et al. *Germany and the Second World War,* Vol. III, p. 676.

151. O'Connell, *Wavell, Scholar and Soldier*, p. 393.

152. IWM AL 1517 Extracts from German diaries and reports, North Africa, 1941.

153. Schraepler, *op. cit.*, p. 76.

154. Neame, *Playing with Strife*, p. 279.

155. Holmes, *The World at War*, p. 162. O'Connor was held prisoner for two years and nine months. His third escape attempt was successful

and he returned to Britain to command VIII Corps during the 1944 Normandy campaign and into the Low Countries.

156. AWM 54 523/7/43 Chester Wilmot's papers, copies and original documents relating to the actions and activities of various units during the siege of Tobruk, April-September 1941, *Narrative of operations in Cyrenaica during the period April 7-14 by Lt-Gen Sir John Lavarack*, p. 5.

157. Gregory & Gehlen, *Two Soldiers, Two Lost Fronts*, p. 145.

158. Holmes, *The World at War*, p. 161.

159. Graham & Mace, *Operations in North Africa and the Middle East 1939-1942*, p. 53.

160. Schmidt, *op. cit.*, 34. In 2015, Gambier-Parry's granddaughter revealed another twist to the goggle saga, namely that the captured general had given Rommel the British goggles that were to adorn his peaked cap throughout the desert campaign. Over dinner, Gambier-Parry had complained to his German host of having had his hat stolen by a German soldier. An incensed Rommel saw that it was returned to its owner. When he spied Gambier-Parry's goggles, the latter agreed that he could keep them.

161. Kittel, 'Capture in the Desert: 3rd Anti-Tank Regiment at Mechili 1941 and Alamein 1942', p. 22.

162. Liddell Hart, *The Rommel Papers*, p. 120.

163. Thompson, *Forgotten Voices*, pp. 42-3.

Chapter Two: Thwarted by Rats

1. Churchill, *The Grand Alliance*, p. 183.

2. Salter, *A Padre with the Rats of Tobruk*, p. 25.

3. Wilmot, *Tobruk*, 1941, p. 99-100.

4. IWM AL 151 Extracts from German diaries and reports, North Africa, 1941

5. Wilmot, *Tobruk 1941*, p. 105.

6. Maughan, *op. cit.*, pp. 117-18.

7. Kennedy, *The Business of War*, pp. 90-91.

8. Day, *Menzies & Churchill at War*, p. 124.

9. Menzies, *Dark and Hurrying Days*, p. 110.

10. Kennedy, p. 91.

11. AWM 3DRL 2632/72 Morshead Papers 1940 to 1944, *Lecture on Tobruch*, pp. 14-15.
12. *Mount Barker and Denmark Record*, 10 July 1941, p. 5
13. Fearnside, *Bayonets Abroad,* p. 88.
14. Flak, *Pages from a Life*. Unpublished memoir.
15. Perversi, *Mirror of Time*, p. 31.
16. AWM 523/7/41 9th Division report on operations Cyrenaica and Tobruk, 1941.
17. CAB 44/421 Fall of Tobruk, June 1942. AWM 523/7/4 2/28 Australian Infantry Battalion, History of the Battalion's activities in Tobruk, March to September 1941. Note that the spelling of this feature varies greatly in wartime and postwar literature, examples including: Midauuar, Ras Medawar, Ras al Mudawwarah, Ras el Mdauuar and Ras al Mudawwarah. The spelling adopted for this thesis is that used in the Australian official history of Tobruk by Maughan.
18. AWM 54 522/7/8 Main movements ordered and made Western Desert and Tobruk with chronology of AIF Units involved in operations – Libya and Tobruk (April-May 1941).
19. Debenham, War Surgery in the Middle East', p. 227.
20. Yindrich, *Fortress Tobruk*, p. 42.
21. McGillvray, *One Man's War*, p. 14.
22. Hartmann, *Panzers in the Sand,* Vol. 1, p. 210.
23. Maughan, *op. cit.*, p. 124.
24. Barber, *The War, the Whores and the Afrika Korps*, pp. 61-3.
25. American Field Service volunteer Andrew Geer noted the aiming procedures of one Tobruk bush battery: 'Two hundred yards in front of each gun on the lip of an escarpment, empty beer bottles were set in a precise geometric pattern. The gunnery officer went to the observation post and watched the first salvo crash into enemy territory. Over the telephone (also enemy equipment) he directed the fire. "Lift eighty yards, sweep two beers to the right."' Geer, *Mercy in Hell*, p. 60.
26. Schmidt, *op. cit.*, p. 37.
27. Ibid.
28. Hartmann, *Panzers in the Sand*, Vol. 1, p. 215.
29. Ibid, p. 216.
30. IWM AL 1517

NOTES

31. Wilmot, *Tobruk 1941*, p. 114

32. Schraepler, *op. cit.*, pp. 78-9.
   Note – General Staff officers had the suffix i.G (im Generalstab) added to their rank.
33. Hartmann, *Panzers in the Sand*, Vol. 1, p. 216.
34. Devine, *The Rats of Tobruk*, p. 72.
35. Wilmot, *Tobruk 1941*, p. 116.
36. Jentz, *Tank Combat in North Africa,* p. 107.
37. Wilmot, *Tobruk*, 1941 p. 121.
38. *The London Gazette* (Supplement), 1 July 1942, pp. 3807-8. Edmondson was posthumously awarded the VC, Australia's first of the war. His citation closed: 'His actions throughout the operations were outstanding for resolution, leadership and conspicuous bravery.'
39. Coombes, *Morshead*, p. 109.
40. Liddell Hart, *The Rommel Papers*, p. 124.
41. IWM AL 1517 Extracts from German diaries and reports, North Africa, 1941.
42. Maughan, *op. cit.*, pp. 150-4.
43. Ibid, pp. 267-8
44. IWM AL 1517 Extracts from German diaries and reports, North Africa, 1941.
45. Ibid.
46. Hartmann, *Panzers in the Sand*, Vol. 1, p. 217.
47. Coombes, *Morshead*, p. 109-10.
48. Winter, *Stalag Australia*, p. 7.
49. Liddell Hart, *The Rommel Papers*, pp. 125-6.
50. AWM 54 522/7/8 Main movements ordered and made Western Desert and Tobruk with chronology of AIF Units involved in operations – Libya and Tobruk (April-May 1941).
51. *The Sun*, 26 April 1941, p. 2.
52. Memo, Halifax [Earl, Ambassador the United States] to Franklin D. Roosevelt, April 17, 1941, Box 35, President's Secretary's File (PSF) Safe Files: State Dept., 1941, Franklin D. Roosevelt Library Digital Archives.
53. AWM 52 8/3/13
54. AWM, 3DRL2632/37 Morshead Papers 1940 to 1944, Translation of Captured German Documents.

55. Churchill, *The Grand Alliance*, p. 186.
56. Low, 'I Saw the Blitzkrieg Stopped at Tobruk.' *Liberty*, June 21, 1941, p. 26.
57. Barber, *The War, the Whores and the Afrika Korps*, p. 73.
58. Schmidt, *op. cit.*, p. 44.
59. Liddell Hart, *The Rommel Papers*, pp. 123-4.
60. Schraepler, *op. cit.*, p. 81. Diary entry, 15 April 1941.
61. Liddell Hart, *The Rommel Papers,* p. 123.
62. Maughan, *op. cit.*, p. 156.
63. Burdick & Jacobson, *The Halder War Diary 1939-1942*, p. 363. Hitler assaulted the Soviet Union with 146 German divisions and some 3 million men; his commitment to North Africa peaked at four divisions and approximately 50,000 men – a commitment of less than two per cent of the Wehrmacht's strength to the desert war. See Bungay, *Alamein*, p. 13.
64. *Mount Barker and Denmark Record*, 10 July 1941, p. 5.
65. *The West Australian*, 18 October 1941, p. 5.
66. *Mount Barker and Denmark Record*, 10 July 1941, p. 5.
67. Liddell Hart, *The Rommel Papers*, p. 126.
68. Maughan *op. cit.*, p. 165.
69. Ibid, p. 166.
70. Wilmot, *op. cit.,* p. 145.
71. Christopherson, *An Englishman at War*, p. 159.
72. Wilmot, *op. cit.,* p. 320.
73. Devine, *op. cit.,* p. 75.
74. AWM. *Lecky's letters: Saturday 26 April 1941.*
75. AWM 54 523/7/29 Reports on 9th Division Operations in Cyrenaica by Lieutenant-Gen. Sir L.J. Morshead, March to October 1941, Parts 1, p. 10. A wartime survey conducted in the Middle East to 'obtain from men first-hand accounts of their reactions to enemy used against them' found that the 'mortar and dive bomber are disliked to an extent out of all proportion to their real effectiveness, while the machine gun, which has about the best performance in causing casualties, is singled out for dislike by few. AWM B5505 Army Training Memorandum (War) (Australia) No. 28.
76. *The Age*, 6 June 1941, p. 6.
77. Heaton & Lewis, *The Star of Africa*, p. 28.
78. Mahlke, *Memoirs of a Stuka Pilot*, p. 196.

79. Auchinleck applauded the efforts of Slater and his gunners: 'They formed the sole means of defence against air attack, as our bases were too distant to allow fighter aircraft to operate over this area. They performed their duties with such efficiency that in spite of continual raids serious damage was rarely inflicted by enemy aircraft, of which several were shot down and many damaged.' *The London Gazette* (Supplement), 21 August 1946, pp. 4221-2.
80. Devine, *op. cit.*, pp. 77-8. *Ladybird* was bombed and sunk on 12 May 1941.
81. Flak, *Pages from a Life*. Private memoir.
82. Schraepler, *op. cit.,* pp. 84-5. Diary entry, 19 April 1941.
83. *Mount Barker and Denmark Record*, 10 July 1941, p. 5.
84. Liddell Hart, *The Rommel Papers*, p. 130.
85. Wade, *A Midshipman's War*, pp. 90-91.
86. Cunningham, *A Sailor's Odyssey*, p. 412.
87. Brigadier Sir Bernard Fergusson, (Wavell's former ADC) recalled, 'There were so many casualties in the Tobruk hospital that the staff could not cope with them, and some poor unknown devil has or had on his conscience the decision to send them back to Egypt on board a non-hospital ship' (Fergusson, *The Trumpet in the Hall*, p. 133). Fergusson continues, '*Chakdina* was not a hospital ship, neither marked nor registered nor illuminated as such; and consequently fair game for the aerial torpedo that sank her' four hours after clearing Tobruk.' Ibid.
88. Gregory-Smith, *Red Tobruk*, p. 63.
89. Coombes, *Morshead*, p. 108. Morshead's experience on the Western Front during WWI commanding the 33rd Battalion meant he was well versed in defensive-offensive strategy and patrolling, experience that served him well throughout the siege.
90. Wilmot, *op. cit.,* p. 138.
91. McGillivray, *One Man's War*, p. 15.
92. Rees, *Desert Boys*, p. 500.
93. AWM PR 3DRL 2632. Papers of Sir Lieutenant General Leslie Morshead.
94. General Auchinleck commended the 'exploits of the innumerable patrols carried out nightly by the cavalry and infantry units of the garrison... Not only did these patrols collect most valuable information and numerous prisoners, but they were in large part

responsible for making it possible to hold a perimeter thirty miles long with only seven battalions and one cavalry regiment in the front line.' *The London Gazette* (Supplement), 21 August 1946, p. 4221.

95. Wilmot, *op. cit.,* p. 148.
96. Schmidt, *op. cit.,* p. 52.
97. Ibid, p. 48.
98. Devine, *op. cit.*, p. 105.
99. Stevens & Hingston, *The Tiger Kills,* p. 22.
100. Riches, 'The Patrolling War in Tobruk', p. 16.
101. AWM 54 523/7/36. Australians on Patrol, Patrol Reports, Tobruk: June-July 1941, pt. 1.
102. Lyman, *The Longest Siege*, p. 212.
103. Stanley, *At the Frontline*, p. 42.
104. Thompson, *Forgotten Voices Desert Victory,* p. 88.
105. Mackenzie-Smith, *Tobruk's Easter Battle 1941,* p. 123. Diary entry, 11 June 1941.
106. Hodson, *War in the Sun,* p. 146.
107. Cox, *A Tale of Two Battles*, p. 141.
108. Reynolds, *Only the Stars Are Neutral*, p. 259. Although Rommel referred to the Desert War as *Krieg ohne Hass* ('War Without Hate'), Hitler's plan to extend the Holocaust into the Middle East was only foiled by the Axis defeat at El Alamein and subsequent surrender in Tunisia.
109. Murray Reid, *The Turning Point*, p. 57.
110. Bernhard, 'Behind the Battle Lines', p. 435
111. The perpetrator later acknowledged his crime arose from the fact that the prisoners were not white. See Bernhard, p. 436.
112. Fielding, *They Sought Out Rommel*, p. 51.
113. Clifford, *Crusader*, p. 61.
114. Wilmot, *Tobruk 1941*, pp. 346-7. Morshead fostered a cohesive spirit within Tobruk: The 'garrison was quickly welded into a team and the team spirit prevailed to a marked degree manifested equally by British, Australians, Indians and later the Poles. Each had confidence in the other and a high regard and everybody played their part.' AWM, 3DRL2632/72 Morshead Papers 1940 to 1944, Lecture on Tobruch part 2.
115. Barrett, *We Were There,* p. 308.

116. Weston, *Nine Lives*, p. 3. 'They were all good Catholics but not a very lovable bunch. We were pleased to see the back of them.' Ibid.
117. Cox, *A Tale of Two Battles*, p. 192.
118. Churchill, *Blood, Toil, Tears, and Sweat,* p. 219.
119. Burdick & Jacobsen, *The Halder War Diary*, p. 374.
120. Wilson, *A Rat's Tale,* p. 20.
121. McGillivray, *One Man's War*, p. 18.
122. McKenzie-Smith, *Tobruk's Easter Battle 1941*, p. 117.
123. Christopherson, *An Englishman at War*, pp. 165-6.
124. IWM AL 1517 Extracts from German diaries and reports, North Africa, 1941.
125. Ibid.
126. Serle, *The Second Twenty-Fourth Australian Infantry Battalion of the 9th Australian Division,* p. 72.
127. Wilmot, *op. cit.,* p. 169.
128. IWM AL 1517 Extracts from German diaries and reports, North Africa, 1941
129. Hurley, *The Diaries of Frank Hurley*, p. 248.
130. Irving, *The Trail of the Fox*, p. 135.
131. Ibid.
132. *The Age,* 'How a Rat's son pieced together two stories of Tobruk', 26 April 2020.
133. IWM AL 1517 Extracts from German diaries and reports, North Africa, 1941.
134. *The West Australian*, 18 October 1941, p. 5.
135. Wilmot, *Tobruk 1941*, p. 203.
136. IWM AL 1517 Extracts from German diaries and reports, North Africa, 1941.
137. *The West Australian*, 18 October 1941, p. 5.
138. *The Telegraph*, 25 July 1942, p. 3.
139. Perversi, *Mirror of Time*, p. 33.
140. Quoted from M. Johnston, *At the Frontline: Experiences of Australian Soldiers in World War II*, p. 32.
141. Bowen, *Back from Tobruk*, p. 102.
142. *The Times*, 29 May 1941, p. 4.
143. *The London Gazette* (Supplement), 21 August 1946, p. 4221.
144. *The British Medical Journal* (4 April 1942) later detailed: Morale, 'built by whatever means, is considered by the German leaders to

be at least as important as weapons. This is all the more impressive when we consider how important they have proved weapons to be.' Fennell, *op. cit.*, pp. 55-6.

145. Wilmot, *Tobruk 1941*, p. 347.

146. According to Field Marshal Thomas Blamey, at the time of the Australian 9th Division's relief the 'condition of the troops was such that any strong attack by the enemy may have endangered the safety of the fortress. Moreover, an offensive was contemplated and plans included operations by the defenders at a later date, which I was certain that they could not have maintained owing to their loss of strength and physical condition…few of them would be able to march eight miles.' NAA: A2684, 556 Relief of 9th Division at Tobruk (1941) also publication of despatch of General Sir Claude Auchinleck (1945-46)

Chapter Three:'Tobruk is relieved, but not as relieved as I am'

1. Burdick & Jacobson, *The Halder War Diary, 1939-1942,* p. 384. Entry dated 7 May 1941.
2. Irving, *The Trail of the Fox*, p. 52.
3. Liddell Hart, *The Rommel Papers*, p. 133.
4. Schreiber, *Germany and the Second World War*, Vol. III, p. 675.
5. D-084, Supplement to 'Reasons for Rommel's Success in Africa, 1941- 42', p. 6.
6. Churchill, *The Grand Alliance*, p. 299.
7. CAB 79/86/2.
8. Ibid, p. 218.
9. One ship had been sunk, SS *Empire Song*, carrying 10 Hurricane fighter aircraft and 57 tanks.
10. Churchill, *The Grand Alliance*, p. 300.
11. Jentz, *Tank Combat in North Africa*, p. 133.
12. 'Italians Bravery Praised by Nazi Chief in Africa', *New York Times*, 5 August 1941.
13. Raugh, *Wavell in the Middle East,* p. 208.
14. Churchill, *The Churchill War Papers*, Vol. III, p. 679.
15. Liddell Hart, *The Rommel Papers*, p. 136.
16. Ibid, p. 137.

17. Ibid, p. 137. Official British losses were 173 men, five Matilda tanks and four 25-pounder guns.
18. Schmidt, *op. cit.*, p. 79.
19. The French Vichy regime under Marshal Philippe Pétain was the nominal government of France in collaboration with Nazi Germany, though never a member of the Axis. France's overseas colonies were originally under Vichy control until a progressive loss to Charles de Gaulle's Allied-orientated Free France.
20. Churchill, *The Grand Alliance*, p. 303.
21. Warner, *Auchinleck*, p. 116.
22. Churchill, p. 303.
23. Ibid, p. 304. Communiqué dated 28 May 1941.
24. Verney, *The Desert Rats*, p. 59.
25. Strawson, *The Battle for North Africa*, p. 81.
26. Developed as an anti-aircraft (*Flugzeugabwehrkanone* or *FlaK*), the formidable 8.8-cm gun was first tested in a ground attack role during the Spanish Civil War. Armour-piercing ammunition was developed, and since no British or French armour fought in Spain, its lethal potential was a nasty surprise to the British in France and North Africa. Although disadvantaged by its high silhouette, the 8.8-cm gun could be brought quickly into action. A fearsome weapon in the hands of an experienced crew, it could knock out the formidably armoured British Matilda at 2,000 yards. A practised crew could fire twenty-five rounds a minute.
27. Under the heading 'Experience gained in the defensive battle of 15-17 June', The War Diary of the 15th Panzer Division noted: 'In order to achieve surprise, all anti-tank weapons will hold their fire until it seems likely to be successful. Even if the Flak 8.8-cm has successfully opened fire, Pak 37- and 50-mms will remain silent in order to escape attention of enemy tanks. They will wait until the heaviest English tanks are only a few hundred metres away before opening fire.' Playfair et al. *The Mediterranean and Middle East*, Vol. II, p. 163.
28. Delaforce, *Monty's Marauders*, p. 20.
29. Ibid.
30. Liddell Hart, *The Rommel Papers*, p. 147.
31. Hartmann, *Panzers in the Sand*, p. 224.
32. Lucas Phillips, *Alamein*, p. 57.

33. Hartmann, *Panzers in the Sand*, p. 226.
34. Liddell Hart, *The Rommel Papers*, p. 145.
35. Churchill, *The Grand Alliance*, p. 307.
36. Thompson, *Forgotten Voices*, p. 62.
37. Liddell Hart, *The Rommel Papers*, p. 146.
38. Schraepler, *op. cit.*, p. 119.
39. Connell, *Wavell, Scholar and Soldier*, p. 502.
40. Churchill, *The Grand Alliance*, p. 309.
41. The *Corpo di Spedizione Italiano in Russia* (Italian Expeditionary Corps), or CSIR, eventually grew to an army of 230,000 men – a much larger force then Rome deployed in North Africa. A Spanish volunteer force of 17,692 men, known as the 'Blue Division', also fought in German uniform. In time one in three men fighting for Hitler against Stalin's Red Army was not a native German.
42. Trevor-Roper, *Hitler's War Directives 1939-1945,* pp. 131-2.
43. Churchill, *The Grand Alliance*, p. 80.
44. Warner, *Auchinleck,* p. 77. Ultra revealed Axis plans for a new offensive in Cyrenaica and the transfer of large-calibre siege artillery from Vichy Tunisia (Hinsley, *British Intelligence in the Second World War*, Vol. II, pp. 280-1). British Intelligence subsequently learned that an Axis attack could not be undertaken before the end of October (Ibid).
45. Warner, *Auchinleck,* p. 86. Auchinleck was generous in his postwar appreciation of Wavell: 'greatly impressed by the solid foundations laid by my predecessor, but I was also able the better to appreciate the vastness of the problems with which he had been confronted and the greatness of his achievements, in a command in which some 40 different languages are spoken by the British and Allied Forces.' *The London Gazette* (Supplement), 21 August 1946, p. 4215.
46. Connell, *Auchinleck,* p. 257.
47. Churchill, p. 361.
48. Ibid.
49. Liddell Hart, *The Rommel Papers*, p. 151.
50. Schmidt, *op. cit.*, p. 93.
51. Irving, *The trail of the Fox*, p. 113.
52. D-424, Command Techniques Employed by Feldmarschall Rommel in Africa, p. 2.

53. Deceptive measures by the British such as a visit by Auchinleck to Palestine further convinced Rommel of no imminent threat. He telephoned Berlin on 14 November to assure Oberstgeneral Alfred Jodl, Chief of the Wehrmacht Operations Staff, that there was no immediate danger of a British operation in his theatre.

54. Schmidt, *op. cit.*, p. 95.

55. Asher, *Get Rommel*, p. 166.

56. Schmidt, *op. cit.*, p. 98. Keyes' VC citation read: 'From the outset Lieutenant-Colonel Keyes deliberately selected for himself the command of the detachment detailed to attack what was undoubtedly the most hazardous of these objectives – the residence and Headquarters of the General Officer Commanding the German forces in North Africa. This attack, even if initially successful, meant almost certain death for those who took part in it… By his fearless disregard of the great dangers which he ran and of which he was fully aware, and by his magnificent leadership and outstanding gallantry, Lieutenant-Colonel Keyes set an example of supreme self-sacrifice and devotion to duty.' *The London Gazette* (Supplement), 16 June 1942, p. 2699.

57. Ministry of Information, *The Eighth Army*, p. 14.

58. Fielding, *They Sought Out Rommel*, p. 3.

59. Ibid, p. 7.

60. Halton, *Ten Years to Alamein*, p. 196.

61. The Italians referred to the battle as the 2nd (British) Offensive; the Germans knew it as the *Winterschlacht* (Winter Battle). Cunningham was presented with two plans for Crusader when he arrived in the Middle East in September from East Africa. He modified the most practical plan and presented it to Auchinleck.

62. Clifford, *The Conquest of North Africa 1940-1943*, p. 137.

63. Churchill, *The Grand Alliance*, p. 493.

64. Fergusson, *The Trumpet in the Hall*, p. 125.

65. The '2-pounder' was named after the weight of the projectile. It was the standard British anti-tank gun until November 1941 when the 6-pounder was introduced in limited quantities.

66. Connell, *Auchinleck*, p. 419.

67. Ibid.

68. Casey, *Personal Experience 1939-1946*, p. 123.

69. Crisp, *Brazen Chariots*, p. 18.

70. Katz, *South Africans versus Rommel*, p. 115.

71. Fielding, *They Sought Out Rommel*, p. 10.

72. von Mellenthin, *Panzer Battles*, p. 78.

73. Owen, *The Desert My Dwelling Place*, p. 109.

74. *The Telegraph*, 25 July 1942, p. 3

75. Churchill, *The Grand Alliance*, p. 504.

76. Clifford, *The Conquest of North Africa 1940-1943*, pp. 145-6.

77. Halton, *Ten Years to Alamein*, p. 199.

78. Crisp, *op. cit.,* p. 44.

79. Lawrence, *The Green Trees Beyond*, pp. 110-11.

80. Roach, *The 8.15 to War,* p. 72.

81. Gardiner, *Freyberg's Circus.* pp. 74-5.

82. Joly, *Take These Men*, pp. 229-30.

83. Moorehead, *Don't Blame the Generals*, p. 67.

84. *The London Gazette* (Supplement), 30 January 1942, p. 545. Campbell's VC citation concludes: 'Throughout these two days his magnificent example and his utter disregard of personal danger were an inspiration to his men and to all who saw him. His brilliant leadership was the direct cause of the very heavy casualties inflicted on the enemy. In spite of his wound he refused to be evacuated and remained with his command, where his outstanding bravery and consistent determination had a marked effect in maintaining the splendid fighting spirit of those under him.'

85. Truck mounted to either fire in mobile action or to be dismounted and fired on the ground.

86. *The London Gazette* (Supplement), 17 April 1942, p. 1741.

87. Gunn's VC citation concludes: 'Second Lieutenant Gunn showed the most conspicuous courage in attacking this large number of enemy tanks with a single unarmoured gun, and his utter disregard for extreme danger was an example which inspired all who saw it. He remained undismayed by intense fire and overwhelming odds, and his gallant resistance only ceased with his death.' Ibid.

88. Beeley's VC citation concludes: 'Rifleman Beeley went to certain death in a gallant and successful attempt to carry the day. His courage and self-sacrifice was a glorious example to his comrades and inspired them to reach their objective, which was eventually captured by them, together with 700 prisoners.' *The London Gazette* (Supplement), 17 April 1942, p. 1741.

89. *The London Gazette* (Supplement), 6 February 1942, p. 645. Gardner's VC citation concludes: 'The courage, determination and complete disregard for his own safety displayed by Captain Gardner enabled him, despite his own wounds, and in the face of intense fire at close range, to save the life of his fellow officer, in circumstances fraught with great difficulty and danger.'

90. Verney, *The Desert Rats*, p. 81.

91. Alexander, *Clive Caldwell*, p. 101-5. Caldwell ended the war as Australia's top-scoring fighter pilot with twenty-two victories in North Africa and is officially credited with 28.5 official kills, six probables and fifteen aircraft damaged.

92. Glass, 'Sidi Rezegh: Reminiscences of the late Gunner Cyril Herbert Glass, 143458, 3rd Field Regiment (Transvaal Horse Artillery).' *Military History Journal*, Vol. 14 No 5 - June 2009.

93. Matthews, 'With the 5th South African Infantry Brigade at Sidi Rezegh.' *Military History Journal*, Vol. 10 No 6 - December 1997.

94. Joly, *Take These Men*, p. 226.

95. von Mellenthin, *op. cit.*, pp. 87-8.

96. Ibid, p. 89.

97. Churchill, *The Grand Alliance*, p. 505.

98. Clifford, *Crusader*, p. 102.

99. comandosupremo.com/siege-of-tobruk/

100. Cunningham flew secretly to Alexandria to see his brother and recoup in a nursing home before returning to Britain where he served as commandant of a staff college for the remainder of the war.

101. Barnett, *op. cit.*, p. 119.

102. Ibid, p. 117.

103. Ibid, p. 118.

104. Reynolds, *Only the Stars Are Neutral*, p. 245. Reynolds wrote that it was a courageous action to fire Cunningham since the 'success of the whole Libyan campaign depended on the co-operation between the Army and the British Navy', commanded by his brother. 'But Alan Cunningham had committed the major military blunder, he had looked over his shoulder. Jockey's don't win Derbies by looking over their shoulders. You don't win battles that way either, so General Cunningham had to take the rap.' Barnett, *op. cit.*, p. 118.

105. Barnett, *op. cit.*, p. 137.

106. McLeave, *A Time to Heal*, p. 97.

107. Aird later wrote, 'I know of no wounded man who, by reason of our preoccupation with abdominal cases, passed untreated through any of the various dressing stations to which I was attached, and who died later as a postponement of his operation. Believing that the first aim of military surgery is the saving of the maximum number of lives, I decided to operate upon all cases whose systolic pressure could be induced to rise to 100 mm of mercury, a level which proved to be attainable in every case of penetrating wound of the abdomen.' Aird, 'Military Surgery in Geographical Perspective', p. 108.
108. *Life*, 19 January 1942. Alan Moorehead, 'Desert Tank Fighting; Columns race across Libya's sands to clash in vast explosions of dust, sound and flame', p. 81.
109. Jackman's VC citation concludes: 'Most of the tank commanders saw him, and his exemplary devotion to duty regardless of danger not only inspired his own men but clinched the determination of the tank crews never to relinquish the position which they had gained. Throughout he coolly directed the guns to their positions and indicated targets to them and at that time seemed to bear a charmed life but later he was killed while still inspiring everyone with the greatest confidence by his bearing.' *The London Gazette* (Supplement), 27 March 1942, p. 1437.
110. Fielding, *They Sought Out Rommel*, p. 19.
111. *Life*, 19 January 1942. Alan Moorehead, 'Desert Tank Fighting; Columns race across Libya's sands to clash in vast explosions of dust, sound and flame.', p. 74.
112. Churchill, *The Grand Alliance*, p. 509.
113. Ibid. Friedrich Wilhelm von Mellenthin notes that 'The Afrika Korps had accomplished nothing decisive on the frontier and was only a fraction of the magnificent force which had entered the battle' on 18 November. Von Mellenthin, *op. cit.*, p. 93.
114. Ibid., p. 92.
115. Murphy, *Relief of Tobruk*, p. 293. The New Zealand Division fought its most costly battle of the war in Operation Crusader with 879 dead and 1,700 wounded.
116. *The Newcastle Sun,* 18 December 1941, p. 2.
117. Fergusson, *The Trumpet in the Hall*, p. 132.
118. Fischer, *Hitler and America*, p. 153.
119. Schraepler, *op. cit.*, p. 184. Diary entry for 7 December 1941.

120. Fielding, *They Sought Out Rommel*, p. 45. Entry dated 13 December.

121. Rodger, *Desert Journey*, p. 143.

122. *Western Morning News*, 28 November 1941, p. 3.

123. Fergusson, *The Trumpet in the Hall*, p. 135.

124. Greene & Massignani, *Rommel's North African Campaign, September 1940-November 1942*, p. 175.

125. Dimbleby, *The Frontiers Are Green*, p. 249.

126. Verney, *The Desert Rats*, p. 102.

127. Schmidt, *op. cit.*, p. 120.

128. Schmidt, *op. cit.*, p. 121.

129. Mussolini violently suppressed the native Libyan population before the war. Approximately 60,000 Libyans perished in concentration camps, shootings, public hangings, large-scale deportations and mass starvation.

130. Peniakoff, *Private Army*, p. 178.

131. In 2002 Germany accepted responsibility for Jews held in Libyan camps at Sidi Azaz, Buq Buq, Giado, Gharyan and Jafara.

132. Liddell Hart, *The Rommel Papers*, p. 175.

133. Schmitt, a First World War veteran, had earlier surrendered to South African forces in 1915 during the German South West African campaign in what today is Namibia.

134. Martin, *The Durban Light Infantry*, p. 69.

135. Martin, *The Durban Light Infantry*, p. 82.

136. Scoullar, *The Battle for Egypt*, p. 1.

137. Connell, *Auchinleck,* p. 445.

138. Ibid, p. 419.

139. Forty, G. *Afrika Korps at War:* Vol. 1, p. 117.

Chapter Four: Counterstroke – Rommel's Reconquest of Cyrenaica

1. Barnett, *op. cit.*, p. 171. In a letter to Ritchie dated 1 January 1942, Auchinleck conceded, 'if our present leaders are too old or too rigid to learn from experience or from the Boche, then we must get others... British soldiers with inferior tools have often beaten thoroughly and decisively enemies much better equipped than they were in the past, and they will do it again if properly led.' Connell, *Auchinleck*, p. 421.

2. Connell, p. 420.
3. Barnett, *op. cit.*, pp. 124-5.
4. Ibid, p. 424.
5. Mindful of the logistical bonds that would again strangle his army, Rommel requested an extra 8,000 trucks – an impossible request given that the four Panzer Armies operating in Russia had only 14,000 vehicles between them!
6. von Mellenthin, *op. cit.*, p. 100.
7. Irving, *The Trail of the Fox*, p. 180.
8. Flicke, 'The Lost Keys to El Alamein', p. 4. Intelligence officer, Hans-Otto Behrendt, declared Fellers' reporting as 'not only strategically but tactically of the utmost usefulness...stupefying in its openness'. Behrendt, *Rommel's Intelligence in the Desert Campaign 1941-1943*, p. 146.
9. Britain's spymaster, Canadian-born Sir William Stephenson (best known by his wartime codename *Intrepid*) wrote after the war that 'the unadvertised tragedy' of Tobruk's June 1942 surrender lay in the intelligence 'innocently' provided to Rommel by Fellers' cables. Stevenson, *A Man Called Intrepid*, p. 404.
10. Hartmann, *Panzers in the Sand,* Vol. 2, pp. 3-4.
11. von Mellenthin, *op. cit.*, p. 104.
12. Ibid, p. 103.
13. Schmidt, *op. cit.*, p. 126.
14. Westphal, *The German Army in the West*, p. 112. After reading a British report of another incident involving Rommel's near capture, Goebbels noted in his diary (5 May 1942) that he is...altogether too careless about his life and security. It would be a terrible national misfortune if he were captured. He should be advised to move about more circumspectly. In any case I shall make the German people learn absolutely nothing about such a possibility.' *Brisbane Telegraph*, 26 May 1948, p. 4.
15. Connell, *Auchinleck*, p. 436.
16. *The Age*, 26 January 1942, p. 2.
17. Connell, *Auchinleck*, p. 441.
18. Forty, *Tank Warfare in World War II*, pp. 198-9. Diary entry for 26 January 1942.
19. Mackenzie, *Eastern Epic*, p. 309.
20. Westphal, *op. cit.*, p. 112.
21. Clifford, *Crusader,* p. 177.

NOTES

22. *The Sydney Morning Herald*, 2 February 1942, p. 6.
23. Churchill, *The Hinge of Fate,* p. 67. General David Belchem later added, this was 'surely without parallel in our annals.' Belchem, *All in the Day's March*, p. 109.
24. IWM AL 1517, p. 11.
25. 'German Psychological Warfare', *British Medical Journal,* 4 April 1942, p. 445.
26. Chutter, *Captivity Captive*, p. 42.
27. Bowen, *Back from Tobruk*, p. 128.
28. *The Illustrated London News*, Vol. 216, Issue 1, 1950.
29. Connell, *Auchinleck*, p. 445. Correspondence with General Arthur Smith, 30 January 1942.
30. Liddell Hart, *The Rommel Papers*, p. 183. Quoted from a letter to his wife, dated 4 February 1942.
31. Mackenzie, *Eastern Epic*, p. 317.
32. von Mellenthin, *op. cit.*, p. 106.
33. Bryant, *The Turn of The Tide,* p. 273.
34. Alanbrooke, *War Diaries 1939-1945*, p. 225.
35. Johnston and Stanley, *Alamein*, pp. 25-6.
36. Stroud, *The Phantom Army of Alamein*, p. 148.
37. Freudenberg, *Churchill and Australia*, p. 294.
38. Jackson, *The Battle for North Africa 1940-1943*, p. 194.
39. Tuker, *Approach to Battle*, p. 81.
40. Fennell, *op. cit.*, p. 196.
41. Moran, *Winston Churchill*, p. 63.
42. FO 954/31B/300 Telegram to the War Office, received 28 February 1942.
43. von Mellenthin, *op. cit.*, p. 110.
44. Bowen, *Back from Tobruk*, p. 115. The AFS ambulance corps sent 800 vehicles and 2,400 volunteer drivers abroad during the war.
45. Geer, *Mercy in Hell*, p. 245.
46. Aylett, *Surgeon at War*, p. 166.
47. Hartmann, *Panzers in the Sand* Vol. 2, p. 10.
48. von Mellenthin: 'Perhaps, fortunately, we underestimated the British strength, for had we known the full facts even Rommel might have balked at an attack on such a greatly superior enemy... Our lack of information is a tribute to the security and camouflage of [the] Eighth Army.' von Mellenthin, *op. cit.*, pp. 111-12.

49. FO 954/31B/300. Telegram to the War Office, received 28 February 1942.
50. Moran, *Winston Churchill,* p. 63.
51. Roberts, *From the Desert to the Baltic*, p. 67.
52. Joly, *Take These Men*, pp. 284-6.
53. Liddell Hart, *The Rommel Papers*, p. 188.
54. Tuker, *op. cit.*, p. 85.
55. D-424, 'Command Techniques Employed by Feldmarschall Rommel in Africa', p. 7.
56. Hart, *The South Notts Hussars*, p. 193.
57. Ibid, p. 194.
58. Forty, *Afrika Korps at War* Vol. 2, p. 19.
59. Warner, *The Lonely Soldier*, p. 144.
60. Naravane, *A Soldier's Life in War and Peace*, p. 85.
61. Bharucha, *The North African campaign, 1940-1943*, p. 367.
62. Barnett, *op. cit.*, p. 140.
63. Hart, *The South Notts Hussars*, p. 203.
64. Forty, *Afrika Korps at War:* Vol. 2., p. 24.
65. Barr, *Pendulum of War*, p. 57.
66. Hart, *op. cit.*, p. 201.
67. von Luck, *op. cit.*, p. 81.
68. *The Courier-Mail*, 8 June 1942, p. 5.
69. George Rock, an AFS ambulance driver, described Bir Hacheim as 'no more than a slight elevation in the vast desert. Once a small fort used for patrols against desert marauders, it was now an area of two to four square miles, heavily mined along its perimeter, containing gun and anti-aircraft emplacements, an operating theatre and tents, Bren carriers, and trenches and dugouts for the 3,000 French troops plus legionnaires, British gunners, and Senegalese soldiers.' Rock, *The History of the American Field Service*, p. 76.
70. Travers, *Tomorrow to be Brave*, p. 153.
71. Carell, *The Foxes of the Desert*, p. 165. Carell was born Paul Schmidt, a Nazi Party member since 1931. From 1940 he became head of the Foreign Ministry's news and press division and the chief spokesman for Joachim von Ribbentrop. He was also responsible for the propaganda magazine *Signal*.
72. Moorehead, *African Trilogy*, p. 332.
73. 'Libya-Successes and Shocks', Movietone News.
74. Liddell Hart, *The Rommel Papers*, p. 196.

75. Roberts, *From the Desert to the Baltic*, p. 104.
76. Merewood, *To War with The Bays,* p. 56.
77. Jones, *op. cit.*, p. 170.
78. Liddell Hart, *The Rommel Papers*, p. 208.
79. Tuker, *op. cit.*, p. 129.
80. Young, *Rommel*, pp. x-xi.
81. Irving, *The Trail of the Fox*, p. 162.
82. Rock, *The History of the American Field Service*, p. 80. The AFS suffered 100 per cent casualties at Bir Hacheim, losing twelve cars and six men.
83. Travers, *Tomorrow to be Brave*, p. 169.
84. Moorehead, *African Trilogy*, p. 332.
85. *The Daily Telegraph* (Sydney), 13 June 1942, p. 3.
86. Irving, *The Trail of the Fox*, p. 254.
87. 'Auchinleck's Report', *Liverpool Evening Express*, p. 4.
88. von Mellenthin, *op. cit.*, p. 106. Kœnig was awarded the DSO by General Alexander. Travers later received the *Croix de Guerre* and the *Ordre du Corps d'Armée*.
89. Eden, *The Reckoning*, p. 384.
90. Young, *Rommel*, pp. x-xi. Desmond Young authored one of the early British postwar biographical works on Rommel.
91. *The London Gazette* (Supplement), 8 September 1942, p. 3954.
92. Roberts, *From the Desert to the Baltic*, pp. 83-4.
93. Joly, *Take These Men*, pp. 295-6.
94. *Time*, Vol. 40, 1942, p. 6
95. Yeide, *Weapons of the Tankers*, p. 52.
96. Aylett, *Surgeon at War,* pp. 183-4. Letter dated 8 June.
97. Hartmann, *Panzers in the Sand,* Vol. 2, pp. 22-3.
98. *Nottingham Journal*, 12 June 1942, p. 1.
99. Fennell, 'War in History', p. 30.
100. Foote's citation concludes: 'Lieutenant-Colonel Foote was always at the crucial point at the right moment, and over a period of several days gave an example of outstanding courage and leadership which it would have been difficult to surpass. His name was a by-word for bravery and leadership throughout the Brigade.' *The London Gazette*, Supplement, 16 May 1944, p. 2269.
101. Boothe, The Battle for Egypt', *Life*, July 13, 1942, p. 73-82.
102. Tuker, *op. cit.*, p. 128.
103. 3squadron.org.au/subpages/Chinchen.htm

104. Liddell Hart, *The Rommel Papers*, p. 225.

105. Ibid, p. 220.

106. *The Times*, 16 June 1942, p. 4.

107. *Daily Advertiser*, 3 June 1942, p. 3.

108. Moseley, *Reporting War*, p. 180.

109. Agar-Hamilton, *Crisis in The Desert*, p. 128.

110. Ibid, p. 113.

111. Ibid, p. 129.

112. Katz, 'The Greatest Military Reversal of South African Arms', footnote, p. 89.

113. Fennell, *op. cit.*, p. 148.

114. Moorehead, *African Trilogy*: *The North African Campaign 1940-43*, p. 346.

115. Horn & Katz, 'The Surrender of Tobruk in 1942: Press Reports and Soldiers' Memories', p. 200.

116. Moorehead, *African Trilogy: The North African Campaign 1940-43*, p. 346.

117. Chutter, *Captivity Captive*, p. 28.

118. Ibid, p. 29.

119. Orpen and Martin, *Salute the Sappers*, Vol. VIII, Part 1, p. 356; Orpen, *War in the Desert*, p. 309.

120. Chutter, *Captivity Captive*, p. 29.

121. Moorehead, *African Trilogy,* p. 347.

122. *The Sun*, July 2, 1942, p. 16.

123. Hartshorn, *Avenge Tobruk*, p. 101.

124. This was especially true of the Egyptian pattern mines. A thorough reconditioning would involve the massive task of searching for individual mines and then remaking the fields.

125. Statement by Lt. Col. G. Bastin, 13th Corps. Court of Enquiry, Vol. II, Part V, p. 64.

126. Court of Enquiry, Vol. I, Part I, p. 5.

127. Mackenzie, *Eastern Epic*, 563; CAB 44/421 Fall of Tobruk, June 1942.

128. Court of Enquiry, Vol. II, pp. 52-4.

129. London was informed by Auchinleck, and his fellow Middle East commanders-in-chief, against holding Tobruk for a second time – their rationale based on the problem of locking up one and a half divisions, the potential cost in shipping, and whether sufficient air cover could be provided.

130. CAB 106/718 Western Desert: Studies on the Decision to Hold Tobruk and the Fall of El Adem 1942; Agar-Hamilton, *Crisis in The Desert*, p. 77. Author's italics.
131. WO 106/2238 A Fall of Tobruk; Court of Enquiry, Vol. I, Part III.
132. The use of the term 'garrison' to describe Tobruk at this point is debatable since there was no unified body of troops inside the perimeter. Furthermore, a significant number of administrative personnel served only to complicate the situation.
133. Churchill, *The Hinge of Fate*, p. 370.
134. Kennedy, *The Business of War*, 242. Diary entry 16 June 1942.
135. Warner, *Auchinleck*, p. 272; PWO 106/2238 A Fall of Tobruk; CAB 106/718 Western Desert: Studies on the Decision to Hold Tobruk and the Fall of El Adem 1942.
136. CAB 106/718 Western Desert: Studies on the Decision to Hold Tobruk and the Fall of El Adem 1942.
137. Court of Enquiry, Vol. I, Part III. Author's italics. Agar-Hamilton, *Crisis in the Desert*, p. 107.
138. Hinsley, *British Intelligence in the Second World War*, Vol. II, p. 385.
139. Liddell Hart, *The Rommel Papers*, p. 225.
140. Cadogan, *The Diaries of Sir Alexander Cadogan,* p. 458.
141. *The Times,* 20 June 1942. p. 4.
142. Liddell Hart, *The Rommel Papers*, p. 230.
143. Playfair, *History of the Second World War,* Vol. III, p. 263.
144. Agar-Hamilton, *Crisis in the Desert*, p. 134.
145. Ibid, p. 128.
146. Liddell Hart, *The Rommel Papers*, p. 225. British Intelligence from Cairo had provided Klopper with details of Rommel's November 1941 plan, which was well known throughout the Eighth Army.
147. Westphal, *op. cit.*, p. 115.
148. Schmidt, *op. cit.*, p. 146.
149. Chutter, *Captivity Captive*, p. 31. A 1943 British study on the effect of enemy weapons on the morale of 300 British soldiers wounded in North Africa found that the Stuka was the 'most disliked' weapon; though 'disliked to an extent out of all proportion to its real effectiveness'.

   Fennell, *Combat and Morale in the North African Campaign*, p. 61. Of the 176 men in question who had experienced dive-bombing, only nine per cent were wounded.
150. *History of the Second World War*, Part 34, 'Tobruk Falls', p. 949.

151. Agar-Hamilton, *Crisis in the Desert*, p. 162; Mackenzie, *Eastern Epic*, p. 564.
152. Schmidt, *op. cit.*, p. 47.
153. Hartmann, *Panzers in the Sand,* Vol. 2, p. 27.
154. Schmidt, *op. cit.*, p. 47.
155. Mackenzie, *Eastern Epic*, p. 566.
156. Statement by Lt. Col. G. Bastin, 13th Corps. Court of Enquiry, Vol. II, Part V, p. 72.
157. Martin, *The Durban Light Infantry*, Vol. II, p. 162.
158. Agar-Hamilton, *Crisis in The Desert*, p. 180.
159. Barnett, *op. cit.*, p. 160.
160. Cooper, *The Police Brigade: 6 S.A. Infantry Brigade 1939-1945*, p. 101.
161. Hartmann, *Panzers in the Sand,* Vol. 2, p. 30.
162. Liddell Hart, *The Rommel Papers*, p. 231.
163. Hartmann, *Panzers in the Sand,* Vol. 2, p. 30.
164. CAB/65/30/22.
165. Cooper, *op. cit.,* p. 101.
166. Ibid, p. 102.
167. Martin, *The Durban Light Infantry*, p. 197.
168. Lewin, *The War on Land*, p. 126.
169. Stewart, 'The "Atomic" Dispatch', p. 91.
170. *The Sun*, June 29, 1942, p. 2.
171. Maughan, *op. cit.,* p. 195. The 7th Gurkhas and Camerons resisted so stubbornly that they became bypassed islands of resistance that refused to surrender. Not until their ammunition and water was exhausted did they surrender, on the morning of 22 June. Unwilling to be taken captive, small bands of men slipped through the Axis cordon and made their way to El Alamein.
172. Moorehead, *African Trilogy*, p. 352.
173. Horn, 'Narratives from North Africa', p. 101.
174. Westphal, *op. cit.*, pp. 115-16.
175. Ministry of Information. *The Eighth Army,* p. 52. Alexander Clifford wrote: 'I think that morning, when we learned of the fall of Tobruk, was the bitterest moment I have known in the desert. At first it was a purely sentimental bitterness – a ridiculous, unwarrantable regret for a ruined, stinking, fly-blown town which had nevertheless come to mean so much to us. But then that was overtaken by a more immediate human bitterness – a sick misery at this futile loss of

so many men and so much materiel, at this gratuitous additional catastrophe in a campaign that was already going badly.' Clifford, *The Conquest of North Africa 1940-1943*, p. 309.

176. Hancock, *Smuts*, p. 375; *The Times*, 23 June 1942, p. 3.

177. FO 954/15A/171

178. Herf, *Nazi Propaganda for the Arab World,* p. 111.

179. Ibid, p. 123.

180. Cook, *The Struggle for Egypt*, p. 115. Sadat later wrote: 'Egypt had been patient. We had suffered insult and provocation, and now we prepared to fight side by side with the Axis to hasten England's defeat.' Sadat, *Revolt on the Nile*, p. 48. Sadat and several associates were subsequently arrested and imprisoned when Rommel was stopped at El Alamein. Sadat's admiration for Rommel led to his establishing a war museum there in his honour. Cook, *op. cit.,* p. 321.

181. Maĭskiĭ, *The Complete Maisky Diaries*, Vol. 3, p. 1286.

182. Ibid. p. 1287.

183. Cooper, *The Police Brigade:* p. 103.

184. Chutter, *Captivity Captive*, p. 36.

185. Martin, *The Durban Light Infantry*, Vol. II, p. 161.

186. Hartshorn, *op. cit.*, p. 138-9. Klopper confronted Smuts in 1948 after reading Auchinleck's dispatches to either exonerate him or accept his resignation. Klopper stated that it 'took seven hours for him to get permission to break out, and by the time it was given his transport in the harbour area was destroyed and useless to his men on the perimeter.' *Herald*, 17 January 1948.

187. Ciano, *op. cit.*, p. 500.

188. Hamilton, *The Mantle of Command*, p. 306.

189. *The New York Times*, June 22, 1942, p. 1.

190. Gallup, *The Gallup Poll*, p. 342. Other reasons included: British won't fight, poor fighters (eight per cent); overconfident British (five per cent); bad government planning (one per cent); miscellaneous (three per cent) and no opinion (thirty-three per cent).

191. *The Sun*, 23 June 1942, p. 2.

192. Bryant, *The Turn of The Tide, p.* 408; Aandahl, *Foreign Relations of the United States*, p. 437.

193. *Daily Mail,* 23 June 1942, p. 4.

194. *The Sun*, 24 June 1942, p. 2; Churchill, *The Hinge of Fate,* p. 386. In a letter to London's *Times*, T.L. Horabin MP wrote: 'Our defeat

at Tobruk has made an impression on people comparable with the [British] public feeling after the failure in Norway. There is now an almost universally-held opinion that the organisation of our war machinery is too loose and inadequate at the top. No confidence can be felt in the conduct of the war while these defects exist at the centre.' *The Argus*, 26 June 1942, p. 1.

195. Gilbert, *Winston S. Churchill*, Vol. VII, p. 140.
196. Churchill, War Speeches, Vol. 2, p. 290.
197. *Daily Mirror*, 23 June 1942, p. 1.
198. Ibid.

Chapter Five: 'Now it is imperative to completely destroy the enemy'

1. Various, *Poems from the Desert*, p. 46.
2. *Birmingham Daily Post*, 1 July 1942, p. 2.
3. Warlimont, *Inside Hitler's Headquarters 1939-1945*, p. 241.
4. Fredborg, *Behind the Steel Wall*, p. 109.
5. Liddell Hart, *The Rommel Papers*, p. 233.
6. Burdick & Jacobson, *The Halder War Diary,* p. 625.
7. Hartmann, *Panzers in the Sand,* Vol. 2, p. 25.
8. Corvaja, *op. cit.*, p. 208.
9. Boog, *Germany and the Second World War*, Vol. 6., p. 726.
10. Scoullar, *The Battle for Egypt*, p. 48.
11. Ibid, p. 78.
12. Moorehead, *African Trilogy*, p. 356.
13. *Dundee Evening Telegraph* in a 'sad meeting' in London meeting on 15 July, Alanbrooke consoled Ritchie, 'I told him that I considered that he had been pushed on much too fast by Auchinleck, to be put in command of Eighth Army in the field when he had never even commanded a division in action.' Alanbrooke, *War Diaries 1939-1945*, p. 280.
14. Barnett, *op. cit.*, p. 171.
15. 'It was through the self-sacrifice and courageous devotion to duty of this infantry anti-tank gunner that the Company was enabled to withdraw and embus in safety.' *The London Gazette* (Supplement), 8 September 1942.
16. Gordon, *A job to Do*, p. 149.

17. Ibid, p. 149.
18. Ibid, p. 151.
19. McLeod, *Myth and Reality*, p. 87. One witness said the Maoris took 'a savage delight in the slaughter they were able to inflict, and they used their bayonets with deadly effect.' See McLeod, 'The New Zealand soldier in World War II: Myth and Reality', p. 102. The DAK war diary recorded 'violations of International Law, such as the slaughter of wounded.' Ibid, p. 134.
20. Liddell Hart, *The Rommel Papers*, p. 281. Clifton explained that the 'bayoneting occurred when the wounded threw grenades' – an explanation Rommel, as reported in a postwar interview, accepted as 'very fair'. 'New Zealand Brigadier's Breezy Chat with Marshal Rommel', *Army News*, 10 April 1945, p. 4.
21. Graham, *Sharpshooters at War*, p. 64.
22. Liddell Hart, *The Rommel Papers*, pp. 238-9.
23. Ciano, *op. cit.*, p. 506.
24. Bowen, *Back from Tobruk*, p. 175.
25. Fennel, 'Steel my soldiers' hearts', p. 7.
26. Ibid.
27. Geer, *Mercy in Hell*. p. 67.
28. Hunt, 'Medical Experiences in North Africa 1943-4', p. 484.
29. Harrison, *Medicine and Victory*, p. 121.
30. Ibid, p. 122.
31. Fennell, 'War in History', p. 1. Since April 1941, there were 291 convictions recorded for desertion and 19 convictions for cowardice in the Middle East. In the 27 days of fighting ending 13 July 1942, 907 instances of absenteeism were reported to the Corps of Military Police, of whom 430 were apprehended.
32. Hammond, *Alamein*, p. 39.
33. Townsend, *Road to Ruin*, p. 4.
34. Sadkovich, *The Italian Navy in World War II*, p. 302.
35. Gorrell, *Soldier of the Press*, p. 207.
36. Moseley, *Reporting War,* p. 180.
37. Boog, *Germany and the Second World War*, Vol. 6., p. 728.
38. Liddell Hart, *The Rommel Papers*, p. 261.
39. Gear, 'Hygiene Aspects of the El Alamein Victory', 1942, p. 348.
40. The label has been challenged by generals and historians alike. Charles Richardson, a senior Eighth Army staff officer, was adamant: 'I can state from my continuous presence as GSO 1

(Plans) that no battle entitled to the name "First Alamein" ever took place.' Latimer, *Alamein*, p. 59. Belchem wrote after the war: 'There was not, as far as we who were present can recall, a "First Battle of El Alamein".' Belchem, *All in a Day's March*, p. 107. The month long period of bitter and often-confused fighting, which some contended as the final act in the Battle of Gazala, is now generally referred to as 'The First Battle of El Alamein'.

41. Stevens & Hingston, *The Tiger Kills*, pp. 231-2.
42. Scoullar, *Battle for Egypt*, p. 161.
43. Ibid.
44. Hartmann, *Panzers in the Sand,* Vol. 2, pp. 36-7.
45. Boog, *Germany and the Second World War*, Vol. 6., p. 728.
46. Hartmann, *Panzers in the Sand,* Vol 2, pp. 35-8.
47. Boog, *Germany and the Second World War*, Vol. 6., p. 732, footnote.
48. Scoullar, *Battle for Egypt*, p. 172.
49. von Mellenthin, *op. cit.*, p. 163.
50. Liddell Hart, *The Rommel Papers*, p. 249.
51. Scoullar, *Battle for Egypt*, p. 197.
52. Murray Reid, *The Turning Point*, p. 67.
53. Boog, *Germany and the Second World War*, Vol. 6., p. 736.
54. P-038 'German Radio Intelligence'.
55. Behrendt, *Rommel's Intelligence in the Desert Campaign 1941-1943,* p. 168.
56. Ibid, p. 170.
57. Flicke, 'The Lost Keys to El Alamein', p. 8.
58. Boog, *Germany and the Second World War*, Vol. 6., p. 746.
59. Bierman & Smith, *The Battle of Alamein,* p. 206. Knight was subsequently awarded the DCM.
60. Gregory & Gehlen. *Two Soldiers, Two Lost Fronts,* p. 167.
61. von Mellenthin, *op. cit.*, p. 167.
62. Scoullar, *Battle for Egypt*, p. 230.
63. Kippenberger, *Infantry Brigadier*, pp. 180.
64. Boog, *Germany and the Second World War*, Vol. 6., p. 746.
65. Ciano, *op. cit.*, p. 507; Boog, *Germany and the Second World War*, Vol. 6., p. 746.
66. Kippenberger, *Infantry Brigadier*, pp. 178-179.
67. Rock, *The History of the American Field Service*, p. 104.

68. *Army News*, 28 April 1945. Upham was liberated from Colditz in 1945 by American forces. His request to be armed and continue fighting in an American unit was denied.

69. Elliott was awarded the VC. His citation concludes: 'Owing to Sergeant Elliott's quick grasp of the situation, great personal courage and leadership, nineteen men who were the only survivors of "B" Company of his Battalion captured and destroyed five machine-guns, one anti-tank gun, killed a great number of the enemy and captured 130 prisoners. Sergeant Elliott sustained only one casualty among his men and brought him back to the nearest advanced dressing station.' *The London Gazette*, Supplement, 24 September 1942, p. 4153.

70. FO 954/16A/156.

71. Brune, 'Gurney, Arthur Stanley (1908–1942)'. *Australian Dictionary of Biography*.

72. Gurney's VC citation commended his 'single-handed act of gallantry in the face of a determined enemy', which enabled his company 'to press forward to its objective, inflicting heavy losses upon the enemy.' *The London Gazette*, Supplement, 11 September 1942, p. 3953.

73. Doherty, *British Armoured Divisions and their Commanders, 1939-1945*, p. 82.

74. Bright, *The Ninth Queen's Royal Lancers, 1936-1945,* p. 104.

75. Townsend, *Road to Ruin*, p. 17.

76. Boog, *Germany and the Second World War*, Vol. 6., p. 741.

77. Warlimont, *Inside Hitler's Headquarters*, p. 247.

78. Connell, *Auchinleck*, p. 938.

79. Barr, *op. cit.*, p. 200.

80. Greacen, *Chink: A Biography,* p. 237.

81. Talbot, *Speaking from the Desert,* p. 24.

82. Gorrell, *Soldier of the Press*, p. 199.

83. Johnston, *Anzacs in the Middle East*, p. 177.

84. Johnston, *That Magnificent 9th*, p. 97.

85. Ministry of Information. *The Eighth Army,* p. 60.

86. Moran, *op. cit.*, p. 68.

87. Churchill, *The Hinge of Fate*, p. 415. Moran noted that while firm in his resolve to install a new commander, privately the 'P.M. hates the thought of removing one of his commanders.' Moran, op. cit., p. 67.

88. Brooke also dismissed Eric Dorman-Smith from his position as Auchinleck's unofficial chief of staff, as well as Tom Corbett. An angry Corbett noted that 'one does not dismiss one's gardener without some explanation.' Barr, *op. cit.*, p. 215.
89. Richardson, *From Churchill's Secret Circle to the BBC*, pp. 117-19.
90. Moran, *op. cit.*, p. 68.
91. Richardson, *op. cit.*, p. 122.
92. Moran, *op. cit.*, pp. 70-71.
93. Ibid, p. 70.
94. Nash, *Strafer Desert General*, pp. 237-8.
95. Montgomery, *The Memoirs of Field Marshal the Viscount Montgomery of Alamein*, p. 93.
96. Fennell, *Combat and Morale in the North African Campaign*, p. 6.
97. Gear, 'Hygiene, Morale and Desert Victory', p. 397.
98. Holmes, *The World at War*, p. 273
99. Fennell, 'Steel my soldiers' hearts', p. 8.
100. Moorehead, *Montgomery*, pp. 123-4.
101. Montgomery, *The Memoirs of Field Marshal the Viscount Montgomery of Alamein K.G.,* p. 102. Montgomery had also lived in Tasmania as a child.
102. Johnston & Stanley, *Alamein*, p. 129.
103. Australian gunners were not impressed: '…wearing a digger hat jammed down on top of his head in a way no self-respecting digger would ever wear it, he must be a prize galah indeed.' Goodhart, *The History of the 2/7th Australian Field Regiment*, Vol. 2, p. 190. Montgomery's slouch hat is today in the collection of the Australian War Memorial, Canberra. Moorehead writes that he 'had no special liking for berets, but it was clear to him that this particular beret was becoming a notable morale builder, since soldiers always liked to see their generals at the front… Twice he was officially asked to discard the beret as something which he was not then entitled to wear and which, moreover, was hardly consonant with the dignity of a commanding general.' Moorehead, *Montgomery*, p. 143.
104. Latimer, *Alamein*, p. 99.
105. Belchem, *All in the Day's March*, p. 111.
106. Moran, *op. cit.*, p. 86.
107. Churchill, *The Hinge of Fate*, p. 515.
108. de Guingand, *Operation Victory*, p. 124.

109. *The Hinge of Fate*, p. 516.
110. See Rasmussen, 'Medical Science and the Military: The Allies' Use of Amphetamine during World War II.'
111. Reifenstein & Davidoff, 'The Psychological Effects of Benzedrine Sulfate', p. 64.
112. Holland, 'Did Stimulants power the Allies to Victory', *The Sunday Telegraph*, 25 August 2019.
113. Rasmussen, *On Speed*, p. 68.
114. Westphal, *op. cit.*, p. 126.
115. Pimlott, *Rommel in His Own Words*, p. 141. 22 August 1942. 'Yesterday I [Rommel] went through a thorough physical check-up. The result: my heart does not function properly, much too low blood pressure, a state of exhaustion, six to eight weeks rest cure recommended. I have asked the High Command to send a substitute.' Quoted from Marshal, *Discovering the Rommel Murder,* p. 82.
116. Liddell Hart, *The Rommel Papers*, p. 270.
117. Talbot, *Speaking from the Desert*, p. 45.
118. Ibid.

Chapter Six: 'Big things at stake'

1. Liddell Hart, *The Rommel Papers*, p. 275.
2. Hartmann, *Panzers in the Sand,* Vol. 2, p. 49.
3. Dovey, 'The False Going Map at Alam Halfa', p. 165.
4. de Guingand, *Operation Victory*, p. 121.
5. Gibson, *op. cit.*, p. 518.
6. Liddell Hart, *The Rommel Papers*, p. 277.
7. In his post-war narrative of the battle, Generalleutnant Fritz Bayerlein wrote: 'Montgomery, as soon as he had arrived in the Western Desert – as we later learned – heavily fortified the most important ridge, Alam el Halfa, and prepared it for defence by placing the greater part of his armour there. He even allowed a map to fall into our hands on which the terrain south of Alam el Halfa was shown as trafficable for armoured vehicles. Actually, it was bottomless sand which would create extreme difficulties for our wheeled vehicles.' Liddell Hart et al. *A Battle Report: Alam Halfa.*
8. Liddell Hart, *The Rommel Papers*, p. 278.

9. Gregory & Gehlen. *Two Soldiers, Two Lost Fronts,* p. 173.

10. Liddell Hart, *The Rommel Papers*, p. 279.

11. Hartmann, *Panzers in the Sand* Vol. 2, p. 50.

12. Kaplan, *Fighter Aces of the Luftwaffe in World War II*, p. 53.

13. von Mellenthin, *op. cit.*, p. 177.

14. Montgomery, *The Memoirs of Field Marshal the Viscount Montgomery of Alamein KG,* p. 103.

15. von Mellenthin, *op. cit.*, p. 172. Rommel was 'no longer the same daring leader', Generalfeldmarschall Albert Kesselring (Wehrmacht Commander-in-Chief South) wrote, worn by 'continual, almost two-year long combat in hot climates coupled with endless friction with the Italians and the disappointment over the failure of his thrust towards Cairo had considerably damaged his health and, particularly, his nerves. Detwiler, D.S. ed. *World War II German Military Studies,* Vol. 14, Part VI, *The Mediterranean Theatre,* p. 68.

16. Liddell Hart, *The Rommel Papers*, p. 283.

17. Schmidt, *op. cit.*, p. 171.

18. 'It was indeed an Empire battle,' Churchill later wrote, 'in which the Mother Country bore the brunt'; of the 1,640 men – 984 British, 257 Australians, 405 New Zealanders, 65 South Africans and 39 Indians. *The Hinge of Fate*, p. 548.

19. Montgomery, *Memoirs,* p. 101.

20. Churchill, *The Hinge of Fate*, p. 548.

21. FO 954/15A/212.

22. D-172, El Alamein Crisis and Its After-Effects in the OKW (23 Oct.-4 Nov. 1942)

23. Gregory & Gehlen. *op. cit.,* p. 175.

24. Schmidt, *op. cit.*, p. 173.

25. Latimer, *Alamein*, p. 125.

26. Marseille was later buried at Derna on 2 October. General Adolf Galland described him as 'the unrivalled virtuoso among the fighter pilots... His achievements were previously considered impossible.'

27. Reuth, *op. cit.,* p. 54.

28. Barkas, *The Camouflage Story*, p. 208.

29. Willkie. *One World*, pp. 14-21.

30. Boog, *Germany and the Second World War*, Vol. 6., p. 770.

31. AWM 54 492/4/77 Stumme to Lower Formations, 20 October 1942, Translation of Appendices to Panzerarmee Afrika War Diary

32. Moorehead, *Montgomery*, p. 134.
33. Orpen, *War in the Desert*, p. 415.
34. Hamilton, *Master of the Battlefield*, p. 50.
35. Moorehead, *Montgomery*, p. 135.
36. Merewood, *To War with The Bays*, p. 66.
37. Ross, *23 Battalion*, p. 197.
38. Reid, *The Turning Point*, p. 181.
39. Gorle, *The Quiet Gunner at War*, p. 78.
40. British Information Services, *African victory with the British forces from El Alamein to Cape Bon*, p. 13.
41. Reid, *op. cit* p. 185.
42. de Guingand, *Operation Victory*, p. 135.
43. British Information Services, *op. cit.*, p. 14.
44. Harper, *The Battle for North Africa*, p. 3.
45. *Warwick and Warwickshire Advertiser*, 10 March 1944, p. 6.
46. Forty, *Afrika Korps at War: Vol. 2*, pp. 71-3.
47. Arthur, *Forgotten Voices of The Second World War*, p. 206.
48. McKenzie, *Gimme the Guns*, p. 49.
49. Latimer, *Alamein*, p. 258.
50. Moran, *op. cit.*, pp. 95-6.
51. Churchill, *The Hinge of Fate*, p. 528.
52. Arthur, *Forgotten Voices of The Second World War*, p. 206.
53. '"Tally Ho" in Tanks', *Warwick and Warwickshire Advertiser*, 10 March 1944, p. 6.
54. Bassett, *Guns and Brooches*, p. 132. The 1st Greek Brigade, part of the Royal Hellenic Army in the Middle East, served under the British 50th during the Second Battle of El Alamein before its transfer to the British 44th Division.
55. Sadler, *El Alamein*, p. 81.
56. de Guingand, *Operation Victory*, p. 166.
57. Boog, *Germany and the Second World War*, Vol. 6., p. 780.
58. Rasmussen, *On Speed*, p. 70.
59. It may be said that Britain's first decisive victory on land was pharmacologically-assisted, even if the extent to which Benzedrine played a part remains unclear.
60. '"Tally Ho" in Tanks', *Warwick and Warwickshire Advertiser*, 10 March 1944, p. 6.
61. Merewood, *To War with The Bays*, p. 68.

62. *The London Gazette* (Supplement), 26 January 1943, pp. 523-4. Gratwick's VC citation concludes: 'By his brave and determined action, which completely unnerved the enemy, and by his successful reduction of the enemy's strength, Private Gratwick's company was able to move forward and mop up its objective. Private Gratwick's unselfish courage, his gallant and determined efforts against the heaviest opposition changed a doubtful situation into the successful capture of his Company's final objective.'

63. von Luck *op. cit.*, p. 94.

64. Schmidt, *op. cit.*, pp. 176-7.

65. Warlimont described El Alamein as 'a typical battle of materiel in which no military genius on the part of the commander, and no amount of courage on the part of the men, could make up for the catastrophic situation brought about by the failure of the overseas [Axis] supply lines.' Jacobsen & Rohwer, *Decisive Battles of World War II*, p. 203.

66. *The Sydney Morning Herald*, 16 January 1943, p. 7. Diary entry for 27 October.

67. Lucas Phillips, *Alamein*, p. 285.

68. Lee, *Up Close and Personal*, p. 115.

69. Ibid, p. 149.

70. Liddell Hart, *The Rommel Papers*, p. 310.

71. *The London Gazette* (Supplement), 20 November 1942, p. 5023. Turner's VC citation concludes: 'His personal gallantry and complete disregard of danger as he moved about encouraging his Battalion to resist to the last, resulted in the infliction of a severe defeat on the enemy tanks. He set an example of leadership and bravery which inspired his whole Battalion and which will remain an inspiration to the Brigade.'

72. Beckett, *Rommel,* p. 105.

73. Weston, *Nine Lives*, p. 6.

74. Ibid.

75. See Giblin, 'Abdominal Surgery in the Alamein Campaign'.

76. Allport, *Browned Off and Bloody-minded*, p. 306.

77. Ibid.

78. Hickey, 'Departing for the Ends of the Earth to do My Humble Part', p. 51.

79. Montgomery, *The Memoirs of Field-Marshal Montgomery*, p. 120.

80. Brooks, *Montgomery and the Eighth Army*, p. 76.

81. *The London Gazette* (Supplement), 26 January 1943, p. 523. Kibby's VC citation concludes: 'Such outstanding courage, tenacity of purpose and devotion to duty was entirely responsible for the successful capture of the Company's objective. His work was an inspiration to all and he left behind him an example and the memory of a soldier who fearlessly and unselfishly fought to the end to carry out his duty.' In his autobiography, Lieutenant General Brian Horrocks acknowledged: 'The success of Supercharge was largely due to the 9th Australian Division who had carried out continuous attacks night after night. After the battle I went to see General Morshead to congratulate him on the magnificent fighting carried out by his division. His reply was the classic understatement of all time: "Thank you, General, the boys were interested".' Horrocks, *A Full life*, p. 140.

82. Liddell Hart, *The Rommel Papers*, p. 316.

83. Latimer, *Alamein*, p. 288.

84. Liddell Hart, *The Rommel Papers*, p. 318.

85. Hammond, *El Alamein: The Battle that Turned the Tide of the Second World War,* p. 261.

86. *The Sydney Morning Herald*, 16 January 1943, p. 7. Diary entry for 3 November 1942.

87. Liddell Hart, p. 319.

88. D-424, Command Techniques Employed by Feldmarschall Rommel in Africa, pp. 8-9.

89. D-172, El Alamein Crisis and Its After-Effects in the OKW (23 Oct.-4 Nov. 1942).

90. von Luck *op. cit.*, p. 95.

91. Beckett, *Rommel*, p. 107.

92. Liddell Hart, *The Rommel Papers*, p. 322. Correspondence dated 3 November 1942.

93. Carell, *The Foxes of the Desert*, p. 324.

94. Liddell Hart, *The Rommel Papers*, p. 324.

95. Hartmann, *Panzers in the Sand,* Vol. 2, p. 63.

96. von Thoma's captor, Captain Grant Singer (Royal Hussars), heir to the Singer Sewing Machine riches, was killed the following day.

97. Brown, *One Man's War*, p. 184.

98. Moorehead, *Montgomery*, p. 141.

99. North, *The Memoirs of Field Marshal Earl Alexander of Tunis 1940-1945,* p. 56.

Index

Also available from David Mitchelhill-Green

Fighting in Ukraine: A Photographer at War

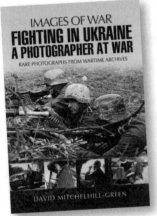

The outcome of the Second World War was decided on the Eastern Front. Denied a swift victory over Stalins Red Army, Hitlers Wehrmacht found itself in a bloody, protracted struggle from late 1941 that it was ill-prepared to fight.

Although many pictorial books have been published on Germanys hapless invasion of the Soviet Union, they are typically a collection of soldiers snapshots or official photographs taken by Propagandakompanien (PK) reporters. This book is different. It contains an extraordinary personal record of the war captured by a professional photographer, Walter Grimm, who served in the German Army in a communications unit.

David Mitchelhill-Green brings Grimms previously unpublished photographs together with a carefully researched introduction. The 300 evocative black and white images provide an absorbing insight into the daily life and privations of the ordinary German soldier amid the maelstrom of historys largest conflict. The Ukrainian people, many of whom initially welcomed the Germans as liberators, freeing them from the yoke of Bolshevik oppression, are also chronicled in this fascinating study of the fighting in Ukraine.

With Rommel in the Desert: Tripoli to El Alamein

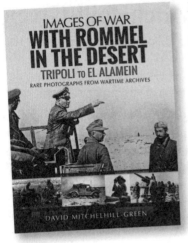

Prior to the outbreak of war in September 1939, the German Army had focused exclusively on the operational, organisational and training preparations needed to wage war in continental Europe. The threat of an Italian collapse in North Africa in early 1941, however, prompted Hitler to reinforce his ally by sending an armoured blocking force to Libya. Not content to merely thwart the British from capturing Tripoli, Lieutenant-General Erwin Rommel harried his inexperienced expeditionary force eastward towards the Nile Delta.

This book is a pictorial narrative of the unfolding conflict from the arrival of the Deutsches Afrikakorps until Rommels departure from the battlefield in March 1943. We view the desert war, with its shifting fortunes and unique challenges, primarily through the lens of ordinary combatants. This is their personal record of serving with Rommel in the desert.

Rommel in North Africa: Quest for the Nile

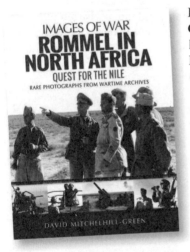

Erwin Rommel is the arguably the most well-known German general of the Second World War. Revered by his troops and applauded by his enemies, the so-called Desert Fox achieved legendary status for his daring exploits and bold manoeuvres during the North African campaign. In this book, richly illustrated with over 400 images, the author examines the privations and challenges Rommel faced in leading his coalition force. Endeavouring to reach the Nile Delta, we find Rommel's Axis soldiers poorly-prepared to undertake such an audacious operation. Much-admired by his men in the front lines, we discover a demanding and intolerant leader, censured by subordinate officers and mistrusted by his superiors in Berlin. Certainly no diplomat, we observe posed interactions with Italian and junior German officers through an official lens.

We note Rommels readiness to take advantage of his enemys weakness and study his extraordinary instinct for waging mobile warfare. We consider his disregard for the decisive factor of supply and view his armys reliance on captured equipment. We learn how this brave and ambitious commander was celebrated by German propaganda when the Wehrmachts fortunes in the East were waning. Conversely, analyse why Winston Churchill honoured him as a daring and skillful opponent. Finally, we picture this energetic, ambitious, at times reckless, commander as he roamed the vast Western Desert battlefield. This is the story of Rommel in North Africa.

Air War Over North Africa – USAAF Ascendant

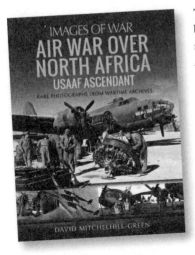

The year 1942 began badly for the Allies. German U-boats were indiscriminately sinking merchant shipping off America's east coast and in the Caribbean. Allied fortunes were no better in the Far East under the relentless Japanese advance. America was struggling to hold the Philippines, while the Soviet Union was fighting a series of bitter winter battles against Hitler's Wehrmacht at the gates of Moscow. General Erwin Rommel's surprise offensive in North Africa brought a renewed threat to the Middle East in mid-1942, which hastened the transfer of U.S. aircraft to Egypt to assist the beleaguered British.

The vast, sprawling deserts of North Africa were a new and strange terrain to American aircrew. Confronted by sand storms, flooding rains, extremes of temperature and primitive living conditions, the United States Army Air Forces were pitted against an experienced and determined enemy. U.S. air power nevertheless played a decisive role in the Allied invasion of Northwest Africa and the subsequent surrender of Axis forces in Tunisia in May 1943. Later bombing missions flown from North Africa struck Axis targets across Europe and supported the Allied invasions of Sicily and mainland Italy.

This book is a pictorial account of U.S. fighter aircraft and bombers — including the iconic B-17 Flying Fortress, P-38 Lightning and B-24 Liberator — and the aircrews that fought to establish ascendancy over North African skies and beyond.

Rommel's Ghost Division: Dash to the Channel – 1940

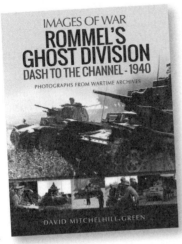

Adolf Hitler invaded Western Europe on 10 May 1940. After breaking through the supposedly 'impenetrable' Ardennes, Erwin Rommel was at the forefront of the Wehrmacht's audacious drive through France. Rommel, who had no prior experience leading an armoured division in combat, moved with such speed and nerve that he frequently surprised French units by arriving far earlier than expected. Crossing the Meuse River, we follow Rommel—in what he referred to as 'practically a lightning Tour de France'—as he pushed through northern France to the English Channel. His spectacular victory at the coastal port of Saint-Valéry-en-Caux was crowned by the capture of Cherbourg. Following the armistice, Rommel was involved in re-enacting certain battles, such as crossing the Somme, for the documentary Sieg im Westen (Victory in the West). This is the story of Rommel and the 7th Panzer Division—the so-called 'Ghost Division'—in France, 1940.